Beginning Programming with Java™

FOR

DUMMIES®

Beginning Programming with Java™ FOR DUMMIES®

by Barry Burd

Wiley Publishing, Inc.

Beginning Programming with Java™ For Dummies®

Published by
Wiley Publishing, Inc.
909 Third Avenue
New York, NY 10022

www.wiley.com

Copyright © 2003 by Wiley Publishing, Inc., Indianapolis, Indiana

Published by Wiley Publishing, Inc., Indianapolis, Indiana

Published simultaneously in Canada

For general information on our other products and services or to obtain technical support, please contact our Customer Care Department within the U.S. at 800-762-2974, outside the U.S. at 317-572-3993, or fax 317-572-4002.

Wiley also publishes its books in a variety of electronic formats. Some content that appears in print may not be available in electronic books.

Library of Congress Control Number: 2003101841

ISBN: 0-7645-2646-4

Manufactured in the United States of America

10 9 8 7 6 5 4 3 2 1

1O/RW/QU/QT/IN

About the Author

Dr. Barry Burd has an M.S. in Computer Science from Rutgers University, and a Ph.D. in Mathematics from the University of Illinois. As a teaching assistant in Champaign-Urbana, Illinois, he was elected five times to the university-wide List of Teachers Ranked as Excellent by their Students.

Since 1980, Dr. Burd has been a professor in the Department of Mathematics and Computer Science at Drew University in Madison, New Jersey. When he's not lecturing at Drew University, Dr. Burd leads training courses for professional programmers in business and industry. He has lectured at conferences in America, Europe, Australia, and Asia. He is the author of several articles and books, including *Java 2 For Dummies* and *Java & XML For Dummies,* both published by Wiley Publishing, Inc.

Dr. Burd lives in Madison, New Jersey, with his wife and two children. For hobbies he enjoys anything that wastes his and everyone else's time.

Dedication

for
Harriet, Sam and Jennie,
Sam and Ruth,
Abram and Katie, Benjamin and Jennie

Author's Acknowledgments

Author's To-Do List, February 13, 2003

Item: Buy a new car for your project editor, Paul Levesque. If he doesn't need a car, then find out what he needs and buy it for him. Since you have no savings, put it all on a credit card. This guy has put up with your nonsense throughout three projects, so he deserves the royal treatment.

Item: Have a plaque erected in honor of Steven Hayes, your acquisitions editor at Wiley. While you dragged your heels, Steve kept on insisting that you write this book. (Sure, you wanted a long vacation instead of a big book project, but who cares? He was right; you were wrong.)

Item: Send thank-you notes and gift baskets to copy editor Jean Rogers and tech editor Jim Kelly. Both helped polish your original work and, miraculously, neither of them made a lot of extra work for you.

Item: Recommend your agent Neil Salkind to other computer book authors. If it weren't for Neil, you'd still be roaming the book exhibits and looking needy at the technology conferences.

Item: Visit Frank Thornton, Bonnie Averbach, and Herbert Putz at Temple University. Thank them for steering you to a career as a professor. In any other career, you'd have no time left to write. (And by the way, while you're in Philly, don't forget to stop for a cheesesteak.)

Item: Send e-mail to Gaisi Takeuti at the University of Illinois, and to William Wisdom and Hughes LeBlanc at Temple University. Thank them for teaching you about Symbolic Logic. It's made your life as a computer scientist and mathematician much richer.

Item: Spend more time with your family. (Remind them that you're the guy who wandered around the house before this book project got started.) Renew your pledge to clean up after yourself. Don't be so high strung, and finish each sentence that you start. Remember that you can never fully return the love they've given you, but you should always keep trying.

Publisher's Acknowledgments

We're proud of this book; please send us your comments through our online registration form located at www.dummies.com/register/.

Some of the people who helped bring this book to market include the following:

Acquisitions, Editorial, and Media Development

Project Editor: Paul Levesque

Senior Acquisitions Editor: Steven Hayes

Copy Editor: Jean Rogers

Technical Editor: Jim Kelly

Editorial Manager: Leah Cameron

Media Development Manager: Laura VanWinkle

Media Development Supervisor: Richard Graves

Editorial Assistant: Amanda Foxworth

Cartoons: Rich Tennant, www.the5thwave.com

Production

Project Coordinator: Maridee Ennis

Layout and Graphics: Carrie Foster, Joyce Haughey, Stephanie D. Jumper, Michael Kruzil, Julie Trippetti

Proofreaders: Andy Hollandbeck, TECHBOOKS Production Services

Indexer: TECHBOOKS Production Services

Publishing and Editorial for Technology Dummies

    Richard Swadley, Vice President and Executive Group Publisher

    Andy Cummings, Vice President and Publisher

    Mary C. Corder, Editorial Director

Publishing for Consumer Dummies

    Diane Graves Steele, Vice President and Publisher

    Joyce Pepple, Acquisitions Director

Composition Services

    Gerry Fahey, Vice President of Production Services

    Debbie Stailey, Director of Composition Services

Contents at a Glance

Table of Contents

Introduction

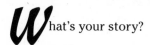hat's your story?

- ✔ Are you a working stiff, interested in knowing more about the way your company's computers work?
- ✔ Are you a student who needs some extra reading in order to survive a beginning computer course?
- ✔ Are you a typical computer user — you've done lots of word processing, and you want to do something more interesting with your computer?
- ✔ Are you a job seeker with an interest in entering the fast-paced, glamorous, high-profile world of computer programming (or at least, the decent-paying world of computer programming)?

Well, if you want to write computer programs, then this book is for you. This book avoids the snobby "of-course-you-already-know" assumptions, describing computer programming from scratch.

The book uses Java — an exciting, relatively new computer programming language. But Java's subtleties and eccentricities aren't the book's main focus. Instead, this book emphasizes a process — the process of creating instructions for a computer to follow. Many highfalutin' books describe the mechanics of this process — the rules, the conventions, and the formalisms. But those other books aren't written for real people. Those books don't take you from where you are to where you want to be.

In this book, I assume very little about your experience with computers. As you read each section, you get to see inside my head. You see the problems that I face, the things that I think, and the solutions that I find. Some problems are the kind that I remember facing when I was a novice; other problems are the kind that I face as an expert. I help you understand, I help you visualize, and I help you create solutions on your own. I even get to tell a few funny stories.

How to Use This Book

I wish I could say, "Open to a random page of this book and start writing Java code. Just fill in the blanks and don't look back." In a sense, this is true. You can't break anything by writing Java code, so you're always free to experiment.

But I have to be honest. If you don't understand the bigger picture, writing a program is difficult. That's true with any computer programming language — not just Java. If you're typing code without knowing what it's about, and the code doesn't do exactly what you want it to do, then you're just plain stuck.

So in this book, I divide programming into manageable chunks. Each chunk is (more or less) a chapter. You can jump in anywhere you want — Chapter 5, Chapter 10, or wherever. You can even start by poking around in the middle of a chapter. I've tried to make the examples interesting without making one chapter depend on another. When I use an important idea from another chapter, I include a note to help you find your way around.

In general, my advice is as follows:

- ✔ If you already know something, don't bother reading about it.

- ✔ If you're curious, don't be afraid to skip ahead. You can always sneak a peek at an earlier chapter if you really need to do so.

Conventions Used in This Book

Almost every technical book starts with a little typeface legend, and *Beginning Programming with Java For Dummies* is no exception. What follows is a brief explanation of the typefaces used in this book:

- ✔ New terms are set in *italics*.

- ✔ When I want you to type something short or perform a step, I use **bold.**

- ✔ You'll also see this `computerese` font. I use the computerese font for Java code, filenames, Web page addresses (URLs), on-screen messages, and other such things. Also, if something you need to type is really long, it appears in computerese font on its own line (or lines).

- ✔ You need to change certain things when you type them on your own computer keyboard. For instance, I may ask you to type

```
class Anyname
```

which means you should type **class** and then some name that you make up on you own. Words that you need to replace with your own words are set in *italicized computerese*.

What You Don't Have to Read

Pick the first chapter or section that has material you don't already know and start reading there. Of course, you may hate making decisions as much as I do. If so, here are some guidelines you can follow:

- ✔ If you already know what computer programming is all about, then skip Chapter 1 and go straight to Chapter 2. Believe me, I won't mind.

- ✔ If your computer has a Java compiler, then you can skip to Chapter 3. To find out if you have a Java compiler, look on your computer for a file named `javac` or `javac.exe`. If it's there, you'll probably find it in a directory named `bin`, and you'll find `bin` in a directory named `j2sdk`, `jdk`, or something like that.

  If, after fishing around a bit, you don't find a `javac` file, then you probably don't have a Java compiler. Even if you find `java.exe` and not `javac.exe`, then you don't have a Java compiler. In this case, you need the sage advice that I offer in Chapter 2.

- ✔ If you've already done a little computer programming, be prepared to skim Chapters 6 through 8. Dive fully into Chapter 9, and see if it feels comfortable. (If so, then read on. If not, re-skim Chapters 6, 7, and 8.)

- ✔ If you feel comfortable writing programs in a language other than Java, then this book isn't for you. Keep this book as a memento, and buy my *Java 2 For Dummies* book, published by Wiley Publishing, Inc.

If you want to skip the sidebars and the Technical Stuff icons, then please do. In fact, if you want to skip anything at all, feel free.

Foolish Assumptions

In this book, I make a few assumptions about you, the reader. If one of these assumptions is incorrect, then you're probably okay. If all these assumptions are incorrect . . . well, buy the book anyway.

- ✔ **I assume that you have access to a computer.** Here's good news. You can run the code in this book on almost any computer. The only computers you can't use to run this code are ancient things that are more than eight years old (give or take a few years). Occasionally, I'm lazy and lapse into Microsoft Windows terminology, but that's only because so many people run Windows.

Java's so versatile that it runs on just about anything — it even runs on PDAs and some household appliances. In Chapter 2, you can find instructions for downloading Java onto your favorite machine.

- ✔ **I assume that you can navigate through your computer's common menus and dialog boxes.** You don't have to be a Windows, Unix, or Macintosh power user, but you should be able to start a program, find a file, put a file into a certain directory . . . that sort of thing. Most of the time, when you practice the stuff in this book, you're typing code on your keyboard, not pointing and clicking your mouse.

  On those rare occasions when you need to drag and drop, cut and paste, or plug and play, I guide you carefully through the steps. But your computer may be configured in any of several billion ways, and my instructions may not quite fit your special situation. So when you reach one of these platform-specific tasks, try following the steps in this book. If the steps don't quite fit, send me an e-mail message, or consult a book with instructions tailored to your system.

- ✔ **I assume that you can think logically.** That's all there is to computer programming — thinking logically. If you can think logically, then you've got it made. If you don't believe that you can think logically, then read on. You may be pleasantly surprised.

- ✔ **I assume that you know little or nothing about computer programming.** This isn't one of those "all things to all people" books. I don't please the novice while I tease the expert. I aim this book specifically toward the novice — the person who has never programmed a computer, or has never felt comfortable programming a computer. If you're one of these people, then you're reading the right book.

How This Book Is Organized

This book is divided into subsections, which are grouped into sections, which come together to make chapters, which are lumped finally into five parts. (When you write a book, you get to know your book's structure pretty well. After months of writing, you find yourself dreaming in sections and chapters when you go to bed at night.) The parts of the book are listed here.

Part 1: Revving Up

The chapters in Part I prepare you for the overall programming experience. In these chapters, you find out what programming is all about and get your computer ready for writing and testing programs.

Part II: Writing Your Own Java Programs

This part covers the basic building blocks — the elements in any Java program, and in any program written using a Java-like language. In this part, you discover how to represent data, and how to get new values from existing values. The program examples are short, but cute.

Part III: Controlling the Flow

Part III has some of my favorite chapters. In these chapters, you make the computer navigate from one part of your program to another. Think of your program as a big mansion, with the computer moving from room to room. Sometimes the computer chooses between two or more hallways, and sometimes the computer revisits rooms. As a programmer, your job is to plan the computer's rounds through the mansion. It's great fun.

Part IV: Using Program Units

Have you ever solved a big problem by breaking it into smaller, more manageable pieces? That's exactly what you do in Part IV of this book. You discover the best ways to break programming problems into pieces and to create solutions for the newly found pieces. You also find out how to use other people's solutions. It feels like stealing, but it's not.

This part also contains a chapter about programming with windows, buttons, and other graphical items. If your mouse feels ignored by the examples in this book, then read Chapter 20.

Part V: The Part of Tens

The Part of Tens is a little beginning programmer's candy store. In the Part of Tens, you can find lists — lists of tips, resources, and all kinds of interesting goodies.

At the end of the Part of Tens is this book's Appendix. I wrote the appendix to help you feel comfortable with Java's documentation. I can't write programs without my Java programming documentation. In fact, no Java programmer can write programs without those all-important docs. These docs are in Web page format, so they're easy to find and easy to navigate. But if you're not used to all the terminology, the documentation can be overwhelming.

Icons Used in This Book

If you could watch me write this book, you'd see me sitting at my computer, talking to myself. I say each sentence several times in my head. When I have an extra thought, a side comment, something that doesn't belong in the regular stream, I twist my head a little bit. That way, whoever's listening to me (usually nobody) knows that I'm off on a momentary tangent.

Of course, in print, you can't see me twisting my head. I need some other way of setting a side thought in a corner by itself. I do it with icons. When you see a Tip icon or a Remember icon, you know that I'm taking a quick detour.

Here's a list of icons that I use in this book.

A tip is an extra piece of information — something helpful that the other books may forget to tell you.

Everyone makes mistakes. Heaven knows that I've made a few in my time. Anyway, when I think of a mistake that people are especially prone to make, I write about the mistake in a Warning icon.

Question: What's stronger than a Tip, but not at strong as a Warning? *Answer:* A Remember icon.

Occasionally, I run across a technical tidbit. The tidbit may help you understand what the people behind the scenes (the people who developed Java) were thinking. You don't have to read it, but you may find it useful. You may also find the tidbit helpful if you plan to read other (more geeky) books about Java.

I know the feeling. When I come to a concept that I don't remember reading about, I get a little cramp in my stomach. Then I remember that no one remembers everything they read (and absolutely no one remembers something that they've skipped over).

If I write a paragraph, and I think an idea in the paragraph may give you a little stomach cramp, I help buffer your pain with a Cross-Reference icon. The Cross-Reference icon tells you which chapter explains that little, cramp-worthy idea.

Where to Go from Here

If you've gotten this far, then you're ready to start reading about computer programming. Think of me (the author) as your guide, your host, your personal assistant. I do everything I can to keep things interesting and, most importantly, help you understand. If you like what you read, then send me a note. My e-mail address, which I created just for comments and questions about this book, is BeginProg@BurdBrain.com.

Part I
Revving Up

"CAREFUL SUNDANCE, THIS ONE'S BEEN LOCKED UP AND FORCED TO BETA-TEST POORLY DOCUMENTED SOFTWARE PRODUCTS ALLLL WEEK AND HE'S ITCHING FOR A FIGHT."

In this part . . .

You have to eat before you can cook. You have to wear before you can sew. You have to ride before you can drive. And you have to run computer programs before you can write computer programs.

In this part of the book, you run computer programs.

Chapter 1

Getting Started

Computer programming? What's that? Is it technical? Does it hurt? Is it politically correct? Does Bill Gates control it? Why would anyone want to do it? And what about me? Can I learn to do it?

What's It All About?

You've probably used a computer to do word processing. Type a letter, print it out, and then send the printout to someone you love. If you have easy access to a computer, then you've probably surfed the Web. Visit a page, click a link, and see another page. It's easy, right?

Well, it's easy only because someone told the computer exactly what to do. If you take a computer right from the factory and give no instructions to this computer, then the computer can't do word processing, the computer can't surf the Web, it can't do anything. All a computer can do is follow the instructions that people give to it.

Now imagine that you're using Microsoft Word to write the great American novel, and you come to the end of a line. (You're not at the end of a sentence, just the end of a line.) As you type the next word, the computer's cursor jumps automatically to the next line of type. What's going on here?

Well, someone wrote a *computer program* — a set of instructions telling the computer what to do. Another name for a program (or part of a program) is *code*. Listing 1-1 shows you what some of Microsoft Word's code may look like.

Listing 1-1   A Few Lines in a Computer Program

```
if (columnNumber > 60)
    wrapToNextLine();
else
    continueSameLine();
```

If you translate Listing 1-1 into plain English, you get something like this:

```
If the column number is greater than 60,
    then go to the next line.
Otherwise (if the column number isn't greater than 60),
    then stay on the same line.
```

Somebody has to write code of the kind shown in Listing 1-1. This code, along with millions of other lines of code, makes up the program called Microsoft Word.

And what about Web surfing? You click a link that's supposed to take you directly to Yahoo.com. Behind the scenes, someone has written code of the following kind:

```
Go to <a href=http://www.yahoo.com>Yahoo</a>.
```

One way or another, someone has to write a program. That someone is called a *programmer.*

Telling a computer what to do

Everything you do with a computer involves gobs and gobs of code. Take a CD-ROM with a computer game on it. It's really a CD-ROM full of code. At some point, someone had to write the game program,:

```
if (person.touches(goldenRing))
    person.getPoints(10);
```

Without a doubt, the people who write programs have valuable skills. These people have two important qualities:

✔ They know how to break big problems into smaller step-by-step procedures.

✔ They can express these steps in a very precise language.

A language for writing steps is called a *programming language,* and Java is just one of several thousand useful programming languages. The stuff in Listing 1-1 is written in the Java programming language.

Pick your poison

This book isn't about the differences among programming languages, but you should see code in some other languages so you understand the bigger picture. For instance, there's another language, named Visual Basic, whose code looks a bit different from code written in Java. An excerpt from a Visual Basic program may look like this:

```
If columnNumber > 60 Then
    Call wrapToNextLine
Else
    Call continueSameLine
End If
```

The Visual Basic code looks more like ordinary English than the Java code in Listing 1-1. But, if you think that Visual Basic is like English, then just look at some code written in COBOL:

```
IF COLUMN-NUMBER IS GREATER THAN 60 THEN
    PERFORM WRAP-TO-NEXT-LINE
ELSE
    PERFORM CONTINUE-SAME-LINE
END-IF.
```

At the other end of the spectrum, you find languages like ISETL. Here's a short ISETL program, along with the program's output:

```
{x | x in {0..100} | (exists y in {0..10} | y**2=x)};
{81, 64, 100, 16, 25, 36, 49, 4, 9, 0, 1};
```

Computer languages can be very different from one another but, in some ways, they're all the same. When you get used to writing IF COLUMN-NUMBER IS GREATER THAN 60, then you can also become comfortable writing if (columnNumber > 60). It's just a mental substitution of one set of symbols for another.

From Your Mind to the Computer's Processor

When you create a new computer program, you go through a multistep process. The process involves three important tools:

✔ **Compiler:** A compiler translates your code into computer-friendly (human-unfriendly) instructions.

✔ **Virtual machine:** A virtual machine steps through the computer-friendly instructions.

✔ **Application programming interface:** An application programming interface contains useful prewritten code.

The next three sections describe each of the three tools.

Translating your code

You may have heard that computers deal with zeros and ones. That's certainly true, but what does it mean? Well, for starters, computer circuits don't deal directly with letters of the alphabet. When you see the word *Start* on your computer screen, the computer stores the word internally as 01010011 01110100 01100001 01110010 01110100. That feeling you get of seeing a friendly looking five-letter word is your interpretation of the computer screen's pixels, and nothing more. Computers break everything down into very low-level, unfriendly sequences of zeros and ones, and then put things back together so that humans can deal with the results.

So what happens when you write a computer program? Well, the program has to get translated into zeros and ones. The official name for the translation process is *compilation*. Without compilation, the computer can't run your program.

I compiled the code in Listing 1-1. Then I did some harmless hacking to help me see the resulting zeros and ones. What I saw was the mishmash in Figure 1-1.

Figure 1-1:
My
computer
understands
these zeros
and ones,
but I don't.

```
11001010 11111110 10111010 10111110 00000000 00000000
00000000 00101110 00000000 00010101 00001010 00000000
00000101 00000000 00010000 00001010 00000000 00000100
00000000 00010001 00001010 00000000 00000100 00000000
00010010 00000111 00000000 00010011 00000111 00000000
00010100 00000001 00000000 00000110 00111100 01101001
01101110 01101001 01110100 00111110 00000001 00000000
00000011 00101000 00101001 01010110 00000001 00000000
00000100 01000001 01101111 01100010 01100101 00000001
00000000 00001111 01001100 01101001 01101110 01100101
01001110 01110101 01101101 01100010 01100101 01110010
01010100 01100001 01100010 01101100 01100101 00000001
00000000 00001011 01100100 01101001 01110011 01110000
01101100 01100001 01111001 01010111 01101111 01110010
01100100 00000001 00000000 00000100 00101000 01001001
00101001 01010110 00000001 00000110 01101110 01101111
01110010 01100001 01110000 01010100 01101111 01101110
01100101 01111000 01110100 01001100 01101001 01101110
01100101 00000001 00000000 01101110 01100110 01101111
01101110 01110100 01101001 01101110 01110101 01100101
01010011 01100001 01101101 01100101 01001100 01101001
01101110 01100101 00000001 00000000 00001010 01010011
01101111 01111101 01110010 01100011 01100101 01000110
```

The compiled mumbo jumbo in Figure 1-1 goes by many different names:

✔ Most Java programmers call it *bytecode.*

✔ I often call it a *.class file.* That's because, in Java, the bytecode gets stored in files named *SomethingOrOther*.class.

✔ To emphasize the difference, Java programmers call Listing 1-1 the *source code,* and refer to the zeros and ones in Figure 1-1 as *object code.*

To visualize the relationship between source code and object code, see Figure 1-2. You can write source code, and then get the computer to create object code from your source code. To create object code, the computer uses a special software tool called a *compiler.*

Figure 1-2:
The
computer
compiles
source code
to create
object code.

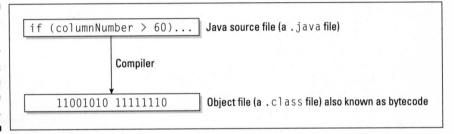

```
if (columnNumber > 60)...
```
Java source file (a .java file)

Compiler

```
11001010 11111110
```
Object file (a .class file) also known as bytecode

Your computer's hard drive may have a file named javac or javac.exe. This file contains that special software tool — the compiler. (Hey, how about that? The word javac stands for "Java compiler!") To build some new object code, you get your computer to run the instructions in the javac file. (For more concrete details, see Chapter 3.)

Running code

Several years ago, I spent a week in Copenhagen. I hung out with a friend who spoke both Danish and English fluently. As we chatted in the public park, I vaguely noticed some kids orbiting around us. I don't speak a word of Danish, so I assumed that the kids were talking about ordinary kids' stuff.

Then my friend told me that the kids weren't speaking Danish. "What language are they speaking?" I asked.

"They're talking gibberish," she said. "It's just nonsense syllables. They don't understand English, so they're imitating you."

Now to return to present day matters. I look at the stuff in Figure 1-1, and I'm tempted to make fun of the way my computer talks. But then I'd be just like the kids in Copenhagen. What's meaningless to me can make perfect sense to my computer. When the zeros and ones in Figure 1-1 percolate through my computer's circuits, the computer "thinks" the thoughts in Figure 1-3.

Everyone knows that computers don't think, but a computer can carry out the instructions depicted in Figure 1-4. With many programming languages (languages like C++ and COBOL, for instance), a computer does exactly what I'm describing. A computer gobbles up some object code, and does whatever the object code says to do.

That's how it works in many programming languages, but that's not how it works in Java. With Java, the computer executes a different set of instructions. The computer executes instructions like the ones in Figure 1-4.

The instructions in Figure 1-4 tell the computer how to follow other instructions. Instead of starting with `Get columnNumber from memory`, the computer's first instruction is, "Do what it says to do in the bytecode file." (Of course, in the bytecode file, the first instruction happens to be `Get columnNumber from memory`.)

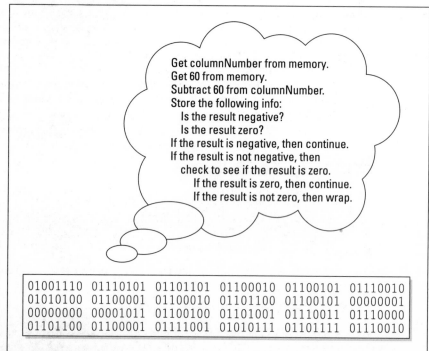

Figure 1-3:
What the computer gleans from a bytecode file.

Get columnNumber from memory.
Get 60 from memory.
Subtract 60 from columnNumber.
Store the following info:
    Is the result negative?
    Is the result zero?
If the result is negative, then continue.
If the result is not negative, then
    check to see if the result is zero.
        If the result is zero, then continue.
        If the result is not zero, then wrap.

```
01001110  01110101  01101101  01100010  01100101  01110010
01010100  01100001  01100010  01101100  01100101  00000001
00000000  00001011  01100100  01101001  01110011  01110000
01101100  01100001  01111001  01010111  01101111  01110010
```

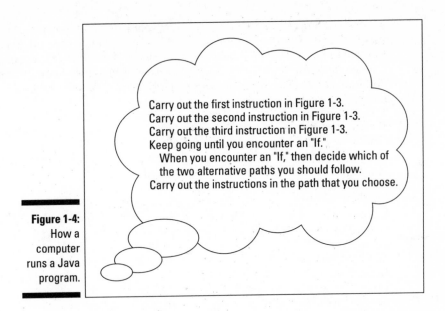

Figure 1-4:
How a
computer
runs a Java
program.

There's a special piece of software that carries out the instructions in Figure 1-4. That special piece of software is called the *Java Virtual Machine* (JVM). The JVM walks your computer through the execution of some byte-code instructions. When you run a Java program, your computer is really running the Java Virtual Machine. That JVM examines your bytecode, zero by zero, one by one, and carries out the instructions described in the bytecode.

Many good metaphors can describe the Java Virtual Machine. Think of the JVM as a proxy, an errand boy, a go-between. One way or another, you have the situation shown in Figure 1-5. On the (a) side is the story you get with most programming languages — the computer runs some object code. On the (b) side is the story with Java — the computer runs the JVM, and the JVM follows the bytecode's instructions.

Your computer's hard drive may have a file named `java` or `java.exe`. This file contains the instructions illustrated previously in Figure 1-4 — the instructions in the Java Virtual Machine. To set a Java program in motion, you command your computer to run the instructions in the `java` file. (For more concrete details, see Chapter 3.)

Code you can use

During the early 1980s, my cousin-in-law Chris worked for a computer software firm. The firm wrote code for word processing machines. (At the time, if you wanted to compose documents without a typewriter, you bought a "computer" that did nothing but word processing.) Chris complained about being asked to write the same old code over and over again. "First, I write a search-and-replace program. Then I write a spell checker. Then I write another search-and-replace program. Then, a different kind of spell checker. And then, a better search-and-replace."

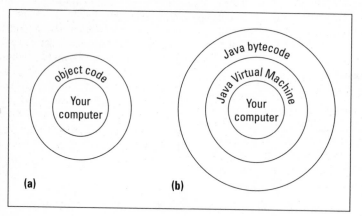

Figure 1-5:
Two ways
to run a
computer
program.

How did Chris manage to stay interested in his work? And how did Chris's employer manage to stay in business? Every few months, Chris had to reinvent the wheel. Toss out the old search-and-replace program, and write a new program from scratch. That's inefficient. What's worse, it's boring.

For years, computer professionals were seeking the Holy Grail — a way to write software so that it's easy to reuse. Don't write and rewrite your search-and-replace code. Just break the task into tiny pieces. One piece searches for a single character, another piece looks for blank spaces, a third piece substitutes one letter for another. When you have all the pieces, just assemble these pieces to form a search-and-replace program. Later on, when you think of a new feature for your word processing software, you reassemble the pieces in a slightly different way. It's sensible, it's cost efficient, and it's much more fun.

The late 1980s saw several advances in software development, and by the early 1990s, many large programming projects were being written from prefab components. Java came along in 1995, so it was natural for the language's founders to create a library of reusable code. The library included about 250 programs, including code for dealing with disk files, code for creating windows, and code for passing information over the Internet. Since 1995, this library has grown to include more than 2,700 programs. This library is called the *API* — the *Application Programming Interface*.

What is bytecode, anyway?

Look at Listing 1-1, and at the listing's translation into bytecode in Figure 1-1. You may be tempted to think that a bytecode file is just a cryptogram — substituting zeros and ones for the letters in words like if and else. But it doesn't work that way at all. In fact, the most important part of a bytecode file is the encoding of a program's logic.

The zeros and ones in Figure 1-1 describe the flow of data from one part of your computer to another. I've illustrated this flow in the following figure. But remember, this figure is just an illustration. Your computer doesn't look at this particular figure, or at anything like it. Instead, your computer reads a bunch of zeros and ones to decide what to do next.

Don't bother to absorb the details in my attempt at graphical representation in the figure. It's not worth your time. The thing you should glean from my mix of text, boxes, and arrows is that bytecode (the stuff in a .class file) contains a complete description of the operations that the computer is to perform. When you write a computer program, your source code describes an overall strategy — a big picture. The compiled bytecode turns the overall strategy into hundreds of tiny, step-by-step details. When the computer "runs your program," the computer examines this bytecode and carries out each of the little step-by-step details.

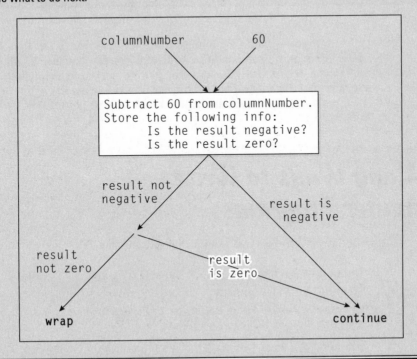

Write Once, Run Anywhere™

When Java first hit the tech scene in 1995, the language became popular almost immediately. This happened in part because of the Java Virtual Machine. The JVM is like a foreign language interpreter, turning Java bytecode into whatever native language a particular computer understands. So if you hand my Windows computer a Java bytecode file, then the computer's JVM interprets the file for the Windows environment. If you hand the same Java bytecode file to my colleague's Macintosh, then the Macintosh JVM interprets that same bytecode for the Mac environment.

Look again at Figure 1-5. Without a virtual machine, you need a different kind of object code for each operating system. But with the JVM, just one piece of bytecode works on Windows machines, Unix boxes, Macs, or whatever. This is called *portability*, and in the computer programming world, portability is a very precious commodity. Think about all the people using computers to browse the Internet. These people don't all run Microsoft Windows, but each person's computer can have its own bytecode interpreter — its own Java Virtual Machine.

The marketing folks at Sun Microsystems call it the *Write Once, Run Anywhere*™ model of computing. I call it a great way to create software.

Every Java program, even the simplest one, calls on code in the Java API. This Java API is both useful and formidable. It's useful because of all the things you can do with the API's programs. It's formidable because the API is so extensive. No one memorizes all the features made available by the Java API. Programmers remember the features that they use often, and look up the features that they need in a pinch.

So Many Ways to Write Computer Programs

To write Java programs, you need three tools:

- ✔ **You need a Java compiler.** (See the section entitled, "Translating your code.")

- ✔ **You need a Java Virtual Machine.** (See the section entitled, "Running code.")

- ✔ **You need the Java API.** (See the section entitled, "Code you can use.")

You have at least two ways to get these tools:

- ✔ **You can download these tools from the Sun Microsystems Web site.**

  Chapter 2 has all the details.

✔ **You can use the tools that come with a commercial product.**

If you own a copy of Borland JBuilder, Metrowerks CodeWarrior, IBM Visual Age for Java, or IBM WebSphere Studio Application Developer (WSAD), then you already have the tools that you need.

In this book, most of the step-by-step instructions assume that you've taken the first alternative — that you've downloaded the tools from the Sun Microsystems Web site. (In fact, Chapter 2 tells you exactly how to download and install these tools.) Why have I written the book this way? Well, I considered a few factors (both pro and con):

✔ **The download from Sun Microsystems is free.** Products like JBuilder, CodeWarrior, and WSAD are not free.

✔ **The download from Sun Microsystems comes with no fancy development tools.** When you type a program, you use any old text editor. (You use Windows Notepad, for instance.) Then, to run a Java program, you type a command. How crude!

In contrast, a product like JBuilder or WSAD is called an *integrated development environment (IDE)*. An IDE provides point-and-click, drag-and-drop, plug-and-play, hop-skip-and-jump access to your Java programs. If you want your program to display a text box, then you click a text box icon and drag it to the workspace on your screen, as shown in Figure 1-6.

With JBuilder and WSAD, you touch the keyboard as little as possible. You do much of your work with the mouse. But . . .

✔ **Unlike the download from Sun Microsystems, the tools in JBuilder and WSAD require their own sets of skills.** Figuring out how to use an IDE involves some special tricks, and these tricks can distract you from the main goal — the goal of learning to write computer programs.

So that settles it. The program examples (the listings) in this book work with almost any collection of Java tools, including Sun's version, JBuilder, CodeWarrior, and WSAD. But when you read an instruction about pressing a key, or opening a window, the instruction works with the simple, no-frills software that you can get for free from Sun Microsystems.

Two bags of goodies

Sun's Web site bundles the basic Java tools in two different ways:

✔ **The Java Runtime Environment (JRE):** This bundle includes a Java Virtual Machine and the Application Programming Interface. With the JRE, you can run existing Java programs. That's all. You can't create new Java programs, because you don't have a Java compiler.

✔ **The Software Development Kit (SDK):** This bundle includes all three tools — a Java compiler, a Java Virtual Machine, and the Application Programming Interface. With the SDK, you can create and run your own Java programs.

For specifics on downloading the SDK, see Chapter 2.

An older name for the Java SDK is the *JDK* — the *Java Development Kit.* Some people still use the JDK acronym, even though the folks at Sun Microsystems don't use it anymore. I confess, though time has passed, I still speak of the JDK.

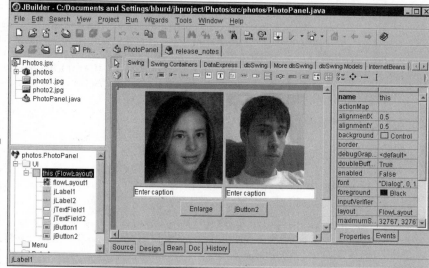

Figure 1-6:
The JBuilder integrated development environment.

How do you type this stuff?

A computer program is a big piece of text. So to write a computer program, you need a *text editor* — a tool for creating text documents. A text editor is a lot like Microsoft Word, or like any other word processing program. The big difference is that the documents that you create with a text editor have no formatting whatsoever. They have no bold, no italic, no distinctions among fonts. They have nothing except plain old letters, numbers, and other familiar keyboard characters. That's good, because computer programs aren't supposed to have any formatting.

A document with no formatting is called a *plain text* document.

I try not to be a Windows chauvinist, but I tend to think in terms of Windows operating environment. So this book has plenty of Windows-centric sentences. "Open an ordinary text editor — an editor like Windows Notepad." If you're a Unix, Linux, or Macintosh user, then please don't be offended. All the material in this book applies to you, too. You just have to use a different text editor. If you're a Mac user, you can use SimpleText or TextEdit. If you're a Linux buff, you can use KWrite. If you're a rough and tough Unix user then, by all means, use Emacs or vi. Have a ball!

Documents without formatting are fairly simple things, so a typical text editor is easier to use than a word processing program. (Text editors are a lot cheaper than word processing programs, and they're lightning fast. Even better, text editors take very little space on your hard drive.)

You can use a word processor, like Microsoft Word, to create program files. But, by default, word processors insert formatting into your document. This formatting makes it impossible for a Java compiler to do its job. I don't recommend using word processors to write Java programs. But, if you must use a word processor, be sure to save your source files with the .java extension. (Call a file *SomeName*.java.) Remember, also, to use the Save As command to save with the plain text file type.

Using a customized editor

Even if you don't use an integrated development environment, you can use other tools to make your programming life easy. Think, for a moment, about an ordinary text editor — an editor like Windows Notepad. With Notepad you can

- ✔ Create a document that has no formatting
- ✔ Find and replace characters, words, and other strings
- ✔ Copy, cut, and paste
- ✔ Print
- ✔ Not much else

Notepad is fine for writing computer programs. But if you plan to do a lot of programming, you may want to try a customized editor. These editors do more than Windows Notepad. They have

- ✔ Syntax highlighting
- ✔ Shortcuts for compiling and running programs
- ✔ Explorer-like views of your works in progress
- ✔ Code completion
- ✔ Other cool stuff

When it comes to choosing a custom editor, my two favorites are JCreator (www.jcreator.com) and TextPad (www.textpad.com). JCreator has lots of cool features, including tools to write some boilerplate Java code, as shown in Figure 1-7. TextPad has fewer Java-specific features, but TextPad is a great general-purpose text editor.

In the next chapter, you get off to a running start. You install a Java compiler on your computer. Get ready, get set, go!

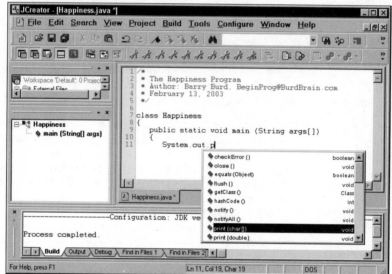

Figure 1-7:
Using
JCreator to
create Java
programs.

Chapter 2

Setting Up Your Computer

••

In This Chapter

▶ Downloading the Java compiler

▶ Installing the Java compiler

▶ Configuring your computer to run Java programs

••

You've arrived home, fresh from your local computer store. You have a brightly colored box (a box with software in it). You tear open the box, take out a CD-ROM, and put the CD-ROM into your computer. In a few minutes (or maybe a few hours), you're off and running. The software is installed and you're typing your heart out. This scenario is typical for software that you buy at your neighborhood computer store.

But what about the software you need to begin writing your own computer programs? This book tells you how to write Java programs, but before you can write Java programs, you need two pieces of software. You need a Java compiler and a Java Virtual Machine (JVM, for short). You can get this software in a brightly colored box, but it's easier (and cheaper) to download the software from the Sun Microsystems Web site at `java.sun.com`. In fact, the Java compiler and the JVM from Sun Microsystems are free. They come as one download, called the Java Software Development Kit (the Java SDK). Who needs another brightly colored box anyway?

Should You Skip This Chapter?

Chapter 1 describes two ways to write Java programs:

✔ You can use an integrated development environment (an IDE).

✔ You can use Sun's freely downloadable Java SDK.

If you're using a fancy integrated development environment, like JBuilder, WSAD, or CodeWarrior, then you don't need to download anything from Sun's Web site. You can skip this whole chapter, because your development environment has its own particular menus and procedures.

Of course, there's another reason why you may not need to visit Sun's Web site. You may be working with a computer that already has Sun's Java SDK. If so (and if your version of the SDK isn't very, very old), then you probably don't need to download the SDK again. (SDK version 1.2 or higher is just fine. You can work with earlier SDK versions, but if you do, some programs in this book may need to be tweaked a bit.)

The numbering of Java's SDK versions is really confusing. First comes "JDK 1.0," then "JDK 1.1," then "Java 2 SDK 1.2," "Java 2 SDK 1.3," and "Java 2 SDK 1.4." Yes, the "Java 2" numbering overlaps partially with the "1.x" numbering. That's what happens when you let marketing people call the shots.

Here are some ways to find out if your computer has Sun's SDK on it:

✔ Poke around for a directory named `jdk-something` or `j2sdk-such-and-such`.

✔ Search for a file named `javac`. If you find such a thing, it should be in a directory named `bin`. The `bin` directory has other files with names like `java`, `javah`, `javap`, and `javaw` in it. (There's no `javaj` file, but they're working on it.)

✔ Jump to the section about compiling and running a program in Chapter 3. See if the steps outlined in that section work on your computer. If they all work, including the `javac` step (Step 3), then your computer already has a Java compiler on it. You can skip this whole chapter.

Seeing the word "Java" on your computer screen doesn't guarantee that your computer has the required SDK. Most computers have all the software they need for running existing Java programs. What you need is the software for creating brand new Java programs.

Downloading the Software You Need

You can download the Java SDK from the Sun Microsystems Web site. Just follow these steps:

1. **Visit** `java.sun.com`.

2. **Poke around for a J2SE download page.**

   The folks who design the Sun Microsystems Web site keep changing things around. Last month, I had to click four links. But this month, I can get close to the correct page by finding a Popular Downloads box and clicking a <u>J2SE 1.4.1</u> link inside that box. Oddly enough, clicking this link doesn't take me straight to the J2SE download page. I still have to click a link that's labeled <u>Download J2SE 1.4.1 Now</u>. When all is said and done, I'm at a page with address `java.sun.com/j2se/1.4.1/download.html`.

In addition to numbers like 1.4.1, you may also see version numbers, such as 1.3.1 and 1.4.1_01. You want the highest J2SE version number that's available at the Web site.

The acronym J2SE stands for Java 2 Standard Edition. Avoid the J2EE (Java 2 Enterprise Edition), unless you know something about the Enterprise Edition and you have a special reason for downloading it.

3. Click the link corresponding to your computer's operating environment (your computer's operating system).

You may find yourself on a page with a big table full of links. The table's headings include rows like Windows (All Languages, Including English), and columns like JRE and SDK. Most people want to click the <u>Download</u> link in the Windows (All Languages, Including English) row and the SDK column, but some people run Java on non-Windows machines. Either way, click a link in the SDK column, not in the JRE column.

Sun's regular J2SE page has links for Windows, Linux, and Solaris users. If your favorite operating environment isn't Windows, Linux, or Solaris, don't despair. Visit `java.sun.com/cgi-bin/java-ports.cgi` for a list of vendors who have converted Java to other environments. If you're a Macintosh user, go straight to `developer.apple.com/java`, and make sure you download the MRJ SDK.

When you click a particular download link, you're taken to the ever-present license agreement page.

4. Do whatever you normally do with license agreements.

I'm not advising that you click the ACCEPT button without reading the license agreement. Of course, I've downloaded the SDK at least a hundred times, and I've never read the Sun license agreement. It's okay. I searched the agreement's text for the phrase "take your firstborn," and I found no such wording.

5. Click the ACCEPT button to start the download.

As you begin downloading the software, note the directory on your hard drive where the software is being deposited.

6. Find a link to the API documentation for the version of Java that you just downloaded.

As a Java programmer, you won't survive without a copy of the API documentation by your side. You can bookmark the documentation at the Sun Microsystems Web site and revisit the site whenever you need to look up something. But in the long run (and in the not-so-long run), you can save time by downloading your own copy of the API docs.

The way the Sun Microsystems Web site is currently set up, it's not too hard to find the API documentation. In fact, the download links for the Java SDK and the Java API documentation are on the same page. This may not be true by the time you read *Beginning Programming with Java For Dummies,* but it's certainly true while I'm writing this book.

The download page has a big table with the words Download J2SE v 1.4.1 on it. Scroll down in the table, and you find a J2SE 1.4.1 Documentation heading with an option to download the docs.

A language like Java comes with many sets of docs. The documentation that you want is called the "API documentation," or the "J2SE documentation." If you see links to the "Java Language Specification" or the "Java Virtual Machine Specification," then ignore these links for now.

7. Download the API documentation.

The API docs are in Web-page format. After you've downloaded the docs, you can view them with your favorite Web browser.

Reading and understanding Java's API documentation is an art, not a science. For tips on making the most of these docs, take a look at this book's Appendix.

Using a Command Prompt Window

In this book, I use the cheapest, the quickest, the most commonly available tools that I can find. I look at folks who use fancy integrated development environments and say, "Hey, whatever happened to typing commands and code?" You may not agree with me, and that's okay. If you like to use a handy drag-and-drop IDE tool, then please feel free to use it. But if you're big and tough like me, you can use your system's command prompt.

If you're not familiar with your system's command prompt window, you should check it out right away. Table 2-1 explains how.

Table 2-1	Finding Your System's Command Prompt Window
If Your Operating System Is	*Do This*
Windows 95 or 98	Choose Start⇨Programs⇨MS-DOS Prompt.
Windows 2000	Choose Start⇨Programs⇨Accessories⇨ Command Prompt.
Windows XP	Choose Start⇨All Programs⇨Accessories⇨ Command Prompt.
Windows Me	Choose Start⇨Programs⇨Accessories⇨ MS-DOS Prompt.
Windows NT	Choose Start⇨Programs⇨Command Prompt.

If Your Operating System Is	Do This
Linux	Click the icon that looks like a computer monitor.
Mac OS X	Run the Terminal application, which is in the Utilities folder. (The Utilities folder is inside the Applications folder.)
Mac Classic	(Sorry, the Macintosh Classic OS doesn't have a command prompt that's of much use for running Java programs. See the Macintosh-specific notes that appear later in this chapter.)

The command prompt window is a place where geeks type cryptic instructions for the computer to follow. For instance, instead of double-clicking the Outlook Express icon, you can go to your command prompt window and type the **msimn** command. When you do this, Outlook Express opens its own beautiful-looking window on your screen, as shown in Figure 2-1.

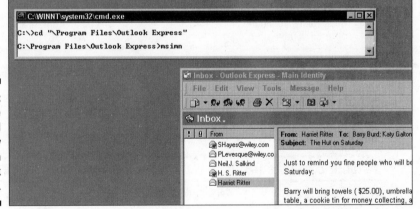

Figure 2-1:
Using the command window to open Outlook Express.

The test program that you run in Chapter 3 is very different from Outlook Express. The test program doesn't open its own window. While the program runs, anything you type appears in the command prompt window along with anything that the program displays, as shown in Figure 2-2. A program that operates completely in the command prompt window is called a *text-based program*. (In contrast, a program that displays windows on the screen uses a *GUI — a Graphical User Interface*.)

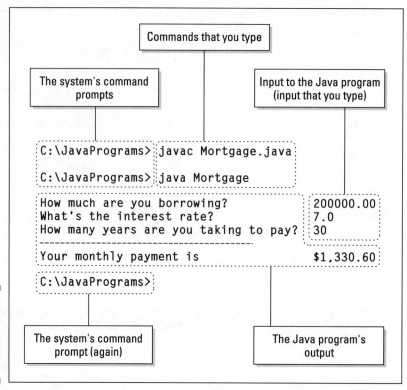

Figure 2-2:
Compiling
and running
a text-based
program.

Figure 2-2 contains four different kinds of text. I summarize these four flavors in Table 2-2.

Table 2-2	**Four Things You Find in a Command Prompt Window**	
	Communicating with the Computer's Operating System	**Communicating with Your Own Java Program**
Text That the Computer Displays for You	The system's command prompt	Output of your Java program
Text That You Type	Commands that you type	Input to your Java program

Here's a more thorough description of the four kinds of text:

✔ **The system's command prompt**

With the text `C:\JavaPrograms>`, the computer invites you (prompts you) to type a command.

✔ **Commands that you type**

By typing `javac Mortgage.java`, you command the system to compile the contents of your `Mortgage.java` file. Then, by typing `java Mortgage`, you command the system to run the compiled version of the `Mortgage` program.

✔ **Your input to the Java program (while the program runs)**

You feed information to the program while the program is running. In Figure 2-2, you type the numbers `200000.00`, `7.0`, and `30`.

For some other program, your input may consist of words rather than numbers, as shown in Figure 2-3. For a program that displays a window, your input may include all kinds of things, such as mouse clicks, voice dictation, and images from your hard drive.

✔ **The output of the Java program (while the program runs)**

While the program runs, the computer displays things such as `How much are you borrowing?` and `What's the interest rate?` Eventually, the computer displays a monthly payment amount, such as `$1,330.60`.

Figure 2-3:
A text
program
with non-
numeric
input.

```
C:\JavaPrograms>javac Authenticator.java
C:\JavaPrograms>java Authenticator
Username: bburd
Password: ******
Sorry, pal. You can't log in.
```

Throughout this book, I abuse some terminology. When I write about "the `javac` command in Figure 2-2," I'm on solid ground. But when I refer to a kind of command called "the `javac` command," I'm committing fraud. Neither `javac` nor `java` are built into the Windows or Unix systems. Both `javac` and `java` are things that you add to your computer's toolkit. So technically, Windows doesn't have special kinds of commands called the `javac` and `java` commands. It doesn't matter. I'll write about "the `javac` command" and "the `java` command" whenever I darn well feel like it. And I'll be in good company too. (Most authors slur the terminology this way.)

The system prompt in Figures 2-2 and 2-3 is `C:\JavaPrograms`. This means that `C:\JavaPrograms` is currently the *working directory*. The working directory is the first place where the computer looks for things that you type in your commands. For instance, in Figure 2-3, you tell the computer to compile the `Authenticator.java` file. Because `C:\JavaPrograms` is your working directory, the computer looks for `Authenticator.java` in the `C:\JavaPrograms` directory. (See Chapter 3 for more details about working directories.)

After you've made friends with the command prompt window, you're ready to work with the Java SDK.

Installing the Java SDK

On most systems, 99 percent of the work of installing the Java Software Development Kit (a.k.a. the Java SDK) is a breeze. Just explore to the directory where you downloaded the SDK and find the icon for the stuff that you downloaded. (It's the download that's described earlier in this chapter. The icon's name is probably `j2sdksomething-or-other`.) Then double-click the icon. This double-clicking opens up a wizard, which does most of the installation for you.

During the Java SDK installation, watch for the name of the directory in which the SDK is being installed. On my computer, that directory's name is `C:\j2sdk1.4.0`, but on your computer, the name may be slightly different. This directory called your *Java home* directory. (That's not too surprising. It's where the Java SDK lives on your computer.) Write down the directory's name, because you'll need that name for stuff that comes later in this chapter.

If you don't catch the Java home directory's name during the SDK installation, then search your computer's hard drive for something named `j2sdk` *something-or-other*. Write down the directory's name and keep the name in your back pocket.

When the install wizard is finished doing its thing, you should have a Java home directory and a *Java bin* directory. On your hard drive's folder tree, the Java bin directory comes directly underneath the Java home directory. (See Figure 2-4.) On my Windows computer, the Java bin directory's name is `C:\j2sdk1.4.0\bin`. On my Linux computer, the Java bin directory's name is `/usr/java/j2sdk1.4.1_01/bin`.

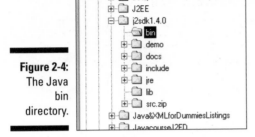

Figure 2-4:
The Java
bin
directory.

When the automated part of the installation is done, you have one lingering task to complete that's not always easy. You have to set your system's environment variables. In particular, you have to set the PATH and CLASSPATH. The next section tells you how to do it.

Tinkering with your system's environment variables

Every operating system stores certain items that are available all the time, no matter what you're doing, and no matter what program you happen to be running. Some of these items are called system-wide *environment variables*. Before you can write Java programs, two of these variables must have certain special values. The trouble is, the automatic Java SDK installation doesn't set these values for you. Instead, you have to set these values yourself.

The variables whose values you set are called the PATH and the CLASSPATH:

✔ The PATH tells the computer where to look for the Java compiler and the Java Virtual Machine.

✔ The CLASSPATH tells the compiler and the JVM where to look for all the Java programs that you write.

Here's what happens (a dramatization!) when you prepare to run a new Java program:

You: Computer, please compile my new Java program; it's named SomeProg.java.

Computer: Okay. To compile the program, I need to run the Java compiler. Where do you keep the Java compiler? I know . . . I'll look at the list of directories in my PATH variable. Hah! I found it.

You: (Saying nothing but waiting patiently. . . .)

Computer: Yo! I started running the Java compiler, and I'm compiling your `SomeProg.java` program. The trouble is, your `SomeProg.java` program calls on another program that you wrote — a program named `OtherProg.java`. Now where do I look for `OtherProg.java`?

You: (Saying nothing, and still waiting patiently. . . .)

Computer: Never mind! I already found `OtherProg.java`. It's in a directory that's listed in the `CLASSPATH` variable.

So much for the dialogue between you and your computer. One way or another, you have to set values for your `PATH` and `CLASSPATH` variables. The good news is, you need to set these values only once. After you've done it, the computer remembers these new values. You can reboot your computer, and the computer still remembers the new values.

Setting the PATH and the CLASSPATH

The way you set your system's environment variables depends on a few different things. Mainly, it varies from one operating system to another. If you're running Unix, it varies with your choice of shell.

This section has instructions for setting the `PATH` and the `CLASSPATH` in several different operating systems. (If you've done this kind of thing before, and you're comfortable setting environment variables, then just do it without reading the rest of this section.)

Windows 2000

To set the `PATH` and `CLASSPATH` in Windows 2000, complete the following steps:

1. **Choose Start⇨Settings⇨Control Panel⇨System.**

   The System Properties dialog box appears.

2. **In the System Properties dialog box, click the Advanced tab. Then click the Environment Variables button.**

   The Environment Variables dialog box appears.

3. **In the Environment Variables dialog box, check to see if there's a variable named `CLASSPATH`.**

   The name is not case-sensitive. It could be `classpath`, `cLaSsPaTh`, or anything spelled that way.

A. If the Environment Variable dialog box doesn't already have a variable named CLASSPATH, then click either of the New buttons. (One New button creates a variable for you alone. The other New button, if it's available, creates a variable for all users on the system.)

A New Variable dialog box is opened. For the variable name, type **CLASSPATH**. For the value, type a dot (a period), as shown in Figure 2-5.

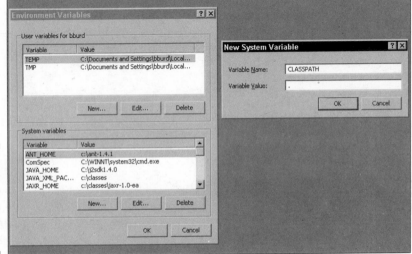

Figure 2-5:
Creating a
CLASSPATH
variable in
Windows
2000.

When you're setting the CLASSPATH variable's value, the single dot refers to your working directory. This dot follows you around wherever you go. For instance, in Figure 2-3, the command prompt is C:\Java Programs. So a dot in the CLASSPATH stands for the C:\JavaPrograms directory. If you move to another directory, say the C:\RawFish directory, then the dot in the CLASSPATH stands for the C:\RawFish directory.

B. If there's already a variable named CLASSPATH, then select the CLASSPATH line in the Environment Variables dialog box. Click the Edit button that's below the CLASSPATH line.

An Edit Variable dialog box opens. First, make sure that the little Variable Name field has the word CLASSPATH in it. Then in the Variable Value field, type a dot. To separate your new dot from what's already in the Variable Value field, type a semicolon. (See Figure 2-6.)

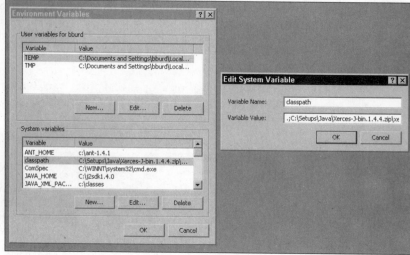

Figure 2-6:
Adding a
dot to the
CLASSPATH
(Windows
2000).

4. Repeat Step 3 for the PATH variable.

I'd be surprised to find a system that doesn't already have a PATH variable. Select the PATH line in the Environment Variables dialog box. Click the Edit button that's below the PATH line.

When the Edit Variable dialog box opens, make sure that the little Variable Name field has the word PATH in it. Then, in the Variable Value field, type the name of your Java bin directory. To separate your new addition from what's already in the Variable Value field, type a semicolon.

For instance, in Figure 2-7, I need to add c:\j2sdk1.4.0\bin to the path. So, in the Variable Value field, I type **c:\j2sdk1.4.0\bin**, followed by a semicolon.

If you're not sure about the name of your Java bin directory, see the explanation that accompanies Figure 2-4.

5. Click OK in every dialog box that's been opened.

Click OK in the Edit Variable or New Variable dialog box, in the Environment Variables dialog box, and in the System Properties dialog box.

6. Close any command prompt windows that you currently have open.

Those old command prompt windows don't use the updated PATH and CLASSPATH values. So type the word **exit** in each old command prompt window. Thereafter, any new command prompt windows will carry the updated values.

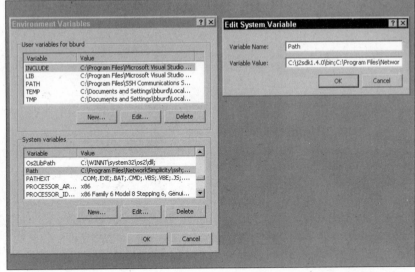

Windows XP

You set the PATH and CLASSPATH in Windows XP by following these steps:

1. **Choose Start➪Control Panel➪Performance & Maintenance➪System.**

   The System Properties dialog box appears.

2. **Follow the preceding instructions for Windows 2000 (starting with Step 2).**

   The Windows XP Environment Variables dialog box is just like its counterpart in Windows 2000. The only difference is that Windows XP dialog boxes and windows come in dazzling candy-like colors instead of neutral blues and grays. To protect your eyesight, please wear sunglasses.

Windows NT

To set the PATH and CLASSPATH in Windows NT, follow these steps:

1. **Choose Start➪Settings➪Control Panel➪System.**

   The System Properties dialog box appears.

2. **In the System Properties dialog box, click the Environment tab.**

3. **To set the CLASSPATH variable, follow Step 3 in the preceding Windows 2000 instructions.**

   At this point in the process, the only difference between Windows NT and Windows 2000 is that Windows 2000 displays a separate New Variable or Edit Variable dialog box. With Windows NT, the variable's name and value are displayed right in the old System Properties dialog box, as shown in Figure 2-8.

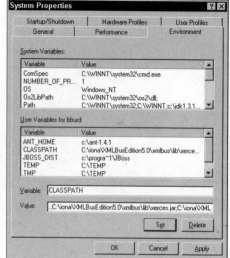

4. **To set the** `PATH` **variable, follow Step 4 in the preceding Windows 2000 instructions.**

With Windows NT, the variable's name and value are displayed in the System Properties dialog box, as shown in Figure 2-9.

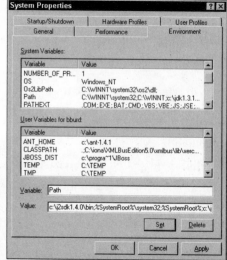

5. **In the System Properties dialog box, click the Set button, and then click the OK button.**

6. **Close any command prompt windows that you currently have open.**

    Type the word **exit** in each old command prompt window. Thereafter, any new command prompt windows will carry the updated values.

It's easy to forget to click the Set button in Step 5. If you don't click the Set button, any changes that you entered have no effect. This can drive you crazy. (I ought to know. I'm crazy.)

Windows 95, 98, or Me

You set the PATH and CLASSPATH in Windows 95, 98, or Me by following these steps:

1. **Choose Start⇨Programs⇨Accessories⇨Notepad.**

    This sequence opens Windows Notepad.

2. **Choose File⇨Open. In the File name box, type \autoexec.bat, and click the Open button.**

    This little ritual opens the \autoexec.bat file, as you can see in Figure 2-10.

Figure 2-10:
Editing the
\autoexec.
bat file
(Windows
95, 98, or
Me).

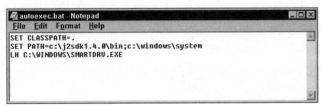

3. **Set the CLASSPATH in the \autoexec.bat file.**

    A. If the file has nothing about a CLASSPATH in it, then you need an additional line to the \autoexec.bat file. (It doesn't matter if you put the line in the beginning, the middle, or the end of the file.) Your new CLASSPATH variable's value should be nothing but a dot. So add the line

    ```
    SET CLASSPATH=.
    ```

    to the \autoexec.bat file.

B. If the file has a line that starts with CLASSPATH or SET CLASSPATH, then add a dot to the start of the CLASSPATH. To separate your new dot from what's already in the CLASSPATH, type a semicolon. Your \autoexec.bat file ends up having a line of the following kind:

```
SET CLASSPATH=.;C:\classes;C:\Program Files\Tomcat
```

4. **Set the PATH in the \autoexec.bat file.**

The \autoexec.bat file probably has a line that starts with PATH or with SET PATH. Add your Java bin directory to start of the PATH. To separate your Java bin directory from what's already in the PATH, type a semicolon. Your \autoexec.bat file ends up having a line of the following kind:

```
SET PATH=c:\j2sdk1.4.0\bin;c:\windows\system
```

To find the name of your Java bin directory, see the explanation that accompanies Figure 2-4.

5. **Choose File⇨Save.**

Congratulations! You just modified your \autoexec.bat file.

6. **Choose Start⇨Shut Down⇨Restart.**

The changes don't take effect until you reboot your system.

Unix and Linux

What you do to set the CLASSPATH in a Unix-like operating system depends on several things, including the kind of command shell that you're using. For instance, if you're using the Bourne shell (sh) or the Korn shell (ksh), then add lines of the following kind to your ~/.profile file:

```
PATH=/usr/java/j2sdk1.4.0/bin:$PATH;    export PATH
CLASSPATH=.;    export CLASSPATH
```

If you're using the Bourne-Again shell (bash), then add lines of that kind to either your ~/.bashrc, ~/.bash_profile, ~/.bash_login, or ~/.profile file. Your choice of file depends on the way in which you use the command shell, and on which of these files already exist. (For more details, check the bash man pages.)

If you're running the C shell (csh), then add lines like the following to the ~/.cshrc file:

```
set PATH="${PATH}:/usr/java/j2sdk1.4.0/bin"
set CLASSPATH=.
```

On some versions of the C shell, you use a setenv command in the ~/.cshrc file:

```
setenv PATH "${PATH}:/usr/java/j2sdk1.4.0/bin"
setenv CLASSPATH .
```

Macintosh OS X

Mac's OS X is based on Unix, so most of the previous section's advice applies to the OS X Terminal. (For information on opening a Terminal window, see Table 2-1.)

When choosing which of the previous section's commands to use, try the C shell commands first. (Macs use `tcsh` — the TENEX C shell — so all the C shell commands should work.) Just add lines from the previous section to your `/etc/csh.cshrc`, `~/.tcshrc`, or `~/.cshrc` file.

Macintosh Classic

For a Mac Classic user, these instructions come in a slightly different order. Even though it's a bit tangled, I assume that you've already created a `Java Programs` directory (something that I describe in Chapter 3). Anyway, here's what you do:

- ✔ Find the `MRJ SDK` folder.

- ✔ Inside the `MRJ SDK` folder, find the `tools` folder.

- ✔ Inside the `tools` folder, look for the `JDK tools` folder.

- ✔ Inside the `JDK tools` folder, find the `javac` icon. Double click that icon to run the `javac` program.

- ✔ Drag your `JavaPrograms` folder to the `javac` program's Classpath pane.

- ✔ Close the `javac` program.

- ✔ Back in the original `tools` folder, look for the `Application Builders` folder.

- ✔ In the `Application Builders` folder, find the `JBindery` folder.

- ✔ Inside the `JBindery` folder, find the `JBindery` icon. Double-click that icon to run the `JBindery` program. (This `JBindery` program is what I call the `java` command in most of this book.)

- ✔ On the left side of the `JBindery` program's window, click the Classpath icon. This opens the Classpath panel.

- ✔ Drag your `JavaPrograms` folder to the Classpath panel's Additions to Classpath pane.

- ✔ Close the `JBindery` program.

Is That All There Is to It?

If you're reading this paragraph, then you've probably followed some of the instructions in this chapter — instructions for installing a Java compiler on your computer. So the burning question is, have you done the installation correctly? The answer to that question lies in Chapter 3, because in that chapter, you use the compiler on a brand new computer program.

Chapter 3

Running Programs

*I*f you're a programming newbie then, for you, running a program probably means clicking a mouse. Double-click the icon for Internet Explorer, or maybe you choose Internet Explorer from the Start menu. That's all there is to it.

Well, when you create your own programs, the situation is a bit different. With a new program, the programmer (or someone from the programmer's company) creates the icons. Before that, a perfectly good program may not have an icon at all. On top of all this, the icon-clicking situation varies from one system to another. In Windows, an icon is a shortcut. In Linux, an icon is a link. In Joe's Operating System, it's a who-knows-what.

As an aspiring programmer, you can rise above all the chaos by starting programs from the command prompt window. This chapter shows you how to do it.

If you use an integrated development environment, like JBuilder, WSAD, or CodeWarrior, then this chapter's material isn't for you. Check your product's documentation instead.

Creating a Directory

First, you need a Java program. You use this program to test your Java compiler. You can get a program by visiting this book's Web site at either www. dummies.com/extras or at www.BurdBrain.com. At either site, you can download the whole bundle (all the programs listed in this book), or you can download a single program named Mortgage.java.

Where do you put this `Mortgage.java` test program? I recommend keeping all your Java programs in one tidy place. I created a directory on my hard drive named `JavaPrograms`. I put the downloaded `Mortgage.java` file in my `JavaPrograms` directory.

Throughout this book, I refer to files that you put in your `JavaPrograms` directory. If you put your Java programs in some other place (a directory named `CleanLaundry`, for instance), then just think of your `CleanLaundry` directory whenever I refer to a `JavaPrograms` directory.

If you become a professional programmer and start working in a big programming team, then don't tell anyone about putting all your files in a single `JavaPrograms` directory. If you do, they'll think you're nuts. This single-directory business becomes awkward when you start writing larger programs, but for the beginning programmer, it's just fine.

If you're handy with your computer's file system, then you can create a `JavaPrograms` directory by pointing and clicking. (In Windows, you can use Windows Explorer.) But you can also create a directory with the system's command prompt. Here's how:

✔ **To create a directory in Windows, issue the following command:**

```
md \JavaPrograms
```

This command creates a new `JavaPrograms` directory directly below your hard drive's top-level (root) directory. Later, when you want to run Java programs, you can get to this directory by issuing the following command:

```
cd \JavaPrograms
```

This command makes `\JavaPrograms` your working directory.

The two letters in the md command stand for the words *make directory*. The letters in the cd command stand for *change directory*.

✔ **To create a directory in Unix or Linux, issue the following command:**

```
mkdir ~/JavaPrograms
```

This command creates a new `JavaPrograms` directory directly below your user home directory. Later, when you want to run Java programs, you can get to your `JavaPrograms` directory by issuing the following command:

```
cd ~/JavaPrograms
```

✔ **To create a directory in Mac OS X, do the following:**

Go to the Utilities subfolder of the Applications folder. In the Utilities subfolder, find the Terminal icon. Double-click this icon to open a Terminal window. Then follow the preceding Unix/Linux directions.

✔ **To create a directory in the Mac Classic OS, do the following:**

Open the Finder, then click anywhere on your desktop. In the Finder's File menu, select New Folder. When a new folder icon appears on your desktop, name the folder JavaPrograms.

Compiling and Running a Program

Are you ready to compile and run Java programs? Here's the acid test.

With Windows, Linux, and all other systems (except Mac Classic)

1. **Put my** Mortgage.java **file (downloadable either from** www.dummies. com/extras **or** www.BurdBrain.com**) in your** JavaPrograms **directory.**

2. **In a command prompt window, follow the instructions from the previous section to move to the** JavaPrograms **directory.**

   Type **cd \JavaPrograms** or **cd ~/JavaPrograms**, whichever is right for your system.

3. **In the same command prompt window, type the following command:**

   ```
   javac Mortgage.java
   ```

   This command tells the computer to compile the Mortgage.java program. If all goes well, the computer responds with very little fanfare. As you can see in Figure 3-1, you get no special messages. After a brief delay, you see yet another command prompt. (You see something like C:\JavaPrograms>.)

Figure 3-1: Compiling a Java program.

```
C:\JavaPrograms>javac Mortgage.java
C:\JavaPrograms>
```

4. **In the same command prompt window, type the following command:**

   ```
   java Mortgage
   ```

   The command tells the computer to run the Mortgage program. If all goes well, the computer starts firing questions at you, as shown in Figure 3-2. You type a dollar amount (like 200000.00), an interest rate

(like 7.0) and a number of years (like 30). After each entry, you press
Enter. After you answer the number-of-years question, the computer displays your monthly payment (a number like $1,330.60).

```
C:\JavaPrograms>java Mortgage

How much are you borrowing?           200000.00
What's the interest rate?             7.0
How many years are you taking to pay? 30

Your monthly payment is               $1,330.60


C:\JavaPrograms>
```

Figure 3-2:
Running
a Java
program.

When you type the `javac` command (in Step 3), you use a complete file
name, such as `Mortgage.java`. But, when you type the `java` command
(in Step 4), you don't use a complete file name. You type **java Mortgage**.
You never type **java Mortgage.java**.

Take a careful look at Figure 3-2. When you type the dollar amount **200000.00**,
you don't type a dollar sign. You don't even type a comma between 200 and
000. That's important. If you type either of these things, then the program
just crashes.

I'm a good programmer, but I'm not a financial wizard. Don't use the output of
my Mortgage program to make decisions about real life situations. Check all
the numbers with your local lender. (Better yet, check with someone whose
advice you trust.)

With the Mac Classic OS

1. **Put my** `Mortgage.java` **file (downloadable either from** `www.dummies.`
   `com/extras` **or** `www.BurdBrain.com`**) in your** `JavaPrograms` **directory.**

2. **Drag** `Morgage.java` **to the** `javac` **icon. Then, in the** `javac` **program**
   window, click the Do Javac button.

   This creates a new `Mortage.class` file in your `JavaPrograms` directory.

3. **Drag the** `Mortgage.class` **file to the** `JBindery` **icon.**

   This opens the `JBindery` program window.

4. **In the** `JBindery` **program window, find the Redirect Stdin drop-down**
   list. In this list, select Message Window.

   This step allows you to respond to the Mortgage the program's questions using your computer keyboard.

5. **Click the Run button.**

   A new window appears displaying the question, `How much are you`
   `borrowing?` Answer this and other questions, and you're on your way.

What Could Possibly Go Wrong?

In Figures 3-1 and 3-2, I show you the picture-perfect processing of a Mortgage program. That's fine for us superheroes, but what can the average person do if things don't go smoothly? What if you get an error message or two?

This section tells you how to diagnose some of the more common difficulties. If you can't compile and run the Mortgage program, then this section's tricks will probably get you past the hurdle.

Note: This section of the book is biased toward Microsoft Windows. If you're not a Windows user, you have to translate these tricks into your computer's native language.

The main trick is to enlarge your repertoire of commands. You retype the `javac` and `java` commands from Figures 3-1 and 3-2, but you mix the `javac` and `java` commands with some useful diagnostic commands. Here's what you do:

1. **In a command prompt window, type the command** cd \JavaPrograms.

   By typing this command, you plant yourself squarely in the `C:\Java Programs` directory. Look at the top of Figure 3-3, and notice how the prompt changes. (It changes from `C:\` to `C:\JavaPrograms`.) The directory `C:\JavaPrograms` becomes your working directory.

```
C:\>cd \JavaPrograms

C:\JavaPrograms>set
classpath=.
COMPUTERNAME=GROUCHO
ComSpec=C:\WINNT\system32\cmd.exe
OS=Windows_NT
Path=C:\WINNT;C:\WINNT\System32;C:\j2sdk1.4.0\bin
PATHEXT=.COM;.EXE;.BAT
PROMPT=$_$P$G
USERPROFILE=C:\Documents and Settings\bburd
windir=C:\WINNT


C:\JavaPrograms>dir
 Volume in drive C has no label.
 Volume Serial Number is 2222-2222

 Directory of C:\JavaPrograms

11/24/2002  12:18a    <DIR>          .
11/24/2002  12:18a    <DIR>          ..
11/24/2002  12:01a             1,321 Mortgage.java
               1 File(s)          1,321 bytes
               2 Dir(s)   1,285,787,648 bytes free

C:\JavaPrograms>javac Mortgage.java

C:\JavaPrograms>
```

Figure 3-3: Diagnosing your setup.

If you type this `cd \JavaPrograms` command, and your prompt doesn't become `C:\JavaPrograms`, then you should do a little checking. Here's how:

- Look again at the `cd` command that you typed. Make sure that you typed the command correctly.

- Open Windows Explorer and make sure that you have a `C:\JavaPrograms` directory. If not, go back to the section entitled, "Creating a Directory," earlier in this chapter.

When you've successfully issued the command `cd \JavaPrograms`, any other commands that you type refer automatically to files in that `C:\JavaPrograms` directory.

It doesn't matter where you start. As long as you're working somewhere on the C: drive, the command `cd \JavaPrograms` always changes your working directory to `C:\JavaPrograms`.

If you open several command prompt windows, then each of these windows can have a different working directory. For instance, imagine that you close one command prompt window and open another. Then, to get to the `JavaPrograms` directory in the new window, you have to issue the `cd \JavaPrograms` command again.

2. **Type the `set` command, as shown in Figure 3-3.**

   The computer responds by displaying a big list. The list has lines like

   ```
   classpath=.
   ```

   and

   ```
   Path=C:\WINNT;C:\WINNT\System32;C:\j2sdk1.4.0\bin
   ```

   In fact, when you issue the `set` command, you're checking the value of the CLASSPATH and the PATH.

   - Make sure that the CLASSPATH contains a dot. It can contain more than just a dot, but the dot must be separated from other things by semicolons. For instance, the line

     ```
     classpath=C:\Classes;.;C:\tomcat\servlet.jar
     ```

     indicates a perfectly good CLASSPATH.

     Notice that, on a Windows machine, the uppercase or lowercase spelling of the word `cLASspATh` doesn't matter at all. Any choice of caps and small letters works fine.

   - Make sure that the PATH includes your Java bin directory. For instance, in Figure 3-3, my PATH includes the directory `C:\j2sdk1.4.0\bin`.

Sometimes, when you type the **set** command, the resulting display is so long that the CLASSPATH and PATH lines roll quickly off of your screen. If this happens to you, try typing **set | more**. With this modified command, you see lines like `classpath=.` one screenful at a time.

Those pesky file name extensions

The file names displayed in Windows Explorer can be misleading. You may visit the Java Programs directory and see the name Mortgage. Instead of just Mortgage, the file's full name may be Mortgage.java or Mortgage.txt. (The name Mortgage.java would be fine, but the name Mortgage.txt would be troublesome.) You may even see Mortgage.java, when the file's full name is something like Mortgage.java.txt (a bad name for a Java program file).

The ugly truth is, Windows Explorer can hide a file's extensions. This awful feature tends to confuse Java programmers. So, if you like using Windows Explorer, you should modify the Windows Hide Extensions feature. To do this,

you have to open the Folder Options dialog box. Here's how:

- ✔ **In Windows 95, 98, or NT:** In the Windows Explorer menu bar, choose View➪Folder Options (or just View➪Options).

- ✔ **In Windows Me or 2000:** Choose Start➪ Settings➪Control Panel➪Folder Options.

- ✔ **In Windows XP:** Choose Start➪Control Panel➪Performance and Maintenance➪ File Types.

In the Folder Options dialog box, click the View tab. Then look for an option labeled Hide File Extensions for Known File Types. Make sure that this item's check box is *not* checked.

---

3. **Type the** dir **command, as shown in Figure 3-3.**

   The computer responds by displaying a list of all files in your Java Programs directory. When you issue the dir command, you're looking for the file Mortgage.java. If this file isn't in your JavaPrograms directory, then you'll have trouble issuing the javac Mortgage.java command.

   When you edit a file with Windows Notepad and you use the File➪Save As dialog box, Windows can add the .txt extension to any file name that you type. For instance, if you type **Mortgage.java** in the Save As dialog box's File Name field, then you might inadvertently create a file named Mortgage.java.txt. A file whose name has this .txt extension will not make the javac command happy. To fix this problem, choose File➪Save As again, and type **"Mortgage.java"** (surrounded by double quote marks) in the Save As dialog box's File Name field.

4. **Type the** javac Mortgage.java **command, as shown in Figure 3-3.**

   The computer should respond with very little fanfare. You should see no messages and another prompt. If you see anything else (messages such as cannot read: Mortgage.java or javac: invalid flag), then something's not right. Redo Steps 1 through 3, and make sure that your ducks are all in a row.

If Steps 1 through 3 look good, but Step 4 still fails, then try the `type Mortgage.java` command, as shown in Figure 3-4. The computer responds by displaying all the stuff in the `Mortgage.java` file. If the display that you see isn't a lot like the display in Figure 3-4, then there's something wrong with your `Mortgage.java` file. You should recopy the file from either `www.dummies.com/extras` or `www.BurdBrain.com`.

```
C:\WINNT\system32\cmd.exe                                          _ □ ×

C:\JavaPrograms>type Mortgage.java
import java.io.*;
import java.text.NumberFormat;

public class Mortgage
{

    public static void main(String args[]) throws IOException
    {

        BufferedReader keyboard =
            new BufferedReader(new InputStreamReader(System.in));
        double principal, rate, ratePercent;
        int years, n;
        final int paymentsPerYear = 12;
        final int timesPerYearCalculated = 12;
        double effectiveAnnualRate;
        double payment;
        NumberFormat currency = NumberFormat.getCurrencyInstance();

        System.out.print("How much are you borrowing?          ");
        principal = Double.parseDouble(keyboard.readLine());
        System.out.print("What's the interest rate?            ");
        ratePercent = Double.parseDouble(keyboard.readLine());
        rate = ratePercent/100.00;
        System.out.print("How many years are you taking to pay? ");
        years = Integer.parseInt(keyboard.readLine());
        System.out.println("-----------------------------------");

        n = paymentsPerYear * years;
        effectiveAnnualRate = rate / paymentsPerYear;
        payment = principal*(effectiveAnnualRate /
            (1 - Math.pow(1 + effectiveAnnualRate, -n)));
        System.out.print("Your monthly payment is              ");
        System.out.println(currency.format(payment));
        System.out.println();
    }
}

C:\JavaPrograms>_
```

Figure 3-4: The Mortgage. java file.

5. **Type the** dir **command again, as shown in Figure 3-5.**

    This time around, you're checking for the names of two files — the old `Mortgage.java` file, and its young cousin, the `Mortgage.class` file.

    The new `Mortgage.class` file comes from a successful run of `javac` (in Step 4). This is the bytecode file that's described in Chapter 1. If you issue the `dir` command, and you don't see a `Mortgage.class` file, then Step 4 wasn't as successful as you thought it was. Without a `.class` file, you can't proceed to the `java` command in the next step.

6. **Type the** java Mortgage **command, as shown in Figure 3-5.**

    If all goes well, you should be asked How much are you borrowing? and two other questions. After answering these questions, you should get a monthly payment amount.

If the program doesn't run the way it's shown in Figure 3-5, then go back and try all six of these steps again. Chances are, something simple needs to be fixed.

If you review the six steps, and you still can't figure out what's wrong, then send me a holler. My address for such questions is BeginProg@ BurdBrain.com.

```
C:\JavaPrograms>dir
 Volume in drive C has no label.
 Volume Serial Number is 2222-2222

 Directory of C:\JavaPrograms

11/24/2002  12:19a       <DIR>          .
11/24/2002  12:19a       <DIR>          ..
11/24/2002  12:19a                1,442 Mortgage.class
11/24/2002  12:01a                1,321 Mortgage.java
               2 File(s)          2,763 bytes
               2 Dir(s)   1,285,713,920 bytes free

C:\JavaPrograms>java Mortgage
How much are you borrowing?             150000.00
What's the interest rate?               8.25
How many years are you taking to pay?   15
─────────────────────────────────
Your monthly payment is                 $1,455.21


C:\JavaPrograms>_
```

Figure 3-5:
Continuing
the
diagnosis.

Part II
Writing Your Own Java Programs

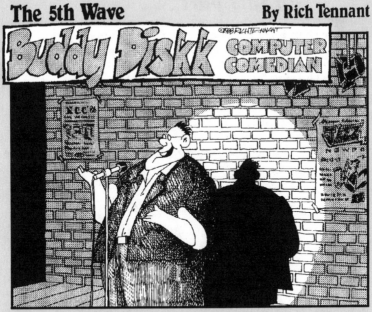

The 5th Wave   By Rich Tennant

Buddy Diskk COMPUTER COMEDIAN

"SO I SAID, 'WAITER! WAITER! THERE'S A BUG IN MY SOUP!' AND HE
SAYS, 'SORRY, SIR, THE CHEF USED TO PROGRAM COMPUTERS.' AHH HAHA
HAHA. THANK YOU! THANK YOU!"

In this part . . .

This part features some of the world's simplest programs. And, as simple as they are, these programs illustrate the fundamental ideas behind all computer code. The ideas include things like variables, values, types, statements, methods, and lots of other important stuff. This part of the book is your springboard, your launch pad, your virtual catapult.

Chapter 4

Exploring the Parts of a Program

In This Chapter

▶ Identifying the words in a Java program

▶ Using punctuation and indentation

▶ Understanding Java statements and methods

1 work in the science building at a liberal arts college. When I walk past the biology lab, I always say a word of thanks under my breath. I'm thankful for not having to dissect small animals. In my line of work, I dissect computer programs instead. Computer programs smell much better than preserved dead animals. Besides, when I dissect a program, I'm not reminded of my own mortality.

In this chapter, I invite you to dissect a program with me. I have a small program, named `ThingsILike`. I cut the program apart, and carefully investigate the program's innards. Get your scalpel ready. Here we go!

Checking Out Java Code for the First Time

I have a confession to make. The first time I look at somebody else's computer program, I feel a bit queasy. The realization that I don't understand something (or many things) in the code makes me nervous. I've written hundreds (maybe thousands) of programs, but I still feel insecure when I start reading someone else's code.

The truth is, figuring out a computer program is a bootstrapping experience. First I gawk in awe of the program. Then I run the program to see what it does. Then I stare at the program for a while, or read someone's explanation of the program and its parts. Then I gawk a little more and run the program again. Eventually, I come to terms with the program. Don't believe the wise guys who say they never go through these steps. Even the experienced programmers approach a new project slowly and carefully.

Behold! A program!

In Listing 4-1, you get a blast of Java code. Like all novice programmers, you're expected to gawk humbly at the code. But *don't be intimidated*. When you get the hang of it, programming is pretty easy. Yes, it's fun too.

Listing 4-1   A Simple Java Program

```
/*
 * A program to list the good things in life
 * Author: Barry Burd, BeginProg@BurdBrain.com
 * February 13, 2003
 */

class ThingsILike
{
    public static void main (String args[])
    {
        System.out.println("Chocolate, royalties, sleep");
    }
}
```

When I run the program in Listing 4-1, I get the result shown in Figure 4-1: The computer displays the words Chocolate, royalties, sleep on the screen. Now I admit that writing and running a Java program is a lot of work just to get the words Chocolate, royalties, sleep to appear on somebody's computer screen, but every endeavor has to start somewhere.

Figure 4-1:
Running the
program in
Listing 4-1.

```
Chocolate, royalties, sleep
```

You can run the code in Listing 4-1 on your computer. Just copy this book's listings from either www.dummies.com/extras or my Web site at www.BurdBrain.com. Then follow the instructions in Chapter 3, especially the instructions in the section about compiling and running a program.

What the program's lines say

If the program in Listing 4-1 ever becomes famous, then someone will write a Cliffs Notes book to summarize the program. The book will be really short, because you can summarize the action of Listing 4-1 in just one sentence. Here's the sentence:

```
Display Chocolate, royalties, sleep on the computer screen.
```

Now compare the sentence above with the bulk in Listing 4-1. Because Listing 4-1 has so many more lines, you may guess that Listing 4-1 has lots of boilerplate code. Well, your guess is correct. You can't write a Java program without writing the boilerplate stuff but, fortunately, the boilerplate text doesn't change much from one Java program to another. Here's my best effort at summarizing all the Listing 4-1 text in 57 words or less:

```
This program lists the good things in life.
Barry Burd wrote this program on February 13, 2003.
Barry realizes that you may have questions about this
code, so you can reach him at BeginProg@BurdBrain.com.

This code defines a Java class named ThingsILike.
    Here's the main starting point for the instructions:
        Display Chocolate, royalties, sleep on the screen.
```

The rest of this chapter (about 4,500 more words) explains the Listing 4-1 code in more detail.

The Elements in a Java Program

That both English and Java are called *languages* is no coincidence. You use a language to express ideas. English expresses ideas to people, and Java expresses ideas to computers. What's more, both English and Java have things like words, names, and punctuation. In fact, the biggest difference between the two languages is that Java is easier to learn than English. (If English were easy, then computers would understand English. Unfortunately, they can't.)

Take an ordinary English sentence and compare it with the code in Listing 4-1. Here's the sentence:

Suzanne says "eh" because, as you know, she lives in Canada.

In your high school grammar class, you worried about verbs, adjectives, and other such things. But in this book, you'll think in terms of keywords and identifiers, as summarized in Figure 4-2.

Keywords:
    Suzanne **says** "eh" **because, as you know, she lives in** Canada.

An identifier that you or I can define:
    Suzanne says "eh" because, as you know, she lives in Canada.

An identifier with a commonly agreed upon meaning:
    Suzanne says "eh" because, as you know, she lives in **Canada**.

A literal:
    Suzanne says **"eh"** because, as you know, she lives in Canada.

Punctuation:
    Suzanne says "eh" because**,** as you know**,** she lives in Canada**.**

A comment:
    Suzanne says "eh" because, as you know, she lives in Canada.

Figure 4-2:
The things
you find in
a simple
sentence.

Suzanne's sentence has all kinds of things in it. They're the same kinds of things that you find in a computer program. So here's the plan: Compare the elements in Figure 4-1 with similar elements in Listing 4-1. You already understand English, so you use this understanding to figure out some new things about Java.

But first, here's a friendly reminder: In the next several paragraphs, I draw comparisons between English and Java. As you read these paragraphs, it's important to keep an open mind. For instance, in comparing Java with English, I may write that "names of things aren't the same as dictionary words." Sure, you can argue that some dictionaries list proper nouns, and that some people have first names like Hope, Prudence, and Spike, but please don't. You'll get more out of the reading if you avoid nitpicking. Okay? Are we still friends? Then read on.

Keywords

A *keyword* is a dictionary word — a word that's built right into a language.

In Figure 4-2, a word like "says" is a keyword, because "says" plays the same role whenever it's used in an English sentence. The other keywords in the Suzanne sentence are "because," "as," "you," "know," "she," "lives," and "in."

Computer programs have keywords, too. In fact, the program in Listing 4-1 uses four of Java's keywords (shown in bold):

```
class ThingsILike
{
    public static void main (String args[])
```

Each Java keyword has a specific meaning — a meaning that remains unchanged from one program to another. For instance, whenever I write a Java program, the word `public` always signals a part of the program that's accessible to any other piece of code.

The Java programming language is *case-sensitive*. This means that, if you change a lowercase letter in a word to an uppercase letter, you change the word's meaning. Changing case can make the entire word go from being meaningful to being meaningless. In Listing 4-1, you can't replace *public* with *Public.* If you do, the whole program stops working.

This chapter has little or no detail about the meanings of the keywords `class`, `public`, `static`, and `void`. You can peek ahead at the material in other chapters, but you can also get along by cheating. When you write a program, just start with

```
class SomethingOrOther
{
```

and paste the text

```
public static void main (String args[])
```

into your code. In your first few programs, this strategy serves you well.

The Cheat Sheet in the front of this book has a complete list of Java keywords.

Here's one thing to remember about keywords: In Java, each keyword has an official, predetermined meaning. The people at Sun Microsystems, who have the final say on what constitutes a Java program, have created all of Java's keywords. You can't make up your own meaning for any of the Java keywords. For instance, you can't use the word `public` in a calculation:

```
//This is BAD, BAD CODE:
public = 6;
```

If you try to use a keyword this way, then the compiler displays an error message and refuses to translate your source code. It works the same way in English. Have a baby, and name it "Because."

> "Let's have a special round of applause for tonight's master of ceremonies — Because O. Borel."

You can do it, but the kid will never lead a normal life.

Identifiers that you or I can define

I like the name Suzanne, but if you don't like traditional names, then make up a brand new name. You're having a new baby. Call her "Deneen" or "Chrisanta." Name him "Belton" or "Merk."

A *name* is a word that identifies something, so I'll stop calling these things names and start calling them *identifiers*. In computer programming, an *identifier* is a noun of some kind. An identifier refers to a value, a part of a program, a certain kind structure, or any number of things.

Listing 4-1 has two identifiers that you or I can define on our own. They're the made-up words `ThingsILike` and `args`.

```
class ThingsILike
{
    public static void main (String args[])
```

Just as the names Suzanne and Chrisanta have no special meaning in English, so the names `ThingsILike` and `args` have no special meaning in Java. In Listing 4-1, I use `ThingsILike` for the name of my program, but I could also have used a name like `GooseGrease`, `Enzyme`, or `Kalamazoo`. I have to put (`String someName[]`) in my program, but I could use (`String args[]`), (`String commandLineArguments[]`), or (`String cheese[]`).

Do as I say, not as I do. Make up sensible, informative names for the things in your Java programs. Names like `GooseGrease` are cute, but they don't help you keep track of your program-writing strategy.

When I name my Java program, I can use `ThinksILike` or `GooseGrease`, but I can't use the word `public`. Words like `class`, `public`, `static`, and `void` are keywords in Java.

The `args` in (`String args[]`) holds anything extra that you type when you issue the command to run a Java program. For instance, if you get the program to run by typing `java ThingsILike won too 3`, then `args` stores the extra values `won`, `too`, and `3`. As a beginning programmer, you don't need to think about this feature of Java. Just paste (`String args[]`) into each of your programs.

Identifiers with agreed upon meanings

Many people are named Suzanne, but only one country is named Canada. That's because there's a standard, well-known meaning for the word "Canada." It's the country with a red maple leaf on its flag. If you start your own country, you should avoid naming it Canada, because naming it Canada would just confuse everyone. (I know, a town in Kentucky is named Canada, but that doesn't count. Remember, you should ignore exceptions like this.)

Most programming languages have identifiers with agreed upon meanings. In Java, almost all of these identifiers are defined in the Java API. Listing 4-1 has five such identifiers. They're the words `main`, `String`, `System`, `out`, and `println`:

```
public static void main (String args[])
{
    System.out.println("Chocolate, royalties, sleep");
}
```

Here's a quick rundown on the meaning of each of these names (more detailed descriptions appear throughout this book):

- **main:** The main starting point for execution in every Java program.

- **String:** A bunch of text; a row of characters, one after another.

- **System:** A canned program in the Java API. (This program accesses some features of your computer that are outside the direct control of the Java Virtual Machine.)

- **out:** Your computer's command prompt window. (See the section about using a command prompt window in Chapter 2.)

- **println:** Display text on your computer screen.

Strictly speaking, the meanings of the identifiers in the Java API are not cast in stone. Although you can make up your own meanings for the words like `System` or `println`, this isn't a good idea. If you did, you would confuse the dickens out of other programmers, who are used to the standard API meanings for these familiar identifier names.

Literals

A *literal* is a chunk of text that looks like whatever value it represents. In Suzanne's sentence (refer to Figure 4-2), "eh" is a literal, because "eh" refers to the word "eh."

Programming languages have literals too. For instance, in Listing 4-1, the stuff in quotes is a literal:

```
System.out.println("Chocolate, royalties, sleep");
```

When you run the `ThingsILike` program, you see the words `Chocolate, royalties, sleep` on the screen. In Listing 4-1, the text `"Chocolate, royalties, sleep"` refers to these words, exactly as they appear on the screen (minus the quotation marks).

Most of the numbers that you use in computer programs are literals. If you put the statement

```
mySalary = 1000000.00;
```

in a computer program, then `1000000.00` is a literal. It stands for the number 1000000.00 (one million).

Punctuation

A typical computer program has lots of punctuation. Take, for instance, the program in Listing 4-1:

```
class ThingsILike
{
    public static void main (String args[])
    {
        System.out.println("Chocolate, royalties, sleep");
    }
}
```

Each bracket, each brace, each squiggle of any kind plays a role in making the program meaningful.

In English, you write all the way across one line, and then you wrap your text to the start of the next line. In programming, you seldom work this way. Instead, the code's punctuation guides the indenting of certain lines. The indentation shows which parts of the program are subordinate to which other parts. It's as if, in English, you wrote Suzanne's sentence like this:

> Suzanne says "eh" because
>
> ,
>
>   as you know
>
> ,
>
> she lives in Canada.

The diagrams in Figures 4-3 and 4-4 show you how parts of the `ThingsILike` program are contained inside other parts. Notice how a pair of curly braces acts like a box. To make the program's structure be visible at a glance, you indent all the stuff inside of each box.

```
class ThingsILIke
{
    public static void main (String args[])
    {
        System.out.printIn("Chocolate, royalties, sleep");
    }
}
```

Figure 4-3:
A pair of
curly braces
acts like
a box.

I can't emphasize this point enough. If you don't indent your code, or if you indent but you don't do it carefully, then your code still compiles and runs correctly. But this successful run gives you a false sense of confidence. The minute you try to update some poorly indented code, you become hopelessly confused. So take my advice: Keep your code carefully indented at every step in the process. Make your indentation precise, whether you're scratching out a quick test program, or writing code for a billionaire customer.

```
Here's a Java class named ThingsILike:

    Here's the main starting point for the instructions:

        Display Chocolate, royalties, sleep on the screen.
```

Figure 4-4:
The ideas in
a computer
program
are nested
inside of
one another.

Comments

A *comment* is text that's outside the normal flow. In Figure 4-2, words "A comment:" aren't part of the Suzanne sentence. Instead, these words are *about* the Suzanne sentence.

The same is true of comments in computer programs. The first five lines in Listing 4-1 form one big comment. The computer doesn't act on this comment. There are no instructions for the computer to perform inside this comment. Instead, the comment tells other programmers something about your code.

Comments are for your own benefit, too. Imagine that you set your code aside for a while and work on something else. When you return later to work on the code again, the comments help you remember what you were doing.

The Java programming language has three different kinds of comments:

- **Traditional comments:** The comment in Listing 4-1 is a *traditional* comment. The comment begins with /* and ends with */. Everything between the opening /* and the closing */ is for human eyes only. Nothing between /* and */ gets translated by the compiler.

  The second, third, and fourth lines in Listing 4-1 have extra asterisks. I call them "extra" because these asterisks aren't required when you create a comment. They just make the comment look pretty. I include them in Listing 4-1 because, for some reason that I don't entirely understand, most Java programmers add these extra asterisks.

- **End-of-line comments:** Here's some code with end-of-line comments:

```
class ThingsILike                    //One thing is missing
{
    public static void main (String args[])
    {
        System.out.println("Royalties, sleep");//Chocolate
    }
}
```

  An *end-of-line* comment starts with two slashes, and goes to the end of a line of type.

  You may hear programmers talk about "commenting out" certain parts of their code. When you're writing a program, and something's not working correctly, it often helps to try removing some of the code. If nothing else, you find out what happens when that suspicious code is removed. Of course, you may not like what happens when the code is removed, so you don't want to delete the code completely. Instead, you turn your ordinary Java statements into comments. For instance, turn System.out. println("Sleep"); into /* System.out.println("Sleep"); */. This keeps the Java compiler from seeing the code while you try to figure out what's wrong with your program.

- **Javadoc comments:** A special *Javadoc* comment is any traditional comment that begins with an extra asterisk.

```
/**
 * Print a String and then terminate the line.
 */
```

This is a cool Java feature. The software that you can download from java.sun.com includes a little program called javadoc. The javadoc program looks for these special comments in your code. The program uses these comments to create a brand new Web page — a customized documentation page for your code. To find out more about Javadoc comments, go to the docs\tooldocs\javadoc subdirectory of your Java home directory.

Understanding a Simple Java Program

The following sections present, explain, analyze, dissect, and otherwise demystify the Java program in Listing 4-1.

What is a method?

You're working as an auto mechanic in an upscale garage. Your boss, who's always in a hurry and has a habit of running words together, says, "FixTheAlternator on that junkyOldFord." Mentally, you run through a list of tasks. "Drive the car into the bay, lift the hood, get a wrench, loosen the alternator belt," and so on. Three things are going on here:

- **You have a name for the thing you're supposed to do.** The name is FixTheAlternator.

- **In your mind, you have a list of tasks associated with the name FixTheAlternator.** The list includes "Drive the car into the bay, lift the hood, get a wrench, loosen the alternator belt," and so on.

- **You have a grumpy boss who's telling you to do all this work.** Your boss gets you working by saying, "FixTheAlternator." In other words, your boss gets you working by saying the name of the thing you're supposed to do.

In this scenario, using the word *method* wouldn't be a big stretch. You have a method for doing something with an alternator. Your boss calls that method into action, and you respond by doing all the things in the list of instructions that you've associated with the method.

Java methods

If you believe all that stuff in the last several paragraphs, then you're ready to read about Java methods. In Java, a *method* is a list of things to do. Every method has a name, and you tell the computer to do the things in the list by using the method's name in your program.

I've never written a program to get a robot to fix an alternator. But, if I did, the program may include a method named `FixTheAlternator`. The list of instructions in my `FixTheAlternator` method would look something like the text in Listing 4-2.

Listing 4-2 A Method Declaration

```
void FixTheAlternator()
{
    DriveInto(car, bay);
    Lift(hood);
    Get(wrench);
    Loosen(alternatorBelt);
    ...
}
```

Somewhere else in my Java code (somewhere outside of Listing 4-2), I need an instruction to call my `FixTheAlternator` method into action. The instruction to call the `FixTheAlternator` method into action may look like the line in Listing 4-3.

Listing 4-3 Calling a Method

```
FixTheAlternator(junkyOldFord);
```

Don't scrutinize Listings 4-2 and 4-3 too carefully. All the code in Listings 4-2 and 4-3 is fake! I made up this code so that it looks a lot like real Java code, but it's not real. What's more important, the code in Listings 4-2 and 4-3 isn't meant to illustrate all the rules about Java. So if you have a grain of salt handy, take it with Listings 4-2 and 4-3.

Almost every computer programming language has something akin to Java's methods. If you've worked with other languages, you may remember things like subprograms, procedures, functions, subroutines, `Sub` procedures, or `PERFORM` statements. Whatever you call it in your favorite programming language, a *method* is a bunch of instructions collected together and given a new name.

The declaration, the header, and the call

If you have a basic understanding of what a method is and how it works, you can dig a little deeper into some useful terminology:

- If I'm being lazy, I refer to the code in Listing 4-2 as a *method*. If I'm not being lazy, I refer to this code as a *method declaration*.

- The method declaration in Listing 4-2 has two parts. The first line (the part with the name `FixTheAlternator` in it) is called a *method header*. The rest of Listing 4-2 (the part surrounded by curly braces) is a *method body*.

✔ The term *method declaration* distinguishes the list of instructions in Listing 4-2 from the instruction in Listing 4-3, which is known as a *method call*.

For a handy illustration of all the method terminology, see Figure 4-5.

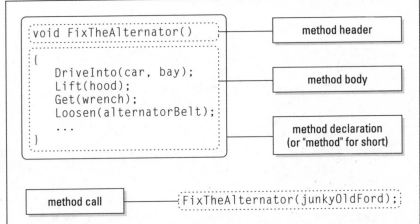

Figure 4-5:
The terminology describing methods.

```
void FixTheAlternator()                    method header

{
    DriveInto(car, bay);                   method body
    Lift(hood);
    Get(wrench);
    Loosen(alternatorBelt);                method declaration
    ...                                    (or "method" for short)
}


method call          FixTheAlternator(junkyOldFord);
```

A method's header and declaration are like an entry in a dictionary. An entry doesn't really use the word that it defines. Instead, an entry tells you what happens if and when you use the word.

> **chocolate** (choc-o-late) *n.* **1.** The most habit-forming substance on earth. **2.** Something you pay for with money from royalties. **3.** The most important nutritional element in a person's diet.

> **FixTheAlternator** () Drive the car into the bay, lift the hood, get the wrench, loosen the alternator belt, and then eat some chocolate.

In contrast, a method call is like the use of a word in a sentence. A method call sets some code in motion.

> "I want some chocolate, or I'll throw a fit."

> "FixTheAlternator on that junkyOldFord."

A *method's declaration* tells the computer what will happen if you call the method into action. A *method call* (a separate piece of code) tells the computer to actually call the method into action. A method's declaration and the method's call tend to be in different parts of the Java program.

The main method in a program

In Listing 4-1, the bulk of the code is the declaration of a method named *main*. (Just look for the word `main` in the code's method header.) For now, don't worry about the other words in the method header — the words `public`, `static`, `void`, `String`, and `args`. I explain these words (on a need-to-know basis) in the next several chapters.

Like any Java method, the `main` method is a recipe:

```
How to make biscuits:
    Preheat the oven.
    Roll the dough.
    Bake the rolled dough.
```

or

```
How to follow the main instructions in the ThingsILike code:
    Display Chocolate, royalties, sleep on the screen.
```

The word `main` plays a special role in Java. In particular, you never write code that explicitly calls a `main` method into action. The word `main` is the name of the method that is called into action automatically when the program begins running.

So have a look at Figure 4-6. Type **java ThingsILike** in the command prompt window to run the `ThingsILike` program. When the `ThingsILike` program runs, the computer automatically finds the program's `main` method and executes any instructions inside the method's body. In the `ThingsILike` program, the `main` method's body has only one instruction. That instruction tells the computer to print `Chocolate, royalties, sleep` on the screen. So in Figure 4-6, you type **java ThingsILike**, and the computer responds immediately with the words `Chocolate, royalties, sleep`.

None of the instructions in a method are executed until the method is called into action. But if you give a method the name `main`, then that method is called into action automatically.

Figure 4-6:
Running the
ThingsILike
program.

```
C:\JavaPrograms>java ThingsILike
Chocolate, royalties, sleep

C:\JavaPrograms>_
```

How you finally tell the computer to do something

Buried deep in the heart of Listing 4-1 is the single line that actually issues a direct instruction to the computer. The line

```
System.out.println("Chocolate, royalties, sleep");
```

tells the computer to display the words Chocolate, royalties, sleep in the command prompt window. I can describe this line in at least two different ways:

- ✔ **It's a statement:** In Java, a direct instruction that tells the computer to do something is called a *statement*. The statement in Listing 4-1 tells the computer to display some text. The statements in other programs may tell the computer to put 7 in certain memory location, or make a window appear on the screen. The statements in computer programs do all kinds of things.

- ✔ **It's a method call:** In the "What is a method?" section, earlier in this chapter, I describe something named a "method call." The statement

  ```
  FixTheAlternator(junkyOldFord);
  ```

  is an example of a method call, and so is

  ```
  System.out.println("Chocolate, royalties, sleep");
  ```

  Java has many different kinds of statements. A method call is just one kind.

Ending a statement with a semicolon

In Java, each statement ends with a semicolon. The code in Listing 4-1 has only one statement in it, so only one line in Listing 4-1 ends with a semicolon.

Take any other line in Listing 4-1, like the method header, for instance. The method header (the line with the word main in it) doesn't directly tell the computer to do anything. Instead, the method header describes some action for future reference. The header announces "Just in case someone ever calls the main method, the next few lines of code tell you what to do in response to that call."

Every complete Java statement ends with a semicolon. A method call is a statement, so it ends with a semicolon, but neither a method header nor a method declaration is a statement.

The method named *System.out.println*

The statement in the middle of Listing 4-1 calls a method named *System. out.println*. This method is defined in the Java API. Whenever you call the `System.out.println` method, the computer displays text on its screen.

Think about names. Believe it or not, I know two people named Pauline Ott. One of them is a nun; the other is physicist. Of course, there are plenty of Paulines in the English-speaking world, just as there are several things named `println` in the Java API. So to distinguish the physicist Pauline Ott from the film critic Pauline Kael, I write the full name "Pauline Ott." And, to distinguish the nun from the physicist, I write "Sister Pauline Ott." In the same way, I write either `System.out.println` or `DriverManager.println`. The first (which you use often) writes text on the computer's screen. The second (which you don't use at all in this book) writes to a database log file.

Just as Pauline and Ott are names in their own right, so `System`, `out`, and `println` are names in the Java API. But to use `println`, you must write the method's full name. You never write `println` alone. It's always `System.out.println` or some other combination of API names.

The Java programming language is case-sensitive. If you change a lowercase letter to an uppercase letter (or vice versa), you change a word's meaning. You can't replace `System.out.println` with `system.out.Println`. If you do, your program won't work.

Methods, methods everywhere

Two methods play roles in the `ThingsILike` program. Figure 4-7 illustrates the situation, and the next few bullets give you a guided tour:

- **There's a declaration for a main method.** I wrote the `main` method myself. This `main` method is called automatically whenever I start running the `ThingsILike` program.

- **There's a call to the System.out.println method.** The method call for the `System.out.println` method is the only statement in the body of the `main` method. In other words, calling the `System.out.println` method is the only thing on the `main` method's to-do list.

  The declaration for the `System.out.println` method is buried inside the official Java API. For a refresher on the Java API, see the Chapter 1.

When I say things like "`System.out.println` is buried inside the API," I'm not doing justice to the API. True, you can ignore all the nitty-gritty Java code inside the API. All you need to remember is that `System.out.println` is defined somewhere inside that code. But I'm not being fair when I make the API code sound like something magical. The API is just another bunch of Java code. The statements in the API that tell the computer what it means to carry out a call to `System.out.println` look a lot like the Java code in Listing 4-1.

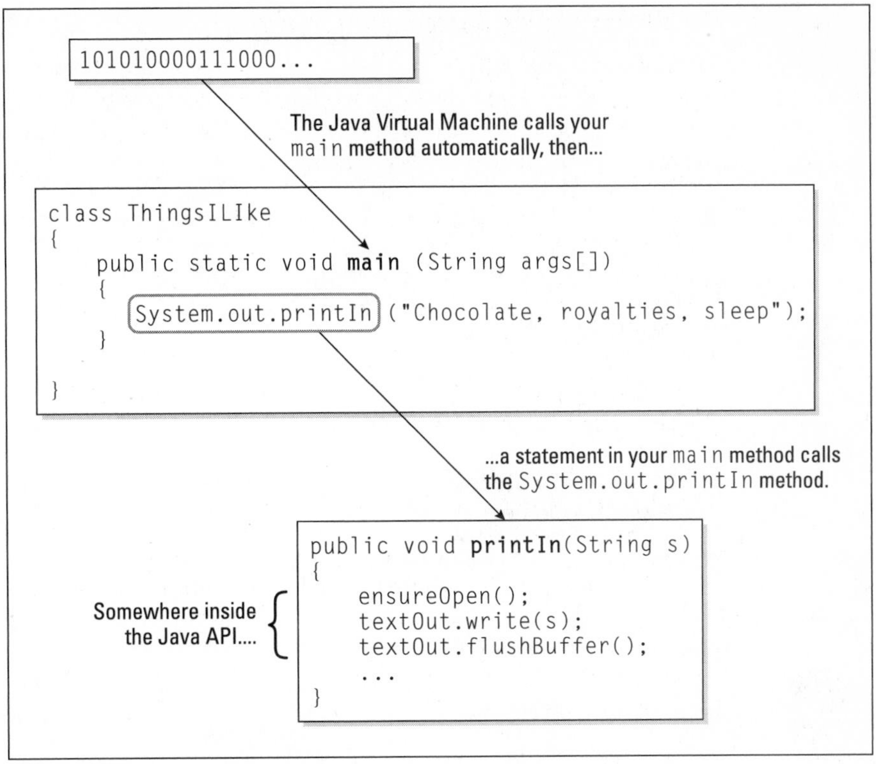

```
101010000111000...
```

The Java Virtual Machine calls your
main method automatically, then...

```
class ThingsILIke
{
    public static void main (String args[])
    {
        System.out.printIn ("Chocolate, royalties, sleep");
    }

}
```

...a statement in your main method calls
the System.out.printIn method.

```
public void printIn(String s)
{
    ensureOpen();
    textOut.write(s);
    textOut.flushBuffer();
    ...
}
```

Somewhere inside
the Java API....

Figure 4-7:
Calling the
System.
out.println
method.

The Java class

Have you heard the term *object-oriented programming* (also known as *OOP*)?
OOP is a way of thinking about computer programming problems — a way
that's supported by several different programming languages. OOP started in
the 1960s with a language called Simula. It was reinforced in the 1970s with
another language named Smalltalk. In the 1980s, OOP took off big time with
the language C++.

Some people want to change the acronym, and call it COP — class-oriented
programming. That's because object-oriented programming begins with
something called a *class*. In Java, everything starts with classes, everything is
enclosed in classes, and everything is based on classes. You can't do anything
in Java until you've created a class of some kind. It's like being on Jeopardy,
hearing Alex Trebek say, "Let's go to a commercial," and then interrupting him
by saying, "I'm sorry, Alex. You can't issue an instruction without putting your
instruction inside a class."

It's important for you to understand what a class really is, so I dare not give a haphazard explanation in this chapter. Instead, I devote much of Chapter 17 to the question, "What is a class?" Anyway, in Java, your `main` method has to be inside a class. I wrote the code in Listing 4-1, so I got to make up a name for my new class. I chose the name `ThingsILike`, so the code in Listing 4-1 starts with the words `class ThingsILike`.

Take another look at Listing 4-1, and notice what happens after the line `class ThingsILike`. The rest of the code is enclosed in curly braces. These braces mark all the stuff inside the class. Without these braces, you'd know where the declaration of the `ThingsILike` class starts, but you wouldn't know where the declaration ends.

It's as if the stuff inside the `ThingsILike` class is in a box. (Refer to Figure 4-3.) To box off a chunk of code, you do two things:

- ✔ **You use curly braces:** These curly braces tell the compiler where a chunk of code begins and ends.

- ✔ **You indent code:** Indentation tells your human eye (and the eyes of other programmers) where a chunk of code begins and ends.

Don't forget. You have to do both.

Chapter 5

Composing a Program

· ·

· ·

*J*ust yesterday, I was chatting with my servant, RoboJeeves. (RoboJeeves is an upscale model in the RJ-3000 line of personal robotic life forms.) Here's how the discussion went:

> *Me:* RoboJeeves, tell me the velocity of an object after it's been falling for three seconds in a vacuum.
>
> *RoboJeeves:* All right, I will. "The velocity of an object after it's been falling for three seconds in a vacuum." There, I told it to you.
>
> *Me:* RoboJeeves, don't give me that smart-alecky answer. I want a number. I want the actual velocity.
>
> *RoboJeeves:* Okay! "A number; the actual velocity."
>
> *Me:* RJ, these cheap jokes are beneath your dignity. Can you or can't you tell me the answer to my question?
>
> *RoboJeeves:* Yes.
>
> *Me:* "Yes," what?
>
> *RoboJeeves:* Yes, I either can or can't tell you the answer to your question.
>
> *Me:* Well, which is it? Can you?
>
> *RoboJeeves:* Yes, I can.
>
> *Me:* Then do it. Tell me the answer.
>
> *RoboJeeves:* The velocity is 153,984,792 miles per hour.

Me: (After pausing to think . . .) RJ, I know you never make a mistake, but that number, 153,984,792, is much too high.

RoboJeeves: Too high? That's impossible. Things fall very quickly on the giant planet Mangorrrrkthongo. Now, if you wanted to know about objects falling on Earth, you should have said so in the first place.

Sometimes that robot rubs me the wrong way. The truth is, RoboJeeves does whatever I tell him to do — nothing more and nothing less. If I say "Feed the cat," then RJ says, "Feed it to whom? Which of your guests will be having cat for dinner?"

Handy as they are, all computers do the same darn thing. They do *exactly* what you tell them to do, and that's sometimes very unfortunate. For instance, in 1962, a Mariner spacecraft to Venus was destroyed just four minutes after its launch. Why? It was destroyed because of a missing keystroke in a FORTRAN program. Around the same time, NASA scientists caught an error that could have trashed the Mercury space flights. (Yup! These were flights with people on board!) The error was a line with a period instead of a comma. (A computer programmer wrote `DO 10 I=1.10` instead of `DO 10 I=1,10`.)

With all due respect to my buddy RoboJeeves, he and his computer cousins are all incredibly stupid. Sometimes they look as if they're second-guessing us humans, but actually they're just doing what other humans told them to do. They can toss virtual coins and use elaborate schemes to mimic creative behavior, but they never really think on their own. If you say, "Jump," then they do what they're programmed to do in response to the letters J-u-m-p.

So when you write a computer program, you have to imagine that a genie has granted you three wishes. Don't ask for eternal love because, if you do, then the genie will give you a slobbering, adoring mate — someone that you don't like at all. And don't ask for a million dollars, unless you want the genie to turn you into a bank robber.

Everything you write in a computer program has to be very precise. Take a look at an example. . . .

A Program to Echo Keyboard Input

Listing 5-1 contains a small Java program. The program lets you type one line of characters on the keyboard. As soon as you press Enter, the program displays a second line that copies whatever you typed.

Listing 5-1   A Java Program

```
class EchoLine
{
    public static void main(String args[])
    {
        System.out.println(DummiesIO.getLine());
    }
}
```

Figure 5-1 shows the compiling and running of the EchoLine code (the code in Listing 5-1). The text in the figure is a mixture of my own typing and the computer's responses. To show you exactly how it works, I ran EchoLine more than once. In Figure 5-2, I finagled things so that anything I type is bold. Everything the computer displays on its own is in regular (non-bold) style.

Figure 5-1:
What part of
the word
"don't" do
you not
understand?

```
C:\>cd \JavaPrograms

C:\JavaPrograms>javac EchoLine.java

C:\JavaPrograms>java EchoLine
Please don't repeat this to anyone.
Please don't repeat this to anyone.

C:\JavaPrograms>_
```

Figure 5-2:
Whatever
you get to
type
appears in
bold print.

```
C:\>cd \JavaPrograms

C:\JavaPrograms>javac EchoLine.java

C:\JavaPrograms>java EchoLine
Please don't repeat this to anyone.
Please don't repeat this to anyone.

C:\JavaPrograms>
```

Here's what happens when you run the code in Listing 5-1:

- ✔ At first, the computer does nothing. You see a cursor on the left edge of the command prompt window, as shown in Figure 5-3. The computer is waiting for you to type something.

- ✔ You type one line of text — any text at all. (See Figure 5-4.)

- ✔ You press Enter, and the computer displays another copy of the line that you typed, as shown in Figure 5-5.

Figure 5-3:
The computer waits for you to type something.

```
C:\JavaPrograms>java EchoLine
-
```

Figure 5-4:
You type a sentence.

```
C:\JavaPrograms>java EchoLine
Hey, there's an echo in here._
```

Figure 5-5:
The computer echoes your input.

```
C:\JavaPrograms>java EchoLine
Hey, there's an echo in here.
Hey, there's an echo in here.

C:\JavaPrograms>_
```

After displaying a copy of your input, the program's run comes to an end. You see the command prompt again. (The command prompt in Figure 5-5 is C:\JavaPrograms>.)

Typing and running a program

You can run the code in Listing 5-1 on your computer. Here's how:

1. **Open a text editor.**

   Windows Notepad works fine.

2. **Type the EchoLine code exactly as it appears in Listing 5-1.**

   You can see me do this in Figure 5-6.

3. **Save your work in your JavaPrograms directory.**

   Be sure to name your file EchoLine.java, as shown in Figure 5-7.

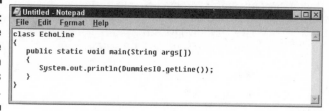

Figure 5-6:
Typing the
EchoLine
code in
Windows
Notepad.

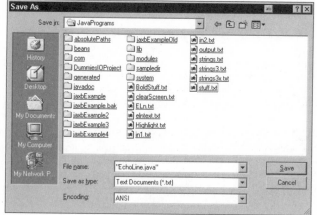

Figure 5-7:
Saving
Echoline.
java.

4. **Copy** `DummiesIO.java` **to your** `JavaPrograms` **directory.**

   You can download `DummiesIO.java` from my Web site (`www.BurdBrain.com`) or the Dummies Web site (`www.dummies.com/extras`). For more information on `DummiesIO.java`, see the "Input and output For Dummies" section, later in this chapter.

5. **Open a command prompt window.**

   For details, see Chapter 2.

6. **Make the JavaPrograms directory your working directory.**

   In Windows, the command to do this is `cd \JavaPrograms`. (Refer to Figure 5-1.)

7. **Compile** `EchoLine.java`.

   Windows or not, the command to compile the code is `javac EchoLine.java`. (Again, refer to Figure 5-1.)

8. **Run** `EchoLine.java`.

   The command to run the code is `java EchoLine`. (Once again, refer to Figure 5-1.)

If this list of steps seems a bit sketchy, you can find much more detail in Chapter 3. (Look first at the section in Chapter 3 about compiling and running a program.) For the most part, the steps here in Chapter 5 are a quick summary of the material in Chapter 3. The big difference is, in Chapter 3, I don't encourage you to type the program yourself.

So what's the big deal when you type the program yourself? Well, lots of interesting things can happen when you apply fingers to keyboard. That's why the second half of this chapter is devoted to troubleshooting.

How the EchoLine program works

When you were a tiny newborn, resting comfortably in your mother's arms, she told you how to send characters to the computer screen:

```
System.out.println(whatever text you want displayed);
```

What she didn't tell you was how to fetch characters from the computer keyboard. There are lots of ways to do it, but the one I recommend in this chapter is:

```
DummiesIO.getLine()
```

Now, here's the fun part. Calling the getLine method doesn't just scoop characters from the keyboard. When the computer runs your program, the computer *substitutes whatever you type on the keyboard* in place of the text DummiesIO.getLine().

To understand this, look at the statement in Listing 5-1:

```
System.out.println(DummiesIO.getLine());
```

When you run the program, the computer sees your call to getLine and stops dead in its tracks (refer to Figure 5-3). The computer waits for you to type a line of text. So (refer to Figure 5-4) you type the line

```
Hey, there's an echo in here.
```

The computer substitutes this entire Hey line for the DummiesIO.getLine() call in your program. The process is illustrated in Figure 5-8.

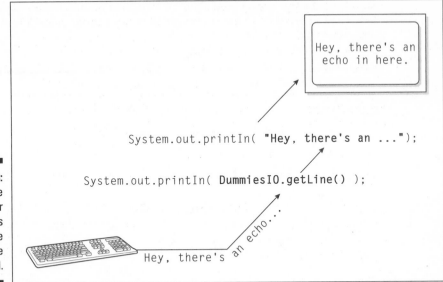

System.out.printIn("Hey, there's an ...");

System.out.printIn(DummiesIO.getLine());

Hey, there's an echo...

Figure 5-8:
The
computer
substitutes
text in place
of the
getLine call.

The call to `DummiesIO.getLine` is nestled inside the `System.out.println` call. So when all is said and done, the computer behaves as if the statement in Listing 5-1 looks like this:

```
System.out.println("Hey, there's an echo in here.");
```

The computer displays another copy of the text `Hey, there's an echo in here.` on the screen. That's why you see two copies of the `Hey` line in Figure 5-5.

Copy my `DummiesIO.java` file to your `JavaPrograms` directory. If you don't, then the Java compiler won't know what `DummiesIO.getLine` means. You can get `DummiesIO.java` at my Web site at `www.BurdBrain.com` or from the Dummies Web site at `www.dummies.com/extras`.

Input and output For Dummies

One of these days, I'll write a letter to the folks at Sun Microsystems. They put more than 2,700 programs in the Standard Java API, but they didn't include programs to read values easily from the computer keyboard. To read just one number from the keyboard, I normally type at least ten lines of code.

To save you the hassle, I've created DummiesIO. With DummiesIO, getting data from the keyboard is a snap. Table 5-1 shows you some of the things you can do.

Table 5-1	Some DummiesIO Methods
To Read This . . .	*. . . Make This Method Call*
A number with no decimal point in it	DummiesIO.getInt()
A number with a decimal point in it	DummiesIO.getDouble()
One character (a letter or a digit, for instance)	DummiesIO.getChar()
A word (ending in a blank space, for instance)	DummiesIO.getString()
A line (or what remains of a line after you've already read some data from the line)	DummiesIO.getLine()

This chapter has only a hit-or-miss introduction to DummiesIO. For a more thorough description, see the documentation that accompanies the DummiesIO code. You can download it from www.BurdBrain.com or from www.dummies.com/extras.

Expecting the Unexpected

Not long ago, I met an instructor with an interesting policy. He said, "Sometimes when I'm lecturing, I compose a program from scratch on the computer. I do it right in front of my students. If the program compiles and runs correctly on the first try, I expect the students to give me a big round of applause."

At first you may think this guy has an enormous ego, but you have to put things in perspective. It's unusual for a program to compile and run correctly the first time. There's almost always a typo or another error of some kind.

So this section deals with the normal, expected errors that you see when you compile and run a program for the first time. Everyone makes these mistakes, even the most seasoned travelers. The key is keeping a cool head. Here's my general advice:

✔ **Don't expect a program that you type to compile the first time.**

Be prepared to return to your editor and fix some mistakes.

✔ **Don't expect a program that compiles flawlessly (with the** `javac` **command) to run correctly (with the** `java` **command).**

Getting a program to compile without errors is the easier of the two tasks.

✔ **Read what's on the screen, not what you assume is on the screen.**

Don't assume that you've typed words correctly, that you've capitalized words correctly, or that you've matched curly braces or parentheses correctly. Compare the code you typed with any sample code that you have. Make sure that every detail is in order.

✔ **Be patient.**

Every good programming effort takes a long time to get right. If you don't understand something right away, then be persistent. Stick with it (or put it away for a while and come back to it). There's nothing you can't understand if you put in enough time.

✔ **Don't become frustrated.**

Don't throw your pie crust. Frustration (not lack of knowledge) is your enemy. If you're frustrated, you can't accomplish anything.

✔ **Don't think you're the only person who's slow to understand.**

I'm slow, and I'm proud of it. (Paul, Chapter 6 will be a week late.)

✔ **Don't be timid.**

If your code isn't working, and you can't figure out why it's not working, then ask someone. Post a message on `groups.google.com`, or send me an e-mail message. (Send it to `BeginProg@BurdBrain.com`.) And don't be afraid of anyone's snide or sarcastic answer. (For a list of gestures you can make in response to peoples' snotty answers, see Appendix Z.)

Diagnosing a problem

The "Typing and running a program" section, earlier in this chapter, tells you how to run the `EchoLine` program. If all goes well, your screen ends up looking like the one shown in Figure 5-1. But things don't always go well. Sometimes your finger slips, inserting a typo into your program. Sometimes you ignore one of the details in Listing 5-1, and you get a nasty error message.

Of course, some things in Listing 5-1 are okay to change. Not every word in Listing 5-1 is cast in stone. So here's a nasty wrinkle — I can't tell you that you must always retype Listing 5-1 exactly as it appears. Some changes are okay; others are not. Keep reading for some "f'rinstances."

Case sensitivity

Java is *case-sensitive*. Among other things, this means that, in a Java program, the letter P isn't the same as the letter p. If you send me some fan mail and start with "Dear barry" instead of "Dear Barry," then I still know what you mean. But Java doesn't work that way.

So change just one character in a Java program, and instead of an uneventful compilation you get a big headache! Change p to P like so:

```
//The following line is incorrect:
System.out.Println(DummiesIO.getLine());
```

When you try to compile and run the program, you get the ugliness shown in Figure 5-9.

Figure 5-9:
The Java
compiler
understands
println, but
not Println.

```
C:\JavaPrograms>javac EchoLine.java
EchoLine.java:5: cannot resolve symbol
symbol  : method Println  (java.lang.String)
location: class java.io.PrintStream
        System.out.Println(DummiesIO.getLine());
                   ^
1 error

C:\JavaPrograms>java EchoLine
Exception in thread "main" java.lang.NoClassDefFoundError: EchoLine

C:\JavaPrograms>_
```

When you get messages like the ones in Figure 5-9, your best bet is to stay calm and read the messages carefully. Sometimes, the messages contain useful hints. (Of course sometimes, they don't.) The messages in Figure 5-9 start with EchoLine.java:5: cannot resolve symbol. In plain English, this means "There's *something* that the Java compiler can't interpret on line 5 of your EchoLine.java file."

"And what may that *something* be?" you ask. The answer is also in Figure 5-9. The second line of the message says symbol : method Println, which means, "The Java compiler can't interpret the word Println." (The message stops short of saying, "It's the word Println, you dummy!" In any case, if the computer says you're one of us Dummies, you should take it as a compliment.)

Now, there are plenty of reasons why the compiler may not be able to understand a word like Println. But, for a beginning programmer, there are two important things that you should check right away:

✔ **Have you spelled the word correctly?**

Did you type `prntlin` instead of `println`?

✔ **Have you capitalized all letters correctly?**

Did you type `Println` or `PrintLn` instead of `println`?

Any of these errors can send the Java compiler into a tailspin. So compare your typing with the approved typing word for word (and letter for letter). When you find a discrepancy, go back to your editor (Windows Notepad, for instance) and fix the problem. Then go back to the command prompt window and reissue the `javac` command.

Before you `javac`, be sure to save your file with all the corrections in it.

When an error message says `EchoLine.java:67`, you don't need to count to the program's 67th line. Just use a customized editor, like the ones described in Chapter 1. These editors have View Line Numbers options, so counting is unnecessary.

Omitting punctuation

In English and in, Java using the; proper! punctuation is important) Take, for instance, the semicolon in Listing 5-1. What happens if you forget to type this semicolon?

```
//The following line is incorrect:
System.out.println(DummiesIO.getLine())
```

If you leave off the semicolon, you get the message shown in Figure 5-10.

Figure 5-10:
A helpful
error
message.

```
C:\JavaPrograms>javac EchoLine.java
EchoLine.java:5: ';' expected
        System.out.println(DummiesIO.getLine())
                                               ^
1 error

C:\JavaPrograms>_
```

A message like the one in Figure 5-10 makes your life much simpler. I don't have to explain the message, and you don't have to puzzle over the message's meaning. Just take the message `';' expected` on its face value. The message says, "I expect to see a semicolon at this point in your program." A caret (a ^ thingy) points to the place in the program where the computer expects to see a semicolon. So do what the message tells you to do. Go back to your `EchoLine.java` file and put a semicolon at the end of the `System.out.println(DummiesIO.getLine())` statement. That settles it.

Is there life after a failed compilation?

Look carefully at Figure 5-9, and notice the progression of messages. In the figure, the programmer tries two things:

☛ **The programmer issues the** `javac` **command.** The command fails because of a capital P. The word should be `println`, with a lower case p.

☛ **The programmer issues the** `java` **command.** At this point, the computer spits out a cheerful `NoClassDefFoundError` message. What does this mean? Well, when you successfully compile the code in Listing 5-1, you end up with two `EchoLine` files on your computer's hard drive. First, you have your `EchoLine.java` file — the file whose text is shown in Listing 5-1. But a successful `javac` gives you another file, named `EchoLine.class`. Sure, this `EchoLine.class` file contains gobbledygook that you can't read with Windows Notepad. But `EchoLine.class` is essential in your running the `java` command. (For more information about the `.class` file, see the section about what could possibly go wrong in Chapter 3.)

Whenever your `javac` command isn't successful, the computer doesn't create a `.class` file. And without this `.class` file, your `java` command isn't successful either.

But sometimes, the story has a peculiar twist. Imagine this unfortunate sequence of events:

☛ **You type Listing 5-1 exactly as it appears in this book.**

☛ **You issue the** `javac` **command, which creates a** `EchoLine.class` **file.** Very nice!

☛ **You issue the** `java` **command, and see the program's output.** Wonderful!

☛ **You make a harmful change to your** `EchoLine.java` **file.** For instance, you turn the p in `println` into a heinous, unwanted capital P.

☛ **You issue the** `javac` **command again.** This gives you your favorite `cannot resolve symbol` error message. The computer *doesn't* create a new `EchoLine.class` file.

☛ **You issue the** `java` **command once again.**

And what happens when you issue the final `java` command? If you guessed that the old `EchoLine` program runs correctly, then you're right. (For a look at the final `javac` and `java` commands, see the following sidebar figure.)

Even though your latest `javac` effort was a failure, your earlier call to `javac` created a good `EchoLine.class` file. That `EchoLine.class` file is still on your hard drive. The file wasn't replaced by the failed attempt to `javac`. So when you issue the `java` command, the computer uses that old `EchoLine.class` file and correctly runs the code in Listing 5-1.

This can be really confusing. When you issue the `java` command, your gut tells you that you're getting the results of your most recent attempt to do `javac`. But your gut can be wrong, wrong, wrong. In the scenario that I just described, an unsuccessful `javac` is followed by what appears to be a successful `java`. It's a mess, so you have to keep your wits about you. If `javac` fails, then don't march on to the `java` command. Go back and figure out why `javac` failed.

```
C:\JavaPrograms>javac EchoLine.java
EchoLine.java:5: cannot resolve symbol
symbol  : method Println (java.lang.String)
location: class java.io.PrintStream
        System.out.Println(DummiesIO.getLine());
                  ^
1 error

C:\JavaPrograms>java EchoLine
The program runs correctly after an unsuccessful attempt to compile!
The program runs correctly after an unsuccessful attempt to compile!

C:\JavaPrograms>_
```

Using too much punctuation

In junior high school, my English teacher said I should use a comma whenever I would normally pause for a breath. This advice doesn't work well during allergy season, when my sentences have more commas in them than words. Even as a paid author, I have trouble deciding where the commas should go, so I often add extra commas for good measure. This makes more work for my copy editor, Jean, who has a recycle bin full of commas by the desk in her office.

It's the same way in a Java program. You can get carried away with punctuation. Take, for instance, the `main` method header in Listing 5-1. This line is a dangerous curve for novice programmers.

For information on the terms *method header* and *method body,* see the section about understanding a simple java program in Chapter 4.

Normally, you shouldn't be ending a method header with a semicolon. But people add semicolons anyway. (Maybe, in some subtle way, a method header looks like it should end with a semicolon.)

```
//The following line is incorrect:
public static void main(String args[]);
```

If you add this extraneous semicolon to the code in Listing 5-1, you get the message shown in Figure 5-11.

Why can't the computer fix it?

How often do you get to finish someone else's sentence? "Please," says your supervisor, "go over there and connect the . . ."

"Wires," you say. "I'll connect the wires." If you know what someone means to say, why wait for them to say it?

This same question comes up in connection with computer error messages. Take a look at the message in Figure 5-10. The computer expects a semicolon at the end of line 5. Well, Mr. Computer, if you know that line 5 should end with a semicolon, then just add the semicolon, and be done with it. Why are you bothering me about it?

The answer is simple. The computer isn't interested in taking any chances. What if you *don't* really want a semicolon at the end of line 5? What if the missing semicolon represents a more profound problem? If the computer added the extra semicolon, it could potentially do more harm than good.

Returning to you and your supervisor . . .

Boom! A big explosion. "Not the wires, you Dummy. The dots. I wanted you to connect the dots."

"Sorry," you say.

Figure 5-11:
A not-so-
helpful error
message.

```
C:\JavaPrograms>javac EchoLine.java
EchoLine.java:3: missing method body, or declare abstract
    public static void main(String args[]);
                      ^
1 error
```

The error message in Figure 5-11 is a bit misleading. Instead of saying extra semicolon should be removed, the message says missing method body, or declare abstract. What the heck does that mean?

Well, when the computer tries to compile the bad code (Listing 5-1 with one too many semicolons), it gets confused. I illustrate the confusion in Figure 5-12. Your eye sees an extra semicolon, but the computer's eye interprets this as a method without a body. So that's the first part of the error message — the computer says missing method body.

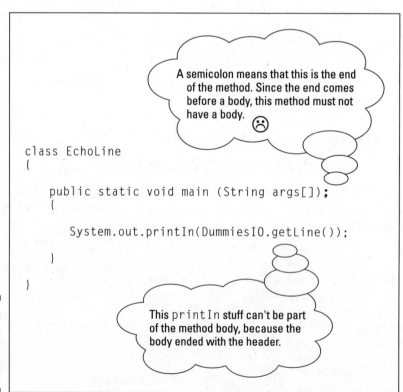

Figure 5-12:
What's
on this
computer's
mind?

We all know that a computer is a very patient, very sympathetic machine. That's why the computer looks at your code, and decides to give you one more chance. The computer remembers that Java has an advanced feature in which you write a method header without writing a method body. When you do this, you get what's called an *abstract method* — something that I don't use at all in this book. Anyway, in Figure 5-11, the computer sees a header with no body. So the computer says to itself, "I know! Maybe the programmer is trying to write an abstract method. The trouble is, an abstract method's header has to have the word abstract in it. I should remind the programmer about that." So the computer displays the declare abstract message in Figure 5-11.

One way or another, you can't interpret the message in Figure 5-11 without reading between the lines. So here are some tips to help you decipher murky messages:

✔ **Avoid the knee-jerk response.**

Some people see the declare abstract message in Figure 5-11 and wonder how they can declare a method to be abstract. Unfortunately, this isn't the right approach. If you don't know what it means to declare abstract then, chances are, you didn't mean to declare anything to be abstract in the first place.

✔ **Stare at the bad line of code for a long, long time.**

If you look carefully at the public static . . . line in Figure 5-11, then eventually you'll notice that it's different from the corresponding line in Listing 5-1. The line in Listing 5-1 has no semicolon, but the line in Figure 5-11 ends with a semicolon.

Of course, you won't always be starting with some prewritten code like the stuff in Listing 5-1. That's where practice makes perfect. The more code you write, the more sensitive your eyes will become to things like extraneous semicolons and other programming goofs.

Often the first message is the best

You're looking for the nearest gas station, so you ask one of the locals. "Go to the first traffic light and make a left," says the local. You go straight for a few streets, and see a blinking yellow signal. You turn left at the signal, and travel for a mile or so. What? No gas station? Maybe you mistook the blinking signal for a real traffic light.

You come to a fork in the road. "The directions said nothing about a fork. Which way should I go?" You veer right, but a minute later you're forced onto a highway. You see a sign that says, "Next Exit 24 Miles." Now you're really lost, and the gas gauge points to "S." (The "S" stands for "Stranded.")

So here's what happened: You made an honest mistake. You shouldn't have turned left at the yellow blinking light. That mistake alone wasn't so terrible. But that first mistake lead to more confusion, and eventually, your choices made no sense at all. If you hadn't turned at the blinking light, you'd never have encountered that stinking fork in the road. Then, getting on the highway was sheer catastrophe.

Is there a point to this story? Of course there is. A computer can get itself into the same sort of mess. The computer notices an error in your program. Then, metaphorically speaking, the computer takes a fork in the road — a fork based on the original error — a fork for which none of the alternatives lead to good results.

Here's an example. You're retyping the code in Listing 5-1, and you forget to type a close parenthesis:

```
//The following line is incorrect:
public static void main (String args[]
```

When you issue the `javac` command, you get the messages shown in Figure 5-13.

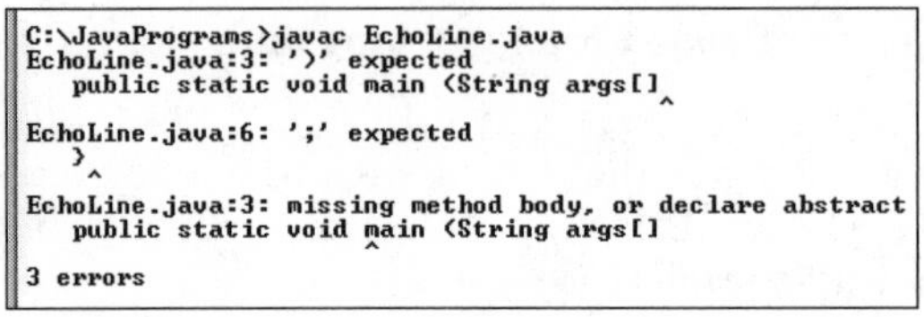

Figure 5-13:
Three error
messages.

```
C:\JavaPrograms>javac EchoLine.java
EchoLine.java:3: ')' expected
        public static void main (String args[]
                                              ^
EchoLine.java:6: ';' expected
        }
         ^
EchoLine.java:3: missing method body, or declare abstract
        public static void main (String args[]
                            ^
3 errors
```

The computer reports three errors — two errors on line 3, and one error on line 6. "Let's see," you say to yourself. "Line 6 is the last line of the `main` method. The message says `';' expected`. Why would I want a semicolon at the end of my `main` method?"

Well, you better take a step backward. In Figure 5-13, the first of the three messages says `')' expected`. That's okay. But after that first message, the computer is really confused. In the second message, the computer suggests that you end the `main` method with a semicolon, as if that would fix anything. The computer is trying to make the best of a bad situation but, at this point, you shouldn't believe a word that the computer says.

The moral to this story is simple. The first of the computer's error messages is often the most reliable. The rest of the messages may be nothing but confusing drivel.

Information overload

Sometimes when you're compiling or running a program, you get lots of error messages — so many messages that they start running off the top of the command prompt window. The computer gets confused and displays a bucket load of messages. The problem is, the first message runs quickly off the screen, and that first message is often the most informative. So what can you do to see the first message again?

If you use Windows NT, 2000, or XP, your problem is already solved. With these operating systems, the command prompt window can have its own scroll bar. You can scroll back to lines that have rolled off the upper edge of the window. You can make the scroll bar appear, make it disappear, make it store fewer lines, or make it store more lines. Just do the following:

1. **Right-click the command prompt window's title bar and select Properties from the context menu.**

2. **On the Properties dialog box that appears, click the Layout tab.**

3. **In the Screen Buffer Size area, change the number in the Height field by using the toggle buttons or by typing a new number in the field.**

   I usually change the number to 200 or 300, but any number between 100 and 500 should serve you well.

If you use Windows 95, 98, or Me, then you need some outside help to get yourself a scroll bar. To do this, I recommend a product named WinOne. The WinOne shell is like the built-in Windows command prompt. But WinOne has multicolored text, smart filename completion, easy access to directories, and (best of all) a scroll bar. For more information on WinOne, visit `www.winone.com.au`.

If you get more than one error message, always look carefully at the first message in the bunch.

Sometimes the first message isn't the best

Earlier, I wrote that the first message in a bunch of error messages is usually the most useful. Well, I wasn't lying to you, but reading and interpreting error messages is an art, not a science.

Here's an example. Take the code in Listing 5-1 and change `public` to `Public` (with a capital P).

```
//The following line is incorrect:
Public static void main(String args[])
```

With this incorrect word `Public`, what happens when you issue the `javac` command? Well, take a look back at Figure 5-9 to see what happens when you incorrectly capitalize the word `println`. In that situation, the `javac` command gives you a `cannot resolve symbol` message. But, when you write `Public` instead of `public`, you get some additional error messages. It's all in Figure 5-14.

Figure 5-14:
Three
messages
for the price
of one.

```
C:\JavaPrograms>javac EchoLine.java
EchoLine.java:3: <identifier> expected
    Public static void main (String args[])
          ^
EchoLine.java:6: ';' expected
    }
     ^
EchoLine.java:3: cannot resolve symbol
symbol  : class Public
location: class EchoLine
    Public static void main (String args[])
    ^
3 errors
```

Of the three messages in Figure 5-14, the last message (not the first) is the most useful. The last message in Figure 5-14 says cannot resolve symbol . . . Public. That's interesting. Because I mistakenly used a capital P, the computer doesn't know what the word Public means.

If you're not used to case-sensitivity, then that last error message may be annoying. But the two earlier error messages in Figure 5-14 are worse than annoying. They're mystifying. The first two messages in Figure 5-14, <identifier> expected and ';' expected, are just weird ramblings on the part of the Java compiler. When it issues these messages, the compiler is thinking that maybe Public is a name that you made up (a name like Echo Line), and that another homegrown name should come after the word Public. This isn't what you intended, but the compiler is doing its best with the information that you've given to it. So my advice is, just ignore the first two messages in Figure 5-14. Change Public to public and then reissue the javac command.

Same kind of error; different kind of message

You've found an old family recipe for deviled eggs (one of my favorites). You follow every step as carefully as you can, but you leave out the salt because of your grandmother's high blood pressure. You hand your grandmother an egg (a finished masterpiece). "Not enough pepper," she says, and she walks away.

The next course is beef bourguignon. You take an unsalted slice to dear old Granny. "Not sweet enough," she groans, and she leaves the room. "But that's impossible," you think. "There's no sugar in beef bourguignon. I left out the salt." Even so, you go back to the kitchen and prepare mashed potatoes. You use unsalted butter, of course. "She'll love it this time," you think.

"Sour potatoes! Yuck!" Granny says, as she goes to the sink to spit it all out. Because you have a strong ego, you're not insulted by your grandmother's behavior. But you're somewhat confused. Why is she saying such different things about three unsalted recipes? Maybe there are some subtle differences that you don't know about.

Well, the same kind of thing happens when you're writing computer programs. You can make the same kind of mistake twice (or at least, make what you think is the same kind of mistake twice), and get different error messages each time. For instance, if you read the earlier stuff in this chapter, you may come to believe that every unrecognized word leads to a `cannot resolve symbol` message. Well, I'm sorry. It just doesn't work that way.

Take, for example, the word `class` in Listing 5-1. Change the lowercase `c` to an uppercase `C`:

```
//The following line is incorrect:
Class EchoLine
```

When it sees this line, the compiler doesn't even bother to tell you that it can't resolve a symbol. The compiler just thinks, "Most programs start with the word `class`, and some start with the word `interface`. This incorrect program starts with a word that I don't understand (because I don't think about the letters `C` and `c` having anything to do with one another). I'll suggest either `class` or `interface`. That should fix it." So the computer sends you the message that's shown in Figure 5-15.

Figure 5-15:
Spelling
"Class"
incorrectly
(with a
capital "C").

```
C:\JavaPrograms>javac EchoLine.java
EchoLine.java:1: 'class' or 'interface' expected
Class EchoLine
^
1 error
```

In fact, that fixes it, because a change from `Class` to `class` gets your code running again.

An *interface* is like a class. But unlike a class, an interface can't stand on its own. For instance, you can't put your `static void main` method in a Java interface. None of the programs in this book use interfaces, so don't worry about interfaces until you advance past the beginning programming stage.

Run-time error messages

Up to this point in the chapter, I describe errors that crop up when you issue the `javac` command. Another category of errors hides until you issue the `java` command. A case in point is the improper capitalization of the word `main`.

Assume that, in a moment of wild abandon, you incorrectly spell `main` with a capital `M`:

```
//The following line is incorrect:
public static void Main (String args[])
```

One message and none very helpful

Look at the following sidebar figure and think about what happened. The computer got all upset because it didn't see one of the words that it expected. The computer expected to see either `class` or `interface`, and it scolded me for not using one of these two words. Oddly enough, the computer was going out on a limb when it suggested the words `class` and `interface`. The fact is, not all programs begin with the word `class` or the word `interface`. Here's an example:

```
import java.lang.*;
class EchoLine
{

    public static void main
    (String args[])
    {

    System.out.println(DummiesI
O.getLine());
    }

}
```

To the code in Listing 5-1, I've added an extra `import` statement — the statement `import java.lang.*`. At this point, you don't have to worry about the meaning of the `import` statement. This statement isn't necessary, but its being there doesn't hurt anything. The new code, `import` statement and all, runs just as flawlessly as the code in Listing 5-1.

Now, what happens if your pinky finger becomes heavy, and you type `Import` instead of `import`?

```
//The following line is incorrect:
Import java.lang.*;
```

Then, much to your dismay, you get the message shown in the accompanying figure. The figure has yet another `'class' or 'interface' expected` message, but this time, the message is all wrong. Sure, you should have typed `import` instead of `Import`. But no, the computer's suggestion that the word `class` or `interface` will fix everything is incorrect.

Now unfortunately, in this particular figure, you don't get a message saying `cannot resolve symbol . . . Import`. And you certainly don't see a message like `'import' expected`. Either of those messages would be more helpful than `'class' or 'interface' expected`, but neither message is destined to appear. That's just the way the cookie crumbles. Computers aren't smart animals, and if someone programs the computer to say `'class' or 'interface' expected`, then that's exactly what the computer says.

Some people say that computers make them feel stupid. For me, it's the opposite. A computer reminds me how dumb a machine can be, and how smart a person can be. I like that.

```
C:\JavaPrograms>javac EchoLine.java
EchoLine.java:1: 'class' or 'interface' expected
Import java.lang.*;

1 error
```

When you compile with the `javac` command, everything is hunky-dory. But then you try to run your program with the `java` command. At this point, the bits hit the fan. The catastrophe is illustrated in Figure 5-16.

Sure, your program has something named `Main`, but does it have anything named `main`? (Yes, I've heard of a famous poet named e. e. cummings, but who the heck is E. E. Cummings?) The computer doesn't presume that your word `Main` means the same thing as the expected word `main`. You need to change `Main` back to `main`. Then everything will be okay.

Figure 5-16:
Whadaya
mean
"NoSuch-
Method-
Error?"

```
C:\JavaPrograms>javac EchoLine.java

C:\JavaPrograms>java EchoLine
Exception in thread "main" java.lang.NoSuchMethodError: main
```

But in the meantime (or in the maintime), why did this improper capitalization make it past the `javac` command? And if the `javac` command likes a capital M, why doesn't the `java` command accept your creative capitalization?

The answer goes back to the different kinds of words in the Java programming language. As it says in Chapter 4, Java has identifiers and keywords.

The keywords in Java are cast in stone. If you change `class` to `Class`, or change `public` to `Public`, then you get something new — something that the computer probably can't understand. That's why the `javac` command chokes on improper keyword capitalizations. It's the `javac` command's job to make sure that all the keywords are used properly.

On the other hand, the identifiers can bounce all over the place. Sure, there's an identifier named `main`, but you can make up a new identifier named `Main`. (You shouldn't do it, though. It's too confusing to people who know Java's usual meaning for the word `main`.) When the compiler sees a mistyped line, like `public static void Main`, the compiler just assumes that you're making up a brand new name. So the `javac` command lets the line pass. You get no complaints from `javac`.

But then, when you issue the `java` command, the computer goes ballistic. The Java Virtual Machine always looks for something spelled `main`, with a small m. If the JVM doesn't see anything named `main`, then the JVM gets upset. "NoSuchMethod . . . main," says the `java` command. So now `java`, and not `javac`, gives you an error message.

What problem? I don't see a problem

I end this chapter on an upbeat note by showing you some of the things you can change in Listing 5-1 without rocking the boat.

The identifiers that you create

If you create an identifier, then that name is up for grabs. For instance, in Listing 5-1, change `EchoLine` to `PleaseRepeat`.

```
class PleaseRepeat
{
    public static void main ... etc.
```

This presents no problem at all, as long as you're willing to be consistent. When you run the program, use the new program name:

```
java PleaseRepeat
```

Spaces and indentation

Java isn't fussy about the use of spaces and indentation. All you need to do is keep your program well-organized and readable. Here's an example:

```
class EchoLine {

    public static void main( String args[] ) {
            System.out.println
                    ( DummiesIO.getLine() );
    }
}
```

How you choose to do things

A program is like a fingerprint. No two programs look very much alike. Say I discuss a programming problem with a colleague. Then we go our separate ways and write our own programs to solve the same problem. Sure, we're duplicating the effort. But will we create the exact same code? Absolutely not. Everyone has his or her own style, and everyone's style is unique.

I asked fellow Java programmer David Herst to write his own EchoLine program without showing him my code from Listing 5-1. Here's what he wrote:

```
import java.io.BufferedReader;
import java.io.InputStreamReader;
import java.io.IOException;

public class EchoLine {
    public static void main(String[] args)
            throws IOException {
        InputStreamReader isr =
            new InputStreamReader(System.in);
        BufferedReader br = new BufferedReader(isr);
        String input = br.readLine();
        System.out.println(input);
    }
}
```

Don't worry about BufferedReader, InputStreamReader, or things like that. Just notice that, like snowflakes, no two programs are written exactly alike, even if they accomplish the same task. That's nice. It means your code, however different, can be as good as the next person's. That's very encouraging.

Chapter 6

Using the Building Blocks: Variables, Values, and Types

*B*ack in 1946, John von Neumann wrote a groundbreaking paper about the newly emerging technology of computers and computing. Among other things, he established one fundamental fact: For all their complexity, the main business of computers is to move data from one place to another. Take a number — the balance in a person's bank account. Move this number from the computer's memory to the computer's processing unit. Add a few dollars to the balance, and then move it back to the computer's memory. The movement of data . . . that's all there is; there ain't no more.

Good enough! This chapter shows you how to move around your data.

Using Variables

Here's an excerpt from a software company's Web site:

> SnitSoft recognizes its obligation to the information technology community. For that reason, SnitSoft is making its most popular applications available for a nominal charge. For just $5.95 plus shipping and handling, you receive a CD-ROM containing SnitSoft's premier products.

Go ahead. Click the <u>Order Now!</u> link. Just see what happens. You get an order form with two items on it. One item is labeled $5.95 (CD-ROM), and the other item reads $25.00 (shipping and handling). What a rip-off! Thanks to SnitSoft's generosity, you can pay $30.95 for ten cents worth of software.

Behind the scenes of the SnitSoft Web page, a computer program does some scoundrel's arithmetic. The program looks something like the code in Listing 6-1.

Listing 6-1   SnitSoft's Grand Scam

```
class SnitSoft
{
    public static void main(String args[])
    {
        double amount;

        amount = 5.95;
        amount = amount + 25.00;

        System.out.print("We will bill $");
        System.out.print(amount);
        System.out.println(" to your credit card.");
    }
}
```

When I run the Listing 6-1 code on my own computer (not the SnitSoft computer), I get the output shown in Figure 6-1.

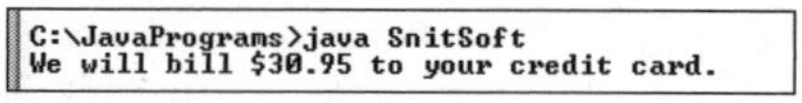

Figure 6-1:
Running the
code from
Listing 6-1.

```
C:\JavaPrograms>java SnitSoft
We will bill $30.95 to your credit card.
```

Using a variable

The code in Listing 6-1 makes use of a variable named amount. A *variable* is a placeholder. You can stick a number like 5.95 into a variable. After you've placed a number in the variable, you can change your mind and put a different number, like 30.95, into the variable. (That's what varies in a variable.) Of course, when you put a new number in a variable, the old number is no longer there. If you didn't save the old number somewhere else, the old number is gone.

Figure 6-2 gives a before and after picture of the code in Listing 6-1. When the computer executes amount = 5.95, the variable amount has the number 5.95 in it. Then, after the amount = amount + 25.00 statement is executed, the variable amount suddenly has 30.95 in it. When you think about a variable, picture a place in the computer's memory where wires and transistors store

5.95, 30.95, or whatever. In Figure 6-2, imagine that each box is surrounded by millions of other such boxes.

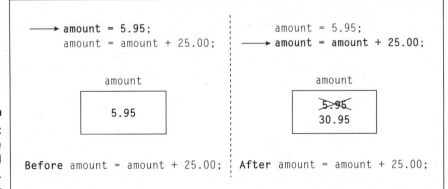

Figure 6-2:
A variable
(before and
after).

Now you need some terminology. (You can follow along in Figure 6-3.) The thing stored in a variable is called a *value*. A variable's value can change during the run of a program (when SnitSoft adds the shipping and handling cost, for instance). The value stored in a variable isn't necessarily a number. (You can, for instance, create a variable that always stores a letter.) The kind of value stored in a variable is a variable's *type*. (You can read more about types in the rest of this chapter and in the next two chapters as well.)

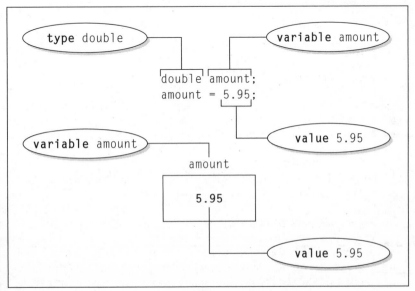

Figure 6-3:
A variable,
its value,
and its type.

There's a subtle, almost unnoticeable difference between a variable and a variable's *name*. Even in formal writing, I often use the word *variable* when I mean *variable name*. Strictly speaking, amount is the variable name, and all the memory storage associated with amount (including the value and type of amount) is the variable itself. If you think this distinction between *variable* and *variable name* is too subtle for you to worry about, join the club.

Every variable name is an identifier — a name that you can make up in your own code (for more about this, see Chapter 4). In preparing Listing 6-1, I made up the name amount.

Understanding assignment statements

The statements with equal signs in Listing 6-1 are called *assignment statements*. In an assignment statement, you assign a value to something. In many cases, this something is a variable.

You should get into the habit of reading assignment statements from right to left. For instance, the first assignment statement in Listing 6-1 says, "Assign 5.95 to the amount variable." The second assignment statement is just a bit more complicated. Reading the second assignment statement from right to left, you get "Add 25.00 to the value that's already in the amount variable and make that number (30.95) be the new value of the amount variable." For a graphic, hit-you-over-the-head illustration of this, see Figure 6-4.

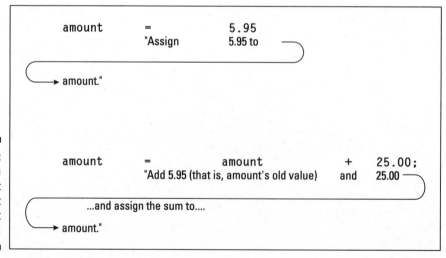

Figure 6-4:
Reading an assignment statement from right to left.

In an assignment statement, the thing being assigned a value is always on the left side of the equal sign.

To wrap or not to wrap?

The last three statements in Listing 6-1 use a neat trick. You want the program to display just one line on the screen, but this line contains three different things:

✔ The line starts with We will bill $.

✔ The line continues with the amount variable's value.

✔ The line ends with to your credit card.

These are three separate things, so you put these things in three separate statements. The first two statements are calls to System.out.print. The last statement is a call to System.out.println.

Calls to System.out.print display text on part of a line and then leave the cursor at the end of the current line. After executing System.out.print, the cursor is still at the end of the same line, so the next System.out.*whatever* can continue printing on that same line. With several calls to print capped off by a single call to println, the result is just one nice-looking line of output, as Figure 6-5 illustrates.

Figure 6-5:
The roles played by System.out. print and System.out. println.

```
C:\JavaPrograms>java SnitSoft
We will bill $ ──print──> 30.95 ──print──> to your credit card. ─┐
 ◄─────────────────────────────────────────────────────────────┘
                                                      println
C:\JavaPrograms>
```

A call to System.out.print writes some things and leaves the cursor sitting at the end of the line of output. A call to System.out.println writes things and then finishes the job by moving the cursor to the start of a brand new line of output.

What Do All Those Zeros and Ones Mean?

Here's a word:

> gift

The question for discussion is, what does that word mean? Well, it depends on who looks at the word. For instance, an English-speaking reader would say that "gift" stands for something one person bestows upon another in a box covered in bright paper and ribbons.

> Look! I'm giving you a **gift**!

But in German, the word "gift" means "poison."

> Let me give you some **gift**, my dear.

And in Swedish, "gift" can mean either "married" or "poison."

> As soon as they got **gift**, she slipped a **gift** into his drink.

Then there's French. In France, there's a candy bar named "Gift."

> He came for the holidays, and all he gave me was a bar of **Gift**.

So what do the letters g-i-f-t really mean? Well, they don't mean anything until you decide on a way to interpret them. The same is true of the zeros and ones inside a computer's circuitry.

Take, for instance, the sequence 01001010. This sequence can stand for the letter J, but it can also stand for the number 74. That same sequence of zeros and ones can stand for $1.0369608636003646\times10^{-43}$. And when interpreted as screen pixels, the same sequence can represent the dots shown in Figure 6-6. The meaning of 01001010 depends entirely on the way the software interprets this sequence.

Figure 6-6:
An extreme close-up of eight black-and-white screen pixels.

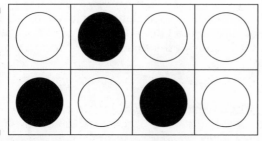

Types and declarations

How do you tell the computer what 01001010 stands for? The answer is in the concept called *type*. The type of a variable describes the kinds of values that the variable is permitted to store.

In Listing 6-1, look at the first line in the body of the `main` method.

```
double amount;
```

This line is called a *variable declaration*. Putting this line in your program is like saying, "I'm declaring my intention to have a variable named `amount` in my program." This line reserves the name `amount` for your use in the program.

In this variable declaration, the word *double* is a Java keyword. This word `double` tells the computer what kinds of values you intend to store in `amount`. In particular, the word `double` stands for numbers between -1.8×10^{308} and 1.8×10^{308}. That's an enormous range of numbers. Without the fancy $\times 10$ notation, the second of these numbers is

```
180000000000000000000000000000000000000000000000000000000000000000
000000000000000000000000000000000000000000000000000000000000000000
000000000000000000000000000000000000000000000000000000000000000000
000000000000000000000000000000000000000000000000000000000000000000
000000000000000000000000000000000000000000000000000000000000000000
0000.0
```

If the folks at SnitSoft ever charge that much for shipping and handling, they can represent the charge with a variable of type `double`.

What's the point?

More important than the humongous range of the `double` keyword's numbers is the fact that a `double` value can have digits to the right of the decimal point. After you declare `amount` to be of type `double`, you can store all sorts of numbers in `amount`. You can store 5.95, 0.02398479, or –3.0. In Listing 6-1, if I hadn't declared `amount` to be of type `double`, then I may not have been able to store 5.95. Instead, I would have had to store plain old 5 or dreary old 6, without any digits beyond the decimal point.

For more info on numbers without decimal points, see Chapter 7.

(This paragraph deals with a really picky point, so skip it if you're not in the mood.) People often use the phrase "decimal number" to describe a number with digits to the right of the decimal point. The problem is, the syllable "dec" stands for the number ten, so the word "decimal" implies a base-10 representation. Because computers store base-2 (not base-10) representations, the word "decimal" to describe such a number is a misnomer. But in this book, I just can't help myself. I'm calling them "decimal numbers" whether the techies like it or not.

Reading Decimal Numbers from the Keyboard

I don't believe it! SnitSoft is having a sale! For one week only, you can get the SnitSoft CD-ROM for the low price of just $5.75! Better hurry up and order one.

No, wait! Listing 6-1 has the price fixed at $5.95. I have to revise the program.

I know. I'll make the code more versatile. I'll input the amount from the keyboard. Listing 6-2 has the revised code, and Figure 6-7 shows a run of the new code.

Listing 6-2   Getting a Double Value from the Keyboard

```
class VersatileSnitSoft
{
    public static void main(String args[])
    {
        double amount;

        System.out.print("What's the price of a CD-ROM? ");
        amount = DummiesIO.getDouble();
        amount = amount + 25.00;

        System.out.print("We will bill $");
        System.out.print(amount);
        System.out.println(" to your credit card.");
    }
}
```

Figure 6-7:
Getting the
value of
a double
variable.

```
C:\JavaPrograms>java VersatileSnitSoft
What's the price of a CD-ROM? 5.75
We will bill $30.75 to your credit card.
```

Though these be methods, yet there is madness in 't

Notice the call to the `DummiesIO.getDouble` method in Listing 6-2. There's nothing special about this `getDouble` method. (It's something I wrote — not part of the standard Java API.) Just remember not to use `DummiesIO.getLine` the way I do in Chapter 5. In Java, each type of input requires its own special method. If you're getting a line of text, then `DummiesIO.getLine` works just fine. But if you're reading stuff from the keyboard, and you want that stuff to be interpreted as a number, you need a method like `DummiesIO.getDouble`. More examples (more `DummiesIO.get`*Something* methods) are in Chapters 7 and 8.

Copy my `DummiesIO.java` file to your `JavaPrograms` directory. If you don't, then the Java compiler won't know what `DummiesIO.getDouble` means. You can get `DummiesIO.java` at my Web site (`www.BurdBrain.com`) or at the Dummies Web site (`www.dummies.com/extras`).

You can find out more about my DummiesIO code by reading the section on input and output in Chapter 5. You can find out even more about my DummiesIO code by visiting Chapter 13.

Methods and assignments

Note how I use `DummiesIO.getDouble` in Listing 6-2. The method `DummiesIO.getDouble` is called as part of assignment statement. If you look in Chapter 5 at the section on how the EchoLine program works, you see that the computer can substitute something in place of a method call. The computer does this in Listing 6-2. When you type `5.75` on the keyboard, the computer turns

```
amount = DummiesIO.getDouble();
```

into

```
amount = 5.75;
```

(The computer doesn't really rewrite the code in Listing 6-2. This `amount = 5.75` line just illustrates the effect of the computer's action.) In the second assignment statement in Listing 6-2, the computer adds 25.00 to the 5.75 that's stored in `amount`.

Some method calls have this substitution effect, and others (like `System.out.println`) don't. To find out more about this, see Chapter 19.

Who does what, and how?

When you write a program, you're called a *programmer,* but when you run a program, you're called a *user.* So when you test your own code, you're being both the programmer and the user.

Say your program contains a DummiesIO.get *Something()* call, like the calls in Listings 5-1 and 6-2. Then your program gets input from the user. But, when the program runs, how does the user know to type something on the keyboard? If the user and the programmer are the same person, and the program is fairly simple, then knowing what to type is no big deal. For instance, when you start running the code in Listing 5-1, you have this book in front of you, and the book says "The computer is waiting for you to type something . . . You type one line of text . . ." So you type the text and press Enter. Everything is fine.

But very few programs come with their own books. In many instances, when a program starts running, the user has to stare at the screen to figure out what to do next. The code in Listing 6-2 works in this stare-at-the-screen scenario. In Listing 6-2, the first call to print puts an informative message (What's the price of a CD-ROM?) on the user's screen. A message of this kind is called a *prompt.* It's a close cousin to the command prompt (C:\JavaPrograms>) that's introduced in Chapter 2.

When you start writing programs, you can easily confuse the roles of the prompt and the user's input. So remember, no preordained relationship exists between a prompt and the subsequent input. To create a prompt, you call print or println. Then, to read the user's input, you call getLine, getDouble, or one of the other DummiesIO get methods. These print and get calls belong in two separate statements. Java has no commonly-used, single statement that does both the prompting and the getting.

As the programmer, your job is to combine the prompting and the getting. You can combine prompting and getting in all kinds of ways. Some ways are helpful to the user, and some ways aren't.

- ✔ **If you don't have a call to** print **or** println, **then the user sees no prompt.** A blinking cursor sits quietly and waits for the user to type something. The user has to guess what kind of input to type. Occasionally that's okay, but usually it isn't.

- ✔ **If you call** print **or** println, **but you don't call a** DummiesIO.get *Something* **method, then the computer doesn't wait for the user to type anything.** The program races to execute whatever statement comes immediately after the print or println.

- ✔ **If your prompt displays a misleading message, then you mislead the user.** Java has no built-in feature that checks the appropriateness of a prompt. That's not surprising. Most computer languages have no prompt-checking feature.

So be careful with your prompts and gets. Be nice to your user. Remember, you were once a humble computer user too.

Variations on a Theme

Look back at Listing 6-1. In that listing, it takes two lines to give the amount variable its first value:

```
double amount;
amount = 5.95;
```

You can do the same thing with just one line:

```
double amount=5.95;
```

When you do this, you don't say that that you're "assigning" a value to the amount variable. The line `double amount=5.95` isn't called an "assignment statement." Instead, this line is called a declaration with an *initialization*. You're *initializing* the amount variable. You can do all sorts of things with initializations, even arithmetic.

```
double gasBill   =  174.59;
double elecBill  =   84.21;
double H2OBill   =   22.88;
double total     = gasBill + elecBill + H2OBill;
```

Moving variables from place to place

It helps to remember the difference between initializations and assignments. For one thing, you can drag a declaration with its initialization outside of a method.

```
//This is okay:
class SnitSoft
{
    static double amount = 5.95;

    public static void main(String args[])
    {
        amount = amount + 25.00;

        System.out.print("We will bill $");
        System.out.print(amount);
        System.out.println(" to your credit card.");
    }
}
```

You can't do the same thing with assignment statements. (See the following code and Figure 6-8.)

```
//This does not compile:
class BadSnitSoftCode
{
    static double amount;
    amount = 5.95;              //Misplaced statement
```

```
    public static void main(String args[])
    {
        amount = amount + 25.00;

        System.out.print("We will bill $");
        System.out.print(amount);
        System.out.println(" to your credit card.");
    }
}
```

Figure 6-8:
A failed
attempt to
compile
BadSnit-
SoftCode.

```
C:\JavaPrograms>javac BadSnitSoftCode.java
BadSnitSoftCode.java:5: <identifier> expected
    amount = 5.95;              //Misplaced statement
           ^
BadSnitSoftCode.java:5: cannot resolve symbol
symbol  : class amount
location: class BadSnitSoftCode
    amount = 5.95;              //Misplaced statement
    ^
2 errors
```

You can't drag statements outside of methods. (Even though a variable declaration ends with a semicolon, a variable declaration isn't considered to be a statement. Go figure!)

The advantage of putting a declaration outside of a method is illustrated in Chapter 19. While you wait impatiently to reach that chapter, notice how I added the word `static` to each declaration that I pulled out of the `main` method. I had to do this because the `main` method's header has the word `static` in it. Not all methods are `static`. In fact, most methods aren't `static`. But, whenever you pull a declaration out of a `static` method, you have to add the word `static` at the beginning of the declaration. All the mystery surrounding the word `static` is resolved in Chapter 18.

Combining variable declarations

The code in Listing 6-1 has only one variable (as if variables are in short supply). You can get the same effect with several variables.

```
class SnitSoftNew
{
    public static void main(String args[])
    {
        double cdPrice;
        double shippingAndHandling;
        double total;
```

```
       cdPrice = 5.95;
       shippingAndHandling = 25.00;
       total = cdPrice + shippingAndHandling;

       System.out.print("We will bill $");
       System.out.print(total);
       System.out.println(" to your credit card.");
    }
 }
```

This new code gives you the same output as the code in Listing 6-1. (Refer to Figure 6-1.)

The new code has three declarations — one for each of the program's three variables. Because all three variables have the same type (the type double), I can modify the code and declare all three variables in one fell swoop:

```
double cdPrice, shippingAndHandling, total;
```

So which is better, one declaration or three declarations? Neither is better. It's a matter of personal style.

You can even add initializations to a combined declaration. When you do, each initialization applies to only one variable. For instance, with the line

```
double cdPrice, shippingAndHandling=25.00, total;
```

the value of shippingAndHandling becomes 25.00, but the variables cdPrice and total get no particular value.

Chapter 7

Numbers and Types

....

....

*N*ot so long ago, people thought computers did nothing but big, number-crunching calculations. Computers solved arithmetic problems, and that was the end of the story.

In the 1980s, with the widespread use of word-processing programs, the myth of the big metal math brain went by the wayside. But even then, computers made great calculators. After all, computers are very fast and very accurate. Computers never need to count on their fingers. Best of all, computers don't feel burdened when they do arithmetic. I hate ending a meal in a good restaurant by worrying about the tax and tip, but computers don't mind that stuff at all. (Even so, computers seldom go out to eat.)

Using Whole Numbers

Let me tell you, it's no fun being an adult. Right now I have four little kids in my living room. They're all staring at me because I have a bag full of gumballs in my hand. With 30 gumballs in the bag, the kids are all thinking "Who's the best? Who gets more gumballs than the others? And who's going to be treated unfairly?" They insist on a complete, official gumball count, with each kid getting exactly the same number of tasty little treats. I must be careful. If I'm not, then I'll never hear the end of it.

With 30 gumballs and four kids, there's no way to divide the gumballs up evenly. Of course, if I get rid of a kid, then I can give ten gumballs to each kid. The trouble is, gumballs are disposable; kids are not. So my only alternative is to divvy up what gumballs I can and dispose of the rest. "Okay, think quick," I say to myself. "With 30 gumballs and four kids, how many gumballs can I promise to each kid?"

I waste no time in programming my computer to figure out this problem for me. When I'm finished, I have the code in Listing 7-1.

Listing 7-1   How to Keep Four Kids from Throwing Tantrums

```java
class KeepingKidsQuiet
{
    public static void main(String args[])
    {
        int gumballs;
        int kids;
        int gumballsPerKid;

        gumballs = 30;
        kids = 4;
        gumballsPerKid = gumballs/kids;

        System.out.print("Each kid gets ");
        System.out.print(gumballsPerKid);
        System.out.println(" gumballs.");
    }
}
```

A run of the KeepingKidsQuiet program is shown in Figure 7-1. If each kid gets seven gumballs, then the kids can't complain that I'm playing favorites. They'll have to find something else to squabble about.

Figure 7-1:
Fair and
square.

```
C:\JavaPrograms>java KeepingKidsQuiet
Each kid gets 7 gumballs.
```

At the core of the gumball problem, I've got whole numbers — numbers with no digits beyond the decimal point. When I divide 30 by 4, I get 7½, but I can't take the ½ seriously. No matter how hard I try, I can't divide a gumball in half, at least not without hearing "my half is bigger than his half." This fact is reflected nicely in Java. In Listing 7-1, all three variables (gumballs, kids, and gumballsPerKid) are of type int. An int value is a whole number. When you divide one int value by another (as you do with the slash in Listing 7-1), you get another int. When you divide 30 by 4, you get 7 — not 7½. You see this in Figure 7-1. Taken together, the statements

```
gumballsPerKid = gumballs/kids;

System.out.print(gumballsPerKid);
```

put the number 7 on the computer screen.

Reading whole numbers from the keyboard

What a life! Yesterday there were four kids in my living room, and I had 30 gumballs. Today there are six kids in my house, and I have 80 gumballs. How can I cope with all this change? I know! I'll write a program that reads the numbers of gumballs and kids from the keyboard. The program is in Listing 7-2, and a run of the program is shown in Figure 7-2.

Listing 7-2   A More Versatile Program for Kids and Gumballs

```java
class KeepingMoreKidsQuiet
{
    public static void main(String args[])
    {
        int gumballs;
        int kids;
        int gumballsPerKid;

        System.out.print("How many gumballs? How many kids? ");

        gumballs = DummiesIO.getInt();
        kids = DummiesIO.getInt();

        gumballsPerKid = gumballs/kids;

        System.out.print("Each kid gets ");
        System.out.print(gumballsPerKid);
        System.out.println(" gumballs.");
    }
}
```

Figure 7-2:
Next thing you know, I'll have seventy kids and a thousand gumballs.

```
C:\JavaPrograms>java KeepingMoreKidsQuiet
How many gumballs? How many kids? 80 6
Each kid gets 13 gumballs.
```

You should notice a couple of things about Listing 7-2. First, you can read an `int` value with my `DummiesIO.getInt` method. Second, you can issue successive calls to `DummiesIO` methods. In Listing 7-2, I call `DummiesIO.getInt` twice. All I have to do is separate the numbers I type by blank spaces. In Figure 7-2, I put one blank space between my 80 and my 6, but more blank spaces would work as well.

This blank space rule applies to many of my `DummiesIO` methods. For instance, here's some code that reads three numeric values:

```
gumballs = DummiesIO.getInt();
costOfGumballs = DummiesIO.getDouble();
kids = DummiesIO.getInt();
```

Figure 7-3 shows valid input for these three `DummiesIO` method calls.

Figure 7-3:
Three
numbers
for three
calls to
Dummies
methods.

```
80                    7.35    6
```

What you read is what you get

When you're writing your own code, you should never take anything for granted. Suppose you accidentally reverse the order of the `gumballs` and `kids` assignment statements in Listing 7-2:

```
//This code is misleading:
System.out.print("How many gumballs? How many kids? ");
kids = DummiesIO.getInt();
gumballs = DummiesIO.getInt();
```

Then, the line `How many gumballs? How many kids?` is very misleading. Because the `kids` assignment statement comes before the `gumballs` assignment statement, the first number you type becomes the value of `kids`, and the second number you type becomes the value of `gumballs`. It doesn't matter that your program displays the message `How many gumballs? How many kids?`. What matters is the order of the assignment statements in the program.

If the `kids` assignment statement accidentally comes first, you can get a strange answer, like the zero answer in Figure 7-4. That's how `int` division works. It just cuts off any remainder. Divide a small number (like 6) by a big number (like 80), and you get 0.

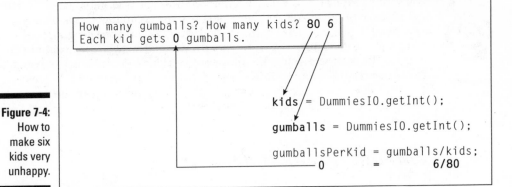

Creating New Values by Applying Operators

What could be more comforting than your old friend, the plus sign? It was the first thing you learned about in elementary school math. Almost everybody knows how to add two and two. In fact, in English usage, adding two and two is a metaphor for something that's easy to do. Whenever you see a plus sign, one of your brain cells says, "Thank goodness, it could be something much more complicated."

So Java has a plus sign. You can use the plus sign to add two numbers:

```
int apples, oranges, fruit;
apples = 5;
oranges = 16;
fruit = apples + oranges;
```

Of course, the old minus sign is available too:

```
apples = fruit - oranges;
```

Use an asterisk for multiplication, and a forward slash for division:

```
double rate, pay, withholding;
int hours;

rate = 6.25;
hours = 35;
pay = rate*hours;
withholding = pay/3.0;
```

TIP

When you divide an `int` value by another `int` value, you get an `int` value. The computer doesn't round. Instead, the computer chops off any remainder. If you put `System.out.println(11/4)` in your program, the computer prints 2, not 2.75. If you need a decimal answer, make either (or both) of the numbers you're dividing `double` values. For instance, if you put `System.out.println(11.0/4)` in your program, the computer divides a `double` value, 11.0, by an `int` value, 4. Because at least one of the two values is `double`, the computer prints 2.75.

Finding a remainder

There's a useful arithmetic operator called the *remainder* operator. The symbol for the remainder operator is the percent sign (%). When you put `System.out.println(11%4)` in your program, the computer prints 3. It does this because 4 goes into 11 who-cares-how-many times, with a remainder of 3.

The remainder operator turns out to be fairly useful. After all, a remainder is the amount you have left over after you divide two numbers. What if you're making change for $1.38? After dividing 138 by 25, you have 13 cents left over, as shown in Figure 7-5.

The code in Listing 7-3 makes use of this remainder idea.

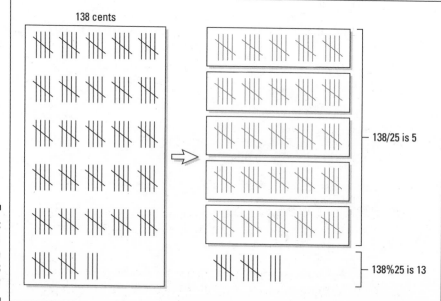

Figure 7-5:
Hey, bud!
Got change
for 138
sticks?

138 cents

138/25 is 5

138%25 is 13

Listing 7-3   Making Change

```
class MakeChange
{
    public static void main(String args[])
    {
        int quarters, dimes, nickels, cents;
        int whatsLeft, total;

        System.out.print("How many cents do you have? ");
        total = DummiesIO.getInt();

        quarters = total/25;
        whatsLeft = total%25;

        dimes = whatsLeft/10;
        whatsLeft = whatsLeft%10;

        nickels = whatsLeft/5;
        whatsLeft = whatsLeft%5;

        cents = whatsLeft;

        System.out.println();
        System.out.println("From " + total + " cents you get");

        System.out.println(quarters + " quarters");
        System.out.println(dimes + " dimes");
        System.out.println(nickels + " nickels");
        System.out.println(cents + " cents");
    }
}
```

A run of the code in Listing 7-3 is shown in Figure 7-6. You start with a total of 138 cents. The statement

```
quarters = total/25;
```

divides 138 by 25, giving 5. That means you can make 5 quarters from 138 cents. Next, the statement

```
whatsLeft = total%25;
```

divides 138 by 25 again, and puts only the remainder, 13, into whatsLeft. Now you're ready for the next step, which is to take as many dimes as you can out of 13 cents.

You keep going like this until you've divided away all the nickels. At that point, the value of whatsLeft is just 3 (meaning 3 cents).

If thine int offends thee, cast it out

The run in Figure 7-6 seems artificial. Why would you start with 138 cents? Why not use the more familiar $1.38? The reason is that the number 1.38 isn't a whole number, and without whole numbers, the remainder operator isn't very useful. For instance, the value of `1.38%0.25` is `0.1299999999999999`. All those nines are tough to work with.

So if you want to input `1.38`, then the program should take your 1.38 and turn it into 138 cents. The question is, how can you get your program do this?

My first idea is to multiply 1.38 by 100:

```
double amount;
int total;
System.out.print("How much
   money do you have? ");
amount = DummiesIO.getDouble();
total = amount*100;   //This
   doesn't quite work.
```

In everyday arithmetic, multiplying by 100 does the trick. But computers are fussy. With a computer, you have to be very careful when you mix `int` values and `double` values. (See the first figure in this sidebar.)

To cram a `double` value into an `int` variable, you need something called *casting*. When you cast a value, you essentially say, "I'm aware that I'm trying to squish a `double` value into an `int` variable. It's a tight fit, but I want to do it anyway."

To do casting, you put the name of a type in parentheses, as follows:

```
total = (int)(amount*100);
   //This works!
```

This casting notation turns the `double` value 138.00 into the `int` value 138, and everybody's happy. (See the second figure in this sidebar.)

```
   double amount:
   int total:
   ...
   total  =  amount*100;

          double   int

According to Java's rules, a
double times an int is a double.
```

Oops! This is an **int**. There's no room to squeeze in a double on this side of the assignment statement.

```
possible loss of precision
found    : double
required : int
     total = amount*100:
```

```
double amount;
int total;
...
total = (int) (amount*100);

                    1.38   100

                    138.00

         138
```

When two or more variables have similar types, you can create the variables with combined declarations. For instance, Listing 7-3 has two combined declarations — one for the variables `quarters`, `dimes`, `nickels`, and `cents` (all of type `int`); another for the variables `whatsLeft` and `total` (both of type `int`). But to create variables of different types, you need separate declarations. For instance, to create an `int` variable named `total` and a `double` variable named `amount`, you need one declaration `int total;` and another declaration `double amount;`.

Listing 7-3 has a call to `System.out.println()` with nothing in the parentheses. When the computer executes this statement, the cursor jumps to a new line on the screen. (I often use this statement to put a blank line in a program's output.)

```
C:\JavaPrograms>java MakeChange
How many cents do you have? 138

From 138 cents you get
5 quarters
1 dimes
0 nickels
3 cents
```

Figure 7-6:
Change
for $1.38.

The increment and decrement operators

Java has some neat little operators that make life easier (for the computer's processor, for your brain, and for your fingers). Altogether there are four such operators — two increment operators and two decrement operators. The increment operators add one, and the decrement operators subtract one. To see how they work, you need some examples.

Using preincrement

The first example is in Figure 7-7.

A run of the program in Figure 7-7 is shown in Figure 7-8. In this horribly uneventful run, the count of gumballs gets displayed three times.

The double plus sign goes under two different names, depending on where you put it. When you put the ++ before a variable, the ++ is called the *preincrement* operator. In the word preincrement, the *pre* stands for *before*. In this setting, the word *before* has two different meanings:

- ✔ You're putting ++ before the variable.
- ✔ The computer adds 1 to the variable's value before the variable gets used in any other part of the statement.

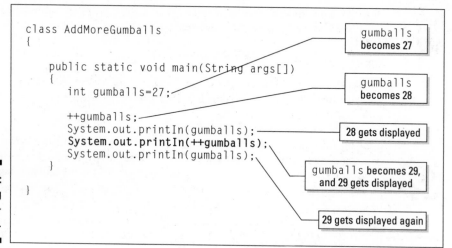

```
class AddMoreGumballs
{

    public static void main(String args[])
    {
        int gumballs=27;

        ++gumballs;
        System.out.printIn(gumballs);
        System.out.printIn(++gumballs);
        System.out.printIn(gumballs);
    }

}
```

gumballs becomes 27

gumballs becomes 28

28 gets displayed

gumballs becomes 29, and 29 gets displayed

29 gets displayed again

Figure 7-7:
Using preincrement.

Figure 7-8:
A run of the preincrement code (the code in Figure 7-7).

```
C:\JavaPrograms>java AddMoreGumballs
28
29
29
```

Figure 7-9 has a slow-motion instant replay of the preincrement operator's action. In Figure 7-9, the computer encounters the System.out.println (++gumballs) statement. First, the computer adds 1 to gumballs (raising the value of gumballs to 29). Then the computer executes System.out. println, using the new value of gumballs (29).

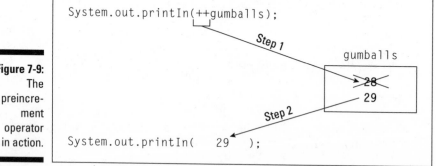

Figure 7-9:
The preincrement operator in action.

System.out.printIn(++gumballs);

Step 1

gumballs

28

29

Step 2

System.out.printIn(29   );

With `System.out.println(++gumballs)`, the computer adds 1 to gumballs *before* printing the new value of gumballs on the screen.

Using postincrement

An alternative to preincrement is *postincrement*. With postincrement, the *post* stands for *after*. The word *after* has two different meanings:

✔ You put ++ after the variable.

✔ The computer adds 1 to the variable's value after the variable gets used in any other part of the statement.

Figure 7-10 has a close-up view of the postincrement operator's action. In Figure 7-10, the computer encounters the `System.out.println` (`gumballs++`) statement. First, the computer executes `System.out.println`, using the *old* value of gumballs (28). Then the computer adds 1 to gumballs (raising the value of gumballs to 29).

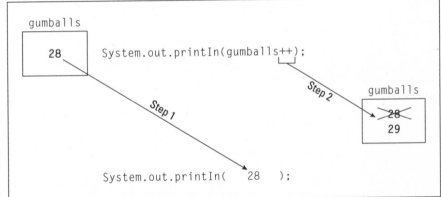

Figure 7-10:
The post-increment operator in action.

Look at the bold line in Figure 7-11. The computer prints the old value of gumballs (28) on the screen. Only after printing this old value does the computer add 1 to gumballs (raising the gumballs value from 28 to 29).

With `System.out.println(gumballs++)`, the computer adds 1 to gumballs *after* printing the old value that gumballs already had.

```
class AddEvenMoreGumballs
{

    public static void main(String args[])
    {
        int gumballs=27;

        gumballs++;
        System.out.println(gumballs);
        System.out.println(gumballs++);
        System.out.println(gumballs);
    }

}
```

gumballs becomes 27

gumballs becomes 28

28 gets displayed

28 gets displayed, **and then** gumballs **becomes 29.**

29 gets displayed

Figure 7-11: Using postincrement.

A run of the code in Figure 7-11 is shown in Figure 7-12. Compare Figure 7-12 with the run in Figure 7-8:

✔ With preincrement in Figure 7-8, the second number that gets displayed is 29.

✔ With postincrement in Figure 7-12, the second number that gets displayed is 28.

In Figure 7-12, the number 29 doesn't show up on the screen until the end of the run, when the computer executes one last System.out. println(gumballs).

Figure 7-12: A run of the postincrement code (the code in Figure 7-11).

```
C:\JavaPrograms>java AddEvenMoreGumballs
28
28
29
```

Are you trying to decide between using preincrement or postincrement? Ponder no longer. Most programmers use postincrement. In a typical Java program, you often see things like gumballs++. You seldom see things like ++gumballs.

In addition to preincrement and postincrement, Java has two operators that use --. These operators are called *predecrement* and *postdecrement:*

✔ With predecrement (`--gumballs`), the computer subtracts 1 from the variable's value before the variable gets used in the rest of the statement.

✔ With postdecrement (`gumballs--`), the computer subtracts 1 from the variable's value after the variable gets used in the rest of the statement.

Assignment operators

If you read the previous section — the section about operators that add 1 — you may be wondering if you can manipulate these operators to add 2, or add 5, or add 1000000. Can you write `gumballs++++`, and still call yourself a Java programmer? Well, you can't. If you try it, then the compiler will give you an error message:

```
unexpected type
required: variable
found    : value
      gumballs++++;
              ^
```

So how can you add values other than 1? As luck would have it, Java has plenty of *assignment operators* you can use. With an assignment operator, you can add, subtract, multiply, or divide by anything you want. You can do other cool operations too.

For instance, you can add 1 to the kids variable by writing

```
kids += 1;
```

Is this better than `kids++` or `kids=kids+1`? No, it's not better. It's just an alternative. But you can add 5 to the kids variable by writing

```
kids += 5;
```

You can't easily add 5 with pre- or postincrement. And what if the kids get stuck in an evil scientist's cloning machine? The statement

```
kids *= 2;
```

multiplies the number of `kids` by 2.

With the assignment operators, you can add, subtract, multiply, or divide a variable by any number. The number doesn't have to be a literal. You can use a number-valued expression on the right side of the equal sign:

```
double amount=5.95;
double shippingAndHandling=25.00, discount=0.15;

amount += shippingAndHandling;
amount -= discount*2;
```

The code above adds 25.00 (`shippingAndHandling`) to the value of `amount`. Then, the code subtracts 0.30 (`discount*2`) from the value of `amount`. How generous!

Statements and expressions

Any part of a computer program that has a value is called an *expression*. If you write

```
gumballs = 30;
```

then 30 is an expression (an expression whose value is the quantity 30). If you write

```
amount = 5.95 + 25.00;
```

then `5.95 + 25.00` is an expression (because 5.95 + 25.00 has the value 30.95). If you write

```
gumballsPerKid = gumballs/kids;
```

then `gumballs/kids` is an expression. (The value of the expression `gumballs/kids` depends on whatever values the variables `gumballs` and `kids` have when the statement with the expression in it is executed.)

This brings us to the subject of the pre- and postincrement and decrement operators. There are two ways to think about these operators: the way everyone understands it, and the right way. The way I explain it in most of this section (in terms of time, with *before* and *after*) is the way everyone understands the concept. Unfortunately, the way everyone understands the concept isn't really the right way. When you see ++ or --, you can think in terms of time sequence. But occasionally some programmer uses ++ or -- in a convoluted way, and the notions of before and after break down. So if you're ever in a tight spot, you should think about these operators in terms of statements and expressions.

First, remember that a statement tells the computer to do something, and an expression has a

value. (Statements are described in Chapter 4, and expressions are described earlier in this sidebar.) Which category does `gumballs++` belong to? The surprising answer is both. The Java code `gumballs++` is both a statement and an expression.

Say that, before executing the code `System.out.println(gumballs++)`, the value of `gumballs` is 28:

- As a statement, `gumballs++` tells the computer to add 1 to `gumballs`.

- As an expression, the value of `gumballs++` is 28, not 29.

So even though `gumballs` gets 1 added to it, the code `System.out.println(gumballs++)` really means `System.out.println(28)`. (See the following figure.)

Now, almost everything you just read about `gumballs++` is true about `++gumballs`. The only difference is, as an expression, `++gumballs` behaves in a more intuitive way. Say that, before executing the code `System.out.println(++gumballs)`, the value of `gumballs` is 28:

- As a statement, `++gumballs` tells the computer to add 1 to `gumballs`.

- As an expression, the value of `++gumballs` is 29.

With `System.out.println(++gumballs)`, the variable `gumballs` gets 1 added to it, and the code `System.out. println(++gumballs)` really means `System.out.println(29)`. (Again, see the following figure.)

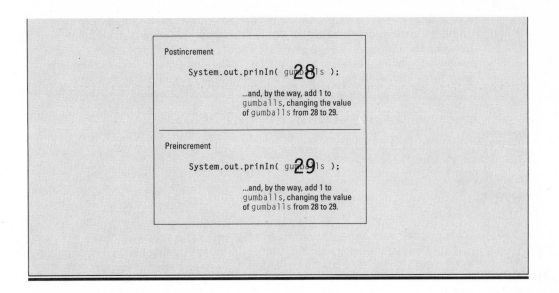

Size Matters

Here are today's new vocabulary words:

> **foregift** (fore-gift) *n.* A premium that a lessee pays to the lessor upon the taking of a lease.

> **hereinbefore** (here-in-be-fore) *adv.* In a previous part of this document.

Now imagine yourself scanning some compressed text. In this text, all blanks have been removed to conserve storage space. You come upon the following sequence of letters:

> hereinbeforegiftedit

The question is, what do these letters mean? If you knew each word's length, you could answer the question.

> here in be foregift edit
>
> hereinbefore gifted it
>
> herein before gift Ed it

A computer faces the same kind of problem. When a computer stores several numbers in memory or on a disk, the computer doesn't put blank spaces between the numbers. So imagine that a small chunk of the computer's memory looks like the stuff in Figure 7-13. (The computer works exclusively with zeros and ones, but Figure 7-13 uses ordinary digits. With ordinary digits, it's easier to see what's going on.)

Figure 7-13:
Storing the
digits 4221.

4	2	2	1

What number or numbers are stored in Figure 7-13? Is it two numbers, 42 and 21? Or is it one number, 4221? And what about storing four numbers, 4, 2, 2, and 1? It all depends on the amount of space each number consumes.

Sometimes you need lots of space. At other times, you want to be stingy with space. Imagine a variable that stores the number of paydays in a month. This number never gets bigger than 31. You can store this small number with just eight zeros and ones. But what about a variable that counts stars in the universe? That number could easily be more than a trillion, and to store one trillion accurately, you need 64 zeros and ones.

At this point, Java comes to the rescue. Java has four types of whole numbers. Just as in Listing 7-1, I declare

```
int gumballsPerKid;
```

I can also declare

```
byte paydaysInAMonth;
short sickDaysDuringYourEmployment;
long numberOfStars;
```

Each of these types (byte, short, int, and long) has its own storage requirements, and each has its own range of possible values. (See Table 7-1.)

Java has two types of decimal numbers (numbers with digits to the right of the decimal point). Just as in Listing 6-1, I declare

```
double amount;
```

I can also declare

```
float monthlySalary;
```

Given the choice between `double` and `float`, I always choose `double`. A variable of type `double` takes up more memory space, but it has a greater possible range of values and much greater accuracy. (See Table 7-1.)

Table 7-1	Java's Primitive Numeric Types	
Type Name	*Storage*	*Range of Values*
Whole Number Types		
`byte`	8 bits	−128 to 127
`short`	16 bits	−32768 to 32767
`int`	32 bits	−2147483648 to 2147483647
`long`	64 bits	−9223372036854775808 to 9223372036854775807
Decimal Number Types		
`float`	32 bits	-3.4×10^{38} to 3.4×10^{38}
`double`	64 bits	-1.8×10^{308} to 1.8×10^{308}

Table 7-1 lists six of Java's *primitive* types (also known as *simple* types). Java has only eight primitive types, so only two of Java's primitive types are missing from Table 7-1.

Have I ever lied to you before (before Table 7-1, that is)? Some of the items in this table are simplifications. (They're not lies. They're simplifications.) Behind the scenes, the Java Virtual Machine plays tricks with storage, and some of the numbers in the table's middle column are more myth than reality. But like many myths, these myths are useful, and you should take them seriously even though they don't tell the whole story.

Chapter 8 describes the two remaining primitive types. Chapter 17 introduces types that aren't primitive.

As a beginning programmer, you don't have to choose among the types in Table 7-1. Just use `int` for whole numbers and `double` for decimal numbers. If, in your travels, you see something like `short` or `float` in someone else's program, just remember the following:

✔ The types `byte`, `short`, `int`, and `long` represent whole numbers.

✔ The types `float` and `double` represent decimal numbers.

Most of the time, that's all you need to know.

Chapter 8

Numbers? Who Needs Numbers?

I don't particularly like fax machines. For one thing, they're high priced. And for another thing, they're inefficient. Send a short fax and what do you have? You have two slices of tree — one at the sending end, and another at the receiving end. You also have millions of dots — dots that scan tiny little lines across the printed page. The dots distinguish patches of light from patches of darkness. What a waste!

Compare a fax with an e-mail message. Using e-mail, I can send a 25 word contest entry with just 2500 zeros and ones, and I don't waste any paper. Best of all, an e-mail message doesn't describe light dots and dark dots. An e-mail message contains codes for each of the letters — a short sequence of zeros and ones for the letter A, a different sequence of zeros and ones for the letter B, and so on. What could be simpler?

Now imagine sending a one-word fax. The word is "true," which is understood to mean, "true, I accept your offer to write *Beginning Programming with Java For Dummies.*" A fax with this message sends a picture of the four letters t-r-u-e, with fuzzy lines where dirt gets on the paper and little white dots where the cartridge runs short on toner.

But really, what's the essence of the "true" message? There are just two possibilities, aren't there? The message could be "true" or "false," and to represent those possibilities, I need very little fanfare. How about 0 for "false" and 1 for "true?"

> They ask, "Do you accept our offer to write *Beginning Programming with Java For Dummies?*"
>
> "1," I reply.

Too bad I didn't think of that a few months ago. Anyway, this chapter deals with letters, truth, falsehood, and other such things.

Characters

In Chapters 6 and 7, you store numbers in all your variables. That's fine, but there's more to life than numbers. For instance, I wrote this book with a computer, and this book contains thousands and thousands of non-numeric things called *characters*.

The Java type that's used to store characters is *char*. Listing 8-1 has a simple program that uses the char type, and a run of the Listing 8-1 program is shown in Figure 8-1.

Listing 8-1   Using the char Type

```
class LowerToUpper
{
    public static void main(String args[])
    {
        char smallLetter, bigLetter;

        smallLetter = 'b';
        bigLetter = Character.toUpperCase(smallLetter);
        System.out.println(bigLetter);
    }
}
```

Figure 8-1:
Converting
lower- to
uppercase.

```
C:\JavaPrograms>java LowerToUpper
B
```

In Listing 8-1, the first assignment statement stores the letter b in the smallLetter variable. In that statement, notice how b is surrounded by single quote marks. In a Java program, every char literal starts and ends with a single quote mark.

When you surround a letter with quote marks, you tell the computer that the letter isn't a variable name. For instance, in Listing 8-1, the incorrect statement smallLetter = b would tell the computer to look for a variable named b. Because there's no variable named b, you'd get a cannot resolve symbol message.

In the second assignment statement of Listing 8-1, the program calls an API method whose name is Character.toUpperCase. The method

Character.toUpperCase does what its name suggests — the method produces the uppercase equivalent of a lowercase letter. In Listing 8-1, this uppercase equivalent (the letter B) is assigned to the variable bigLetter, and the B that's in bigLetter is printed on the screen, as illustrated in Figure 8-2.

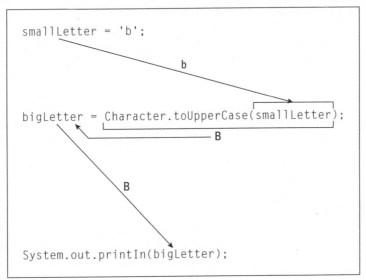

```
smallLetter = 'b';

                                    b

bigLetter = Character.toUpperCase(smallLetter);
                                B

                          B

System.out.printIn(bigLetter);
```

Figure 8-2:
The action
in Listing
8-1.

When the computer displays a char value on the screen, the computer does not surround the character with single quote marks.

I digress . . .

A while ago, I wondered what would happen if I called the Character. toUpperCase method and fed the method a character that isn't lowercase to begin with. I yanked out the Java API documentation, but I found no useful information. The documentation said that toUpperCase "converts the character argument to uppercase using case mapping information from the UnicodeData file." Thanks, but that's not useful to me.

Silly as it seems, I asked myself what I'd do if I were the toUpperCase method. What would I say if someone handed me a capital R and told me to capitalize that letter? I'd say, "Take back your stinking capital R." In the lingo of computing, I'd send that person an error message. So I wondered if I'd get an error message when I applied Character.toUpperCase to the letter R.

I tried it. I cooked up the experiment in Listing 8-2.

Listing 8-2   Investigating the Behavior of toUpperCase

```
class MyExperiment
{
    public static void main(String args[])
    {
        char smallLetter, bigLetter;

        smallLetter = 'R';
        bigLetter = Character.toUpperCase(smallLetter);
        System.out.println(bigLetter);

        smallLetter = '3';
        bigLetter = Character.toUpperCase(smallLetter);
        System.out.println(bigLetter);
    }
}
```

In my experiment, I didn't mix chemicals and blow things up. Here's what I did instead:

✔ **I assigned** `'R'` **to** smallLetter.

The toUpperCase method took the uppercase R and gave me back another uppercase R. (See Figure 8-3.) I got no error message. This told me what the toUpperCase method does with a letter that's already uppercase. The method does nothing.

✔ **I assigned** `'3'` **to** smallLetter.

The toUpperCase method took the digit 3 and gave me back the same digit 3. (See Figure 8-3.) I got no error message. This told me what the toUpperCase method does with a character that's not a letter. It does nothing, zip, zilch, bupkis.

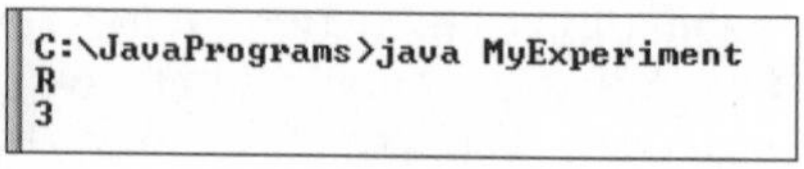

Figure 8-3:
Running the
code in
Listing 8-2.

```
C:\JavaPrograms>java MyExperiment
R
3
```

I write about this experiment to make an important point. When you don't understand something about computer programming, it often helps to write a test program. Make up an experiment, and see how the computer responds.

I guessed that handing a capital R to the toUpperCase method would give me an error message, but I was wrong. See? The answers to questions aren't handed down from heaven. The people who created the Java API made decisions. They made some obvious choices, and but they also made some unexpected choices. No one knows everything about Java's features, so don't expect to cram all the answers into your head.

The Java documentation is great, but for every question that the documentation answers, it ignores three other questions. So be bold. Don't be afraid to tinker. Write lots of short, experimental programs. You can't break the computer, so play tough with it. Your inquisitive spirit will always pay off.

One character only, please

A `char` variable stores only one character. So if you're tempted to write the following statements

```
char smallLetters;
smallLetters = 'barry';  //Don't do this
```

please resist the temptation. You can't store more than one letter at a time in a `char` variable, and you can't put more than one letter between a pair of single quotes. If you're trying to store words or sentences (not just single letters), then you need to use something called a *String*. For a look at Java's `String` type, see Chapter 18.

Variables and recycling

In Listing 8-2, I use `smallLetter` twice and I use `bigLetter` twice. That's why they call these things *variables*. First the value of `smallLetter` is R. Later, I vary the value of `smallLetter` so that the value of `smallLetter` becomes 3.

When I assign a new value to `smallLetter`, the old value of `smallLetter` gets obliterated. For instance, in Figure 8-4, the second `smallLetter` assignment puts 3 into `smallLetter`. When the computer executes this second assignment statement, the old value R is gone.

Is that okay? Can you afford to forget the value that `smallLetter` once had? Yes, in Listing 8-2, it's okay. After you've assigned a value to `bigLetter` with the statement

```
bigLetter = Character.toUpperCase(smallLetter);
```

you can forget all about the existing `smallLetter` value. You don't need to do this:

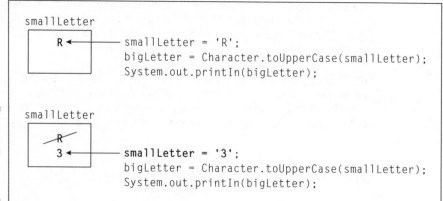

Figure 8-4:
Varying the
value of
small-
Letter.

```
// This code is cumbersome.
// The extra variables are unnecessary.
char smallLetter1, bigLetter1;
char smallLetter2, bigLetter2;

smallLetter1 = 'R';
bigLetter1 = Character.toUpperCase(smallLetter1);
System.out.println(bigLetter1);

smallLetter2 = '3';
bigLetter2 = Character.toUpperCase(smallLetter2);
System.out.println(bigLetter2);
```

You don't need to store the old and new values in separate variables. Instead, you can reuse the variables smallLetter and bigLetter as in Listing 8-2.

This reuse of variables doesn't save you from a lot of extra typing. It doesn't save much memory space either. But reusing variables keeps the program uncluttered. When you look at Listing 8-2, you can see at a glance that the code has two parts, and you see that both parts do roughly the same thing.

The code in Listing 8-2 is simple and manageable. In such a small program, simplicity and manageability don't matter very much. But in a large program, it helps to think carefully about the use of each variable.

When not to reuse a variable

The previous section discusses the reuse of variables to make a program slick and easy to read. This section shows you the flip side. In this section, the problem at hand forces you to create new variables.

Suppose you're writing code to reverse the letters in a four-letter word. You store each letter in its own separate variable. Listing 8-3 shows the code, and Figure 8-5 shows the code in action.

Listing 8-3   Making a Word Go Backwards

```
class ReverseWord
{
    public static void main(String args[])
    {
        char c1, c2, c3, c4;

        c1 = DummiesIO.getChar();
        c2 = DummiesIO.getChar();
        c3 = DummiesIO.getChar();
        c4 = DummiesIO.getChar();

        System.out.print(c4);
        System.out.print(c3);
        System.out.print(c2);
        System.out.print(c1);
        System.out.println();
    }
}
```

Figure 8-5:
Stop those
pots!

```
C:\JavaPrograms>java ReverseWord
pots
stop
```

The trick in Listing 8-3 is as follows:

- Assign values to variables c1, c2, c3, and c4 in that order.
- Display these variables' values on the screen in reverse order: c4, c3, c2, and then c1, as illustrated in Figure 8-6.

If you don't use four separate variables, then you don't get the result that you want. For instance, imagine that you store characters in only one variable. You run the program and type the word pots. When it's time to display the word in reverse, the computer remembers the final s in the word pots. But the computer doesn't remember the p, the o, or the t, as shown in Figure 8-7.

I wish I could give you twelve simple rules to help you decide when and when not to reuse variables. The problem is, I can't. It all depends on what you're trying to accomplish. So how do you figure out on your own when and when not to reuse variables? Like the guy says to the fellow who's trying to get to Carnegie Hall, "Practice, practice."

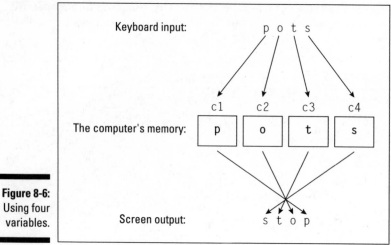

Figure 8-6:
Using four
variables.

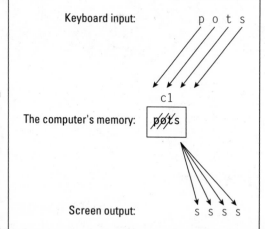

Figure 8-7:
Getting
things
wrong
because
you used
only one
variable.

Reading characters

Notice the format for the input in Figure 8-5. To enter the characters in the word pots, I type four letters, one after another, with no blank spaces between the letters and no quote marks. My DummiesIO.getChar method works that way, but don't blame me or my method. Other developers' character reading methods work the same way. No matter whose methods you use, reading a character differs from reading a number. Here's how:

✔ **With methods like** `getDouble` **and** `getInt`**, you type blank spaces between numbers.**

If I type **80 6**, then two calls to `getInt` read the number 80, followed by the number 6. If I type **806**, then a single call to `getInt` reads the number 806 (eight hundred six), as illustrated in Figure 8-8.

✔ **With method** `getChar`**, you don't type blank spaces between characters.**

If I type **po**, then two calls to `getChar` read the letter p, followed by the letter o. If I type **p o**, then two calls to `getChar` read the letter p, followed by a blank space character. (Yes, the blank space is a character!) Again, see Figure 8-8.

```
firstInt = DummiesIO.getInt();          80   6
secondInt = DummiesIO.getInt();


onlyInt = DummiesIO.getInt();           806


firstChar = DummiesIO.getChar();
secondChar = DummiesIO.getChar();       po


firstChar = DummiesIO.getChar();
secondChar = DummiesIO.getChar();       p   o
```

Figure 8-8:
Reading
numbers
and
characters.

To represent a lone character in the text of a computer program, you surround the character with single quote marks. But, when you type a character as part of a program's input, you don't surround the character with quote marks.

When I created `DummiesIO`, I sacrificed versatility for ease of use. So with `DummiesIO`, you can't read a number followed immediately by any old character. For instance, say that your program calls `getInt`, and then `getChar`. If you type **80x** on the keyboard, you get an error message. (The message says `Cannot read an int value`. My `getInt` method expects you to type a blank space after each `int` value.) Now what happens if, instead of typing

80x, you type **80 x** on the keyboard? Then the program gets 80 for the int value, followed by a blank space for the char value. For the program to get the x, the program has to call getChar one more time. It seems wasteful, but it makes sense in the long run.

The boolean Type

I'm in big trouble. I have 140 gumballs, and 15 kids are running around and screaming in my living room. They're screaming because each kid wants 10 gumballs, and they're running because that's what kids do in a crowded living room. I need a program that tells me if I can give 10 gumballs to each kid.

I need a variable of type *boolean*. A boolean variable stores one of two values — true or false (true, I can give 10 gumballs to each kid; or false, I can't give 10 gumballs to each kid). Anyway, the kids are going berserk, so I've written a short program and put it in Listing 8-4. The output of the program is shown in Figure 8-9.

Listing 8-4   Using the boolean Type

```
class CanIKeepKidsQuiet
{
    public static void main(String args[])
    {
        int gumballs;
        int kids;
        int gumballsPerKid;
        boolean eachKidGetsTen;

        gumballs = 140;
        kids = 15;
        gumballsPerKid = gumballs/kids;

        System.out.print("True or false? ");
        System.out.println("Each kid gets 10 gumballs.");
        eachKidGetsTen = gumballsPerKid>=10;
        System.out.println(eachKidGetsTen);
    }
}
```

Figure 8-9:
Oh no!

```
C:\JavaPrograms>java CanIKeepKidsQuiet
True or false? Each kid gets 10 gumballs.
false
```

In Listing 8-4, the variable eachKidGetsTen is of type boolean. So the value stored in the eachKidGetsTen variable can be either true or false. (I can't store a number or a character in the eachKidGetsTen variable.)

To find a value for the variable eachKidGetsTen, the program checks to see if gumballsPerKid is greater than or equal to ten. (The symbols >= stand for "greater than or equal to." What a pity! There's no _ key on the standard computer keyboard.) Because gumballsPerKid is only nine, gumballsPerKid>=10 is false. So eachKidGetsTen becomes false. Yikes! The kids will tear the house apart! (Before they do, take a look at Figure 8-10.)

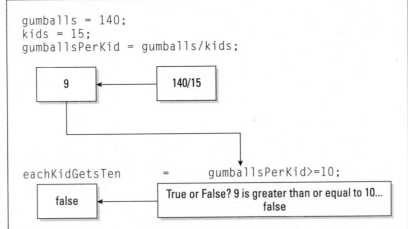

Figure 8-10: Assigning a value to the eachKid-GetsTen variable.

Expressions and conditions

In Listing 8-4, the code gumballsPerKid>=10 is an expression. The expression's value depends on the value stored in the variable gumballsPerKid. On a bad day, the value of gumballsPerKid>=10 is false. So the variable eachKidGetsTen is assigned the value false.

An expression like gumballsPerKid>=10, whose value is either true or false, is sometimes called a *condition*.

Values like true and false may look as if they contain characters, but they really don't. Internally, the Java Virtual Machine doesn't store boolean values with the letters t-r-u-e or f-a-l-s-e. Instead, the JVM stores codes, like 0 for false and 1 for true. When the computer displays a boolean value (as in System.out.println(eachKidGetsTen)), the Java Virtual Machine converts a code like 0 into the five-letter word false.

Comparing numbers; comparing characters

In Listing 8-4, I compare a variable's value with the number 10. I use the >= operator in the expression

```
gumballsPerKid>=10
```

Of course, the greater-than-or-equal comparison gets you only so far. Table 8-1 shows you the operators you can use to compare things with one another.

Table 8-1	Comparison Operators	
Operator Symbol	*Meaning*	*Example*
==	is equal to	`yourGuess == winningNumber`
!=	is not equal to	`5 != numberOfCows`
<	is less than	`strikes < 3`
>	is greater than	`numberOfBoxtops > 1000`
<=	is less than or equal to	`numberOfCows + numberOfBulls <= 5`
>=	is greater than or equal to	`gumballsPerKid >= 10`

With the operators in Table 8-1, you can compare both numbers and characters.

Notice the double equal sign in the first row of Table 8-1. Don't try to use a single equal sign to compare two values. The expression `yourGuess = winningNumber` (with a single equal sign) doesn't compare `yourGuess` with `winningNumber`. Instead `yourGuess = winningNumber` changes the value of `yourGuess`. (It assigns the value of `winningNumber` to the variable `yourGuess`.)

You can compare other things (besides numbers and characters) with the `==` and `!=` operators. But when you do, you have to be careful. For more information, see Chapter 18.

Comparing numbers

Nothing is more humdrum than comparing numbers. "True or false? Five is greater than or equal to ten." False. Five is neither greater than nor equal to ten. See what I mean? Bo-ring.

Comparing whole numbers is an open-and-shut case. But unfortunately, when you compare decimal numbers, there's a wrinkle. Take a program for converting from Celsius to Fahrenheit. Wait! Don't take just any such program; take the program in Listing 8-5.

Listing 8-5   It's Warm and Cozy in Here

```
class CelsiusToFahrenheit
{
    public static void main(String args[])
    {
        double celsius, fahrenheit;

        System.out.print ("Enter the Celsius temperature: ");
        celsius = DummiesIO.getDouble();

        fahrenheit = 9.0/5.0*celsius+32.0;

        System.out.print("Room temperature? ");
        System.out.println(fahrenheit==69.8);
    }
}
```

If you run the code in Listing 8-5 and input the number 21, the computer finds the value of `9.0/5.0*21+32.0`. Believe it or not, you want to check the computer's answer. (Who knows? Maybe the computer gets it wrong!) You need to do some arithmetic, but please don't reach for your calculator. A calculator is just a small computer, and machines of that kind stick up for one another. To check the computer's work, you need to do the arithmetic by hand. What? You say you're math phobic? Well, don't worry. I've done all the math in Figure 8-11.

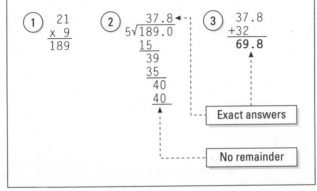

Figure 8-11: The Fahrenheit temperature is exactly 69.8.

If you do the arithmetic by hand, then the value you get for `9.0/5.0*21+32.0` is exactly 69.8. Run the code in Listing 8-5, and give `celsius` the value 21. You should get `true` when you display the value of `fahrenheit==69.8`, right? Well, no. Take a look at the run in Figure 8-12. When the computer evaluates `fahrenheit==69.8`, I get `false`, not `true`. What's going on here?

Figure 8-12:
A run of the code in Listing 8-5.

```
C:\JavaPrograms>java CelsiusToFahrenheit
Enter the Celsius temperature: 21
Room temperature? false
```

A little detective work can go a long way. So review the facts:

- ✓ **Fact:** The value of `fahrenheit` should be exactly 69.8.

- ✓ **Fact:** If `fahrenheit` is 69.8, then `fahrenheit==69.8` is `true`.

- ✓ **Fact:** In Figure 8-12, the computer displays the word `false`. So the expression `fahrenheit==69.8` isn't `true`.

How do you reconcile these facts? There can be little doubt that `fahrenheit==69.8` is `false`, so what does that say about the value of `fahrenheit`? Nowhere in Listing 8-5 is the value of `fahrenheit` displayed. Could that be the problem?

At this point, I use a popular programmer's trick. I add statements to display the value of `fahrenheit`.

```
fahrenheit = 9.0/5.0*celsius+32.0;
System.out.print("fahrenheit: ");       //Added
System.out.println(fahrenheit);         //Added
```

A run of the enhanced code is shown in Figure 8-13. As you can see, the computer misses its mark. Instead of the expected value 69.8, the computer's value for `9.0/5.0*21+32.0` is 69.80000000000001. That's just the way the cookie crumbles. The computer does all its arithmetic with zeros and ones, so the computer's arithmetic doesn't look like the base-10 arithmetic in Figure 8-11. The computer's answer isn't wrong. The answer is just slightly inaccurate.

Figure 8-13:
The fahrenheit variable's full value.

```
C:\JavaPrograms>java CelsiusToFahrenheit
Enter the Celsius temperature: 21
fahrenheit: 69.80000000000001
Room temperature? false
```

So be careful when you compare two numbers for equality (with ==) or for inequality (with !=). When you compare two `double` values, the values are almost never dead-on equal to one another.

If your program isn't doing what you think it should do, then check your suspicions about the values of variables. Add `print` and `println` statements to your code.

Comparing characters

The comparison operators in Table 8-1 work overtime for characters. Roughly speaking, the operator < means "comes earlier in the alphabet." But you have to be careful of the following:

- ✔ Because B comes alphabetically before H, the condition `'B' < 'H'` is true. That's not surprising.

- ✔ Because b comes alphabetically before h, the condition `'b' < 'h'` is true. That's no surprise either.

- ✔ Every uppercase letter comes before any of the lowercase letters, so the condition `'b' < 'H'` is *false*. Now that's a surprise. (See Figure 8-14.)

Figure 8-14:
The
ordering of
the letters.

```
ABCDEFGHIJKLMNOPQRSTUVWXYZabcdefghijklmnopqrstuvwxyz
lesser ◄─────────────────────────────────► greater
```

Automated debugging

If your program isn't working correctly, and you like using fancy software tools, you can try something called a *debugger*. A debugger automatically adds invisible `print` and `println` calls to your suspicious code. In fact, debuggers have all kinds of features to help you diagnose problems. For instance, a debugger can pause a run of your program and accept special commands to display variables' values. With some debuggers, you can pause a run and change a variable's value (just to see if things go better when you do).

Most integrated development environments (including JCreator) come with their own debuggers. The debugger `jdb` comes with the free SDK download from Sun Microsystems. The only problem is, debuggers are complicated. To use a debugger, you have to know two things: how to write computer programs, and how to use the debugger. I've tried using debuggers, and I've never felt that they're worth their weight. In the end, I always revert to the old time-tested practice — manually typing calls to `print` and `println`.

In practice, you seldom have reason to compare one letter with another. But in Chapter 18, you can read about Java's String type. With the String type, you can compare words, names, and other good stuff. At that point, you have to think carefully about alphabetical ordering, and the ideas in Figure 8-14 come in handy.

Under the hood, the letters A through Z are stored with numeric codes 65 through 90. The letters a through z are stored with codes 97 through 122. That's why each uppercase letter is "less than" any of the lowercase letters.

The Remaining Primitive Types

In Chapter 7, I tell you that Java has eight primitive types, but Table 7-1 lists only six out of eight types. Table 8-2 describes the remaining two types — the types char and boolean. Table 8-2 isn't too exciting, but I can't just leave you with the incomplete story in Table 7-1.

Table 8-2	Java's Primitive Non-numeric Types	
Type Name	*Storage*	*Range of Values*
Character Type		
char	16 bits	Thousands of characters, glyphs, and symbols
Logical Type		
boolean	1 bit	Only true or false

Talk about getting your money's worth! Table 8-2 comes with two disclaimers, not just one. The first disclaimer is the same as the one that accompanies Table 7-1: The storage amounts in each table's middle column are somewhat soft. You're the computer programmer, and as far as you're concerned, a boolean value takes up just a tiny zero or one in the computer's memory. But the Java Virtual Machine plays games with storage, and these games can change the picture without your knowing about it. Fortunately, you don't have to know about it.

The second disclaimer for Table 8-2 is about the char type. Java (and many other programming languages) considers char to be a numeric type. That's because the code for the letter A is 65, for B is 66, and so on. But don't worry about all this. The only reason I'm writing about the char type's being numeric is to save face among my techie friends.

Part III

Controlling the Flow

The 5th Wave   By Rich Tennant

WANDA HAD THE DISTINCT FEELING HER HUSBAND'S NEW
SOFTWARE PROGRAM WAS ABOUT TO BECOME INTERACTIVE.

In this part . . .

A computer program is like a role-playing video game. It's not the kind of game that involves shooting, punching, or racing. It's a game that involves strategies. Find the golden ring to open the secret passageway. Save the princess by reciting the magic words. It's that sort of thing.

So in this part of the book, you create passageways. As your program weaves its way from one virtual room to another, the computer gets closer and closer to the solution of an important problem.

Hey, admit it. This sounds like fun!

Chapter 9

Forks in the Road

. . . .

. . . .

Here's an excerpt from *Beginning Programming with Java For Dummies,* Chapter 2:

> **If you're using a fancy integrated development environment,** like JBuilder, WSAD, or CodeWarrior, then you don't need to download anything from Sun's Web site. You can **skip this whole chapter,** because your development environment has its own particular menus and procedures. *

The excerpt illustrates two important points: First, you may not have to read Chapter 2. Second, your choice of action can depend on something's being true or false.

> **If it's true** that you're using an integrated development environment,
>
> > skip Chapter 2.

So picture yourself walking along a quiet country road. You're enjoying a pleasant summer day. It's not too hot, and a gentle breeze from the north makes you feel fresh and alert. You're holding a copy of this book, opened to the start of Chapter 2. You read the paragraph about an integrated development environment (an IDE), and then you look up.

You see a fork in the road. You see two signs — one pointing to the right; the other pointing to the left. One sign reads, "Using an IDE? True." The other sign reads, "Using an IDE? False." You evaluate the IDE situation and march on, veering right or left depending on your software situation. A diagram of this story is shown in Figure 9-1.

* This excerpt is reprinted with permission from Wiley Publishing, Inc. If you can't find a copy of *Beginning Programming with Java For Dummies* in your local bookstore, visit www.wiley.com.

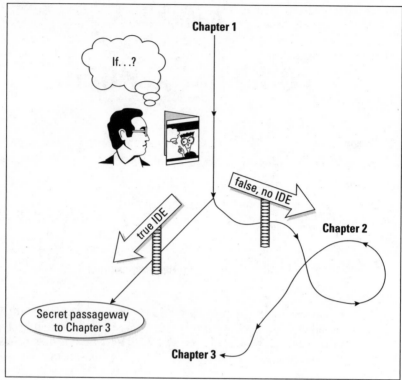

Figure 9-1:
Which way
to go?

Life is filled with forks in the road. Take an ordinary set of directions for heating up a frozen snack:

- **Microwave cooking directions:**

    Place on microwave safe plate.

    Microwave on high for 2 minutes.

    Turn product.

    Microwave on high for 2 more minutes.

- **Conventional oven directions:**

    Preheat oven to 350 degrees.

    Place product on baking sheet.

    Bake for 25 minutes.

Once again, you choose between alternatives. If you use a microwave oven, do this. Otherwise, do that.

In fact, it's hard to imagine useful instructions that don't involve choices. If you're a homeowner with two dependents earning more than $30,000 per year, check here. If you don't remember how to use curly braces in Java programs, see Chapter 4. Did the user correctly type his or her password? If yes, then let the user log in; if no, then kick the bum out. If you think the market will go up, then buy stocks; otherwise, buy bonds. And if you buy stocks, which should you buy? And when should you sell?

This chapter deals with decision-making, which plays a fundamental role in the creation of instructions. With the material in this chapter, you expand your programming power by leaps and bounds.

Making Decisions (Java if Statements)

When you work with computer programs, you make one decision after another. So almost every programming language has a way of branching in one of two directions. In Java (and in many other languages) the branching feature is called an *if statement*. Check out Listing 9-1 to see an if statement.

Listing 9-1   An if Statement

```
if (randomNumber > 5)
    System.out.println("Yes. Isn't it obvious?");
else
    System.out.println("No, and don't ask again.");
```

The if statement in Listing 9-1 represents a branch, a decision, two alternative courses of action. In plain English, this statement has the following meaning:

```
If the randomNumber variable's value is greater than 5,
    display "Yes. Isn't it obvious?" on the screen.
Otherwise,
    display "No, and don't ask again." on the screen.
```

Pictorially, you get the fork shown in Figure 9-2.

Looking carefully at if statements

An if statement can take the following form:

```
if (Condition)
    Statement1
else
    Statement2
```

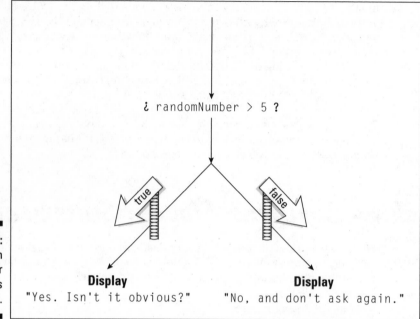

Figure 9-2:
A random
number
decides
your fate.

To get a real-life if statement, you substitute meaningful text for the three placeholders *Condition*, *Statement1*, and *Statement2*. Here's how I make the substitutions in Listing 9-1:

- ✔ I substitute randomNumber > 5 for *Condition*.
- ✔ I substitute System.out.println("Yes. Isn't it obvious?"); for *Statement1*.
- ✔ I substitute System.out.println("No, and don't ask again."); for *Statement2*.

The substitutions are illustrated in Figure 9-3.

Sometimes I need alternate names for parts of an if statement. I call them the *if clause* and the *else clause*.

```
if (Condition)
    if clause
else
    else clause
```

An if statement is an example of a *compound statement* — a statement that includes other statements within it. The if statement in Listing 9-1 includes two println calls and these calls to println are statements.

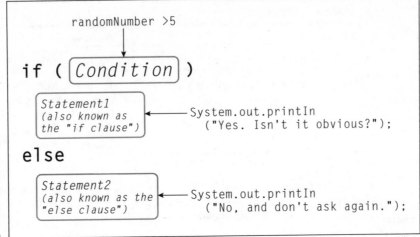

Figure 9-3:
An if
statement
and its
format.

Notice how I use parentheses and semicolons in the `if` statement of Listing 9-1. In particular, notice the following:

- ✔ The condition must be in parentheses.
- ✔ The statement inside the `if` clause ends with a semicolon. So does the statement that's inside the `else` clause.
- ✔ There's no semicolon immediately after the condition.
- ✔ There's no semicolon immediately after the word `else`.

As a beginning programmer, you may think these rules are arbitrary. But they're not. These rules belong to a very carefully crafted grammar. They're like the grammar rules for English sentences, but they're even more logical! (Sorry, Jean.)

Table 9-1 shows you the kinds of things that can go wrong when you break the `if` statement's punctuation rules. The table's last item is the most notorious. When you put a semicolon after the word `else`, the compiler generally doesn't catch the error. This lulls you into a false sense of security. The trouble is, when you run the program, the code's behavior isn't what you expect it to be.

Table 9-1	Common if Statement Error Messages
Error	**Message**
Missing parentheses surrounding the condition	`'(' expected`
Missing semicolon after a statement that's inside the `if` clause or the `else` clause	`';' expected`

(continued)

Table 9-1 *(continued)*

Error	Message
Semicolon immediately after the condition	`'else' without 'if'`
Semicolon immediately after the word else	The program compiles without errors, but the statement after the word else is always executed, whether the condition is `true` or `false`.

As you compose your code, it helps to think of an if statement as one indivisible unit. Instead of typing the whole first line (condition and all), try typing the if statement's skeletal outline.

```
if ()               //To do: Fill in the condition.
                    //To do: Fill in Statement1.
else
                    //To do: Fill in Statement2.
```

With the entire outline in place, you can start working on the items on your to-do list. When you apply this kind of thinking to a compound statement, it's harder to make a mistake.

A complete program

Listing 9-2 contains a complete program with a simple if statement. The listing's code behaves like an electronic oracle. Ask the program a yes or no question, and the program answers you back. Of course, the answer to your question is randomly generated. But who cares? It's fun to ask anyway.

Listing 9-2   I Know Everything

```
class AnswerYesOrNo
{
    public static void main(String args[])
    {
        int randomNumber;

        System.out.print("Type your question, my child:  ");
        DummiesIO.getLine();

        randomNumber = DummiesRandom.getInt();
        if (randomNumber > 5)
            System.out.println("Yes. Isn't it obvious?");
```

```
        else
            System.out.println("No, and don't ask again.");
    }
}
```

Figure 9-4 shows several runs of the program in Listing 9-2. The program's action has four parts:

Figure 9-4:
The all-
knowing
Java
program in
action.

```
C:\JavaPrograms>java AnswerYesOrNo
Type your question, my child:  Will I write a bestseller?
Yes. Isn't it obvious?

C:\JavaPrograms>java AnswerYesOrNo
Type your question, my child:  Will I earn lots of money?
No, and don't ask again.

C:\JavaPrograms>java AnswerYesOrNo
Type your question, my child:  Is "no" the correct answer to this question?
Yes. Isn't it obvious?

C:\JavaPrograms>java AnswerYesOrNo
Type your question, my child:  Fritz ate air meow swimmingly crackers
Yes. Isn't it obvious?
```

1. **Prompt the user.**

   Call System.out.print, telling the user to type a question.

2. **Get the user's question from the keyboard.**

   In Figure 9-4, I run the AnswerYesOrNo program four times, and I type a different question each time. Meanwhile, back in Listing 9-2, the statement

   ```
   DummiesIO.getLine();
   ```

   swallows up my question, and does absolutely nothing with it. This is an anomaly, but you're smart so you can handle it.

   Normally, when a program gets input from the keyboard, the program does something with the input. For instance, the program can assign the input to a variable:

   ```
   amount = DummiesIO.getDouble();
   ```

   Alternatively, the program can display the input on the screen:

   ```
   System.out.println(DummiesIO.getLine());
   ```

   But the code in Listing 9-2 is different. When this AnswerYesOrNo program runs, the user has to type something. (The call to getLine waits for the user to type some stuff, and then press Enter.) But the AnswerYesOrNo program has no need to store the input for further analysis. (The computer does what I do when my wife asks me if I plan to clean up after myself. I ignore the question and make up an arbitrary answer.) So the program doesn't do anything with the user's input. The call to DummiesIO.getLine just sits there in a statement of its own, doing nothing, behaving like a big black hole. It's unusual for a program to do this, but an electronic oracle is an unusual thing. It calls for some slightly unusual code.

3. Get a random number — any int **value from 1 to 10.**

Okay, wise guys. You've just trashed the user's input. How will you answer yes or no to the user's question?

No problem! None at all! You'll display an answer randomly. The user won't know the difference. (Hah, hah!) You can do this as long as you can generate random numbers. The numbers from 1 to 10 will do just fine.

With newer versions of the Java API, you can easily generate random numbers. But for this book, I make the process even easier. I've written my own DummiesRandom.getInt method and posted the code at www.BurdBrain.com and at www.dummies.com/extras. The call to DummiesRandom.getInt in Listing 9-2 gets a number from 1 to 10 and assigns that number to the variable randomNumber. When that's done, you're ready to answer the user's question.

My DummiesRandom.getInt method can generate numbers in ranges other than 1 to 10. For instance, to generate numbers from 1 to 100, call DummiesRandom.getInt(100). Calling DummiesRandom.getInt(), with nothing in parentheses, is like calling DummiesRandom.getInt(10). That's the way I set it up.

4. Answer yes or no.

Calling DummiesRandom.getInt() is like spinning a wheel on a TV game show. The wheel has slots numbered 1 to 10. The if statement in Listing 9-2 turns your number into a yes or no alternative. If you roll a number that's greater than 5, the program answers *yes*. Otherwise (if you roll a number that's less than or equal to 5), the program answers *no*.

You can trust me on this one. I've made lots of important decisions based on my AnswerYesOrNo program.

Indenting if statements in your code

Notice how, in Listing 9-2, the println calls inside the if statement are indented. Strictly speaking, you don't have to indent the statements that are inside an if statement. For all the compiler cares, you can write your whole program on a single line or place all your statements in an artful, misshapen zigzag. The problem is, if you don't indent your statements in some logical fashion, then neither you nor anyone else can make sense of your code. In Listing 9-2, the indenting of the println calls helps your eye (and brain) see quickly that these statements are subordinate to the overall if/else flow.

In a small program, unindented or poorly indented code is barely tolerable. But in a complicated program, indentation that doesn't follow a neat, logical pattern is a big, ugly nightmare.

Always indent your code to make the program's flow apparent at a glance.

Randomness makes me dizzy

When you call my `DummiesRandom.get Int()` method, you get a number from 1 to 10. As a test, I wrote a program that calls the `DummiesRandom.getInt()` twenty times.

```
public static void main(String
    args[])
{
    System.out.println();
    System.out.print(Dummies
    Random.getInt());
    System.out.print(" ");
    System.out.print(Dummies
    Random.getInt());
    System.out.print(" ");
    System.out.print(Dummies
    Random.getInt());
    //...And so on.
```

I ran the program several times, and got the results shown in the figure below. Stare briefly at the figure and notice two trends:

✔ There's no obvious way to predict what number comes next.

✔ No number occurs much more often than any of the others.

The Java Virtual Machine jumps through hoops to maintain these trends. That's because cranking out numbers in a random fashion is a very tricky business. Here are some interesting facts about the process:

✔ Scientists and non-scientists use the term *random number*. But in reality, there's no such thing as a single random number. After all, how random is a number like 9?

A number is *random* only when it's one in a very disorderly collection of numbers. More precisely, a number is *random* if the process used to generate the number follows the two trends listed above. When they're being careful, scientists avoid the term *random number,* and use the term *randomly generated number* instead.

✔ It's hard to generate numbers randomly. Computer programs do the best they can, but ultimately, today's computer programs follow a pattern, and that pattern isn't truly random.

To generate numbers in a truly random fashion, you need a big tub of ping-pong balls, like the kind they use in state lottery drawings. The problem is, most computers don't come with big tubs of ping-pong balls among their peripherals. So strictly speaking, the numbers generated by my `DummiesRandom` code aren't random. Instead, scientists call these numbers *pseudorandom.*

✔ It surprises us all, but knowing one randomly generated value is of no help in predicting the next randomly generated value.

For example, if you toss a coin twice, and get heads each time, are you more likely to get tails on the third flip? No. It's still fifty-fifty.

If you have three sons, and you're expecting a fourth child, is the fourth child more likely to be a girl? No. A child's gender has nothing to do with the genders of the older children. (I'm ignoring any biological effects, which I know absolutely nothing about. Wait! I do know some biological trivia: A newborn child is more likely to be a boy than a girl. For every 21 newborn boys, there are only 20 newborn girls. Boys are weaker, so we die off faster. That's why nature makes more of us at birth.)

```
6 10 3 10 3 13 8 10 6 3 3 8 5 2 6 1 10 8
C:\JavaPrograms>java TestRandom
8 3 5 5 4 8 7 4 7 1 7 4 7 10 1 3 5 3 7 9
C:\JavaPrograms>java TestRandom
10 4 3 7 2 4 7 7 3 7 4 6 9 7 2 9 2 8 9 5
C:\JavaPrograms>java TestRandom
4 2 3 9 4 4 7 3 9 9 2 6 8 9 3 2 8 8 2 3
C:\JavaPrograms>java TestRandom
6 3 1 2 10 10 9 4 5 3 1 8 10 6 4 7 4 3 4 9
C:\JavaPrograms>java TestRandom
10 3 8 2 7 7 4 10 4 1 9 6 9 7 1 7 3 9 1 7
C:\JavaPrograms>java TestRandom
1 2 10 3 3 4 10 6 8 3 10 4 5 6 2 8 10 1 3 6
C:\JavaPrograms>java TestRandom
6 8 3 6 10 8 10 8 4 1 1 9 1 1 4 6 4 3 3 7
C:\JavaPrograms>java TestRandom
9 8 1 2 5 1 4 4 5 4 5 9 10 7 7 6 8
```

Variations on the Theme

I don't like to skin cats. But I've heard that, if I ever need to skin one, I have a choice of several techniques. I'll keep that in mind the next time my cat Histamine mistakes the carpet for a litter box.

Anyway, whether you're skinning kitties or writing computer programs, the same principle holds true. You always have alternatives. Listing 9-2 shows you one way to write an if statement. The rest of this chapter shows you some other useful ways.

. . . Or else what?

You can create an if statement without an else clause. For example, imagine a Web page on which one in ten randomly chosen visitors receives a special offer. To keep visitors guessing, I call my DummiesRandom.getInt method, and make the offer to anyone whose number is lucky 7.

- If DummiesRandom.getInt generates the number 7, display a special offer message.

- If DummiesRandom.getInt generates any number other than 7, do nothing. Don't display a special offer message, and don't display a discouraging, "Sorry, no offer for you," message.

The code to implement such a strategy is shown in Listing 9-3. A few runs of the code are shown in Figure 9-5.

Listing 9-3   Aren't You Lucky?

```
class SpecialOffer
{
    public static void main(String args[])
    {
        int randomNumber = DummiesRandom.getInt();

        if (randomNumber == 7)
            System.out.println("An offer just for you!");

        System.out.println(randomNumber);
    }
}
```

Figure 9-5:
Three runs
of the code
in Listing
9-3.

```
C:\JavaPrograms>java SpecialOffer
4
C:\JavaPrograms>java SpecialOffer
9
C:\JavaPrograms>java SpecialOffer
An offer just for you!
7
```

The if statement in Listing 9-3 has no else clause. This if statement has the following form:

```
if (Condition)
    Statement1
```

When randomNumber is 7, the computer displays An offer just for you!
When randomNumber isn't 7, the computer doesn't display An offer just
for you! The action is illustrated in Figure 9-6.

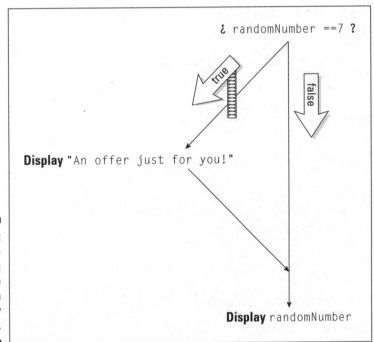

Figure 9-6:
If you have
nothing
good to
say, then
don't say
anything.

Always (I mean *always*) use a double equal sign when you compare two numbers or characters in an `if` statement's condition. Never (that's *never, ever, ever*) use a single equal sign to compare two values. A single equal sign does assignment, not comparison.

In Listing 9-3, I took the liberty of adding an extra `println`. This `println` (at the end of the `main` method) displays the random number generated by my call to `DummiesRandom.getInt`. On a Web page with special offers, you probably wouldn't see the randomly generated number, but I can't test my `SpecialOffer` code without knowing what numbers the code generates.

Anyway, notice that the value of `randomNumber` is displayed in every run. The `println` for `randomNumber` isn't inside the `if` statement. (This `println` comes after the `if` statement.) So the computer always executes this `println`. Whether `randomNumber == 7` is true or false, the computer takes the appropriate `if` action, and then marches on to execute `System.out.println (randomNumber)`.

Packing more stuff into an if statement

Here's an interesting situation: You have two baseball teams — the Hankees and the Socks. You want to display the teams' scores on two separate lines, with the winner's score coming first. (On the computer screen, the winner's score is displayed above the loser's score. In case of a tie, you display the two identical scores, one above the other.) Listing 9-4 has the code, and Figure 9-7 has a few runs of the code.

Listing 9-4   May the Best Team Be Displayed First

```
class TwoTeams
{
    public static void main(String args[])
    {
        int hankees, socks;

        System.out.print("Hankees and Socks scores?  ");
        hankees = DummiesIO.getInt();
        socks = DummiesIO.getInt();
        System.out.println();

        if (hankees > socks)
        {
            System.out.print("Hankees: ");
            System.out.println(hankees);
```

```
            System.out.print("Socks:    ");
            System.out.println(socks);
        }
    else
        {
            System.out.print("Socks:    ");
            System.out.println(socks);
            System.out.print("Hankees: ");
            System.out.println(hankees);
        }
    }
}
```

Figure 9-7:
See? The
code in
Listing 9-4
really
works!

In Listing 9-4, the if clause seems to have more than one statement in it. I make this happen by enclosing four statements in a pair of curly braces. The same is true of the listing's else clause. The curly braces create the forking situation shown in Figure 9-8.

With curly braces, a bunch of print and println calls are tucked away safely inside the if clause. Another group of print and println calls are squished inside the else clause.

To brace or not to brace?

In Listing 9-2, neither the if clause nor the else clause uses curly braces, but in Listing 9-4 both the if clause and the else clause use curly braces. So what's up? When should you brace, and when shouldn't you brace? Here's a summary of the rules:

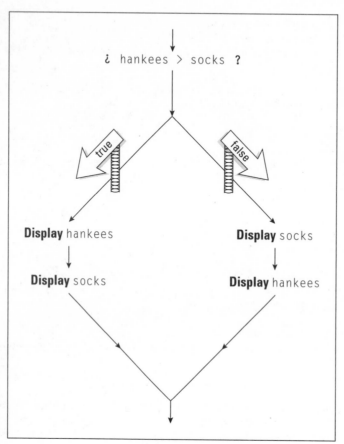

✔ To put several statements inside an `if` clause, you must surround those statements with curly braces. To put several statements inside an `else` clause, you must surround those statements with curly braces.

✔ You can use curly braces in one clause without using curly braces in the other clause. For instance, the following two code fragments are legal:

```
// Big if; small else:
if (randomNumber == 7)
{
    System.out.println("  -------------------------  ");
    System.out.println("|                         |");
    System.out.println("| Coupon worth 10 cents!  |");
    System.out.println("|                         |");
    System.out.println("  -------------------------  ");
}
else
    System.out.println("We like you anyway!");
```

```
// Small if; big else:
if (randomNumber == 7)
    System.out.println("An offer just for you!");
else
{
    System.out.println("Sorry, no offer for you.");
    numberOfLosers++;
}
```

✔ Curly braces are always safe to use. Even with a single statement in an if clause (or a single statement in an else clause), curly braces are okay. For instance, the following code (a variant of the code in Listing 9-1) is great stuff:

```
if (randomNumber > 5)
{
    System.out.println("Yes. Isn't it obvious?");
}
else
{
    System.out.println("No, and don't ask again.");
}
```

Statements and blocks

An elegant way to think about the rule for curly braces in if statements is to remember that you can put only one statement inside each clause of an if statement.

```
if (Condition)
    Statement1
else
    Statement2
```

On first reading of this one-statement rule, you're probably thinking that there's a misprint. After all, in Listing 9-4, each clause (the if clause and the else clause) seems to contain four statements, not just one.

But technically, the if clause in Listing 9-4 has only one statement, and the else clause in Listing 9-4 has only one statement. The trick is, when you surround a bunch of statements with curly braces, you get what's called a *block,* and a block behaves, in all respects, like a single statement. In fact, the official Java documentation lists a block as a kind of statement (one of many different kinds of statements). So in Listing 9-4, the block

```
{
    System.out.print("Hankees: ");
    System.out.println(hankees);
    System.out.print("Socks: ");
    System.out.println(socks);
}
```

is a single statement. It's a statement that has, within it, four smaller statements. So this big block, this single statement, serves as the one and only statement inside the if clause in Listing 9-4.

That's how the one-statement rule works. In an if statement, when you want the computer to execute several statements, you combine those statements into one big statement. To do this, you make a block using curly braces.

Making a dent

When you write if statements, you may be tempted to chuck all the rules about curly braces out the window and just rely on indentation. Unfortunately, this seldom works.

Try some experiments. Say you indent four statements in an if clause, and you forget to enclose those statements in curly braces:

```
//This code doesn't compile:
if (hankees > socks)
    System.out.print("Hankees: ");
    System.out.println(hankees);
    System.out.print("Socks:    ");
    System.out.println(socks);
else
{
    System.out.print("Socks:    ");
    System.out.println(socks);
    System.out.print("Hankees: ");
    System.out.println(hankees);
}
```

When you try to compile, you get the error message shown in Figure 9-9.

Figure 9-9:
The word
"else"
doesn't like
being alone.

```
C:\JavaPrograms>javac BadTwoTeamsCode.java
BadTwoTeamsCode.java:17: 'else' without 'if'
        else
        ^
1 error
```

Remember, the compiler doesn't give a hoot about indentation. In spite of all your indentation, the compiler thinks that your if clause has only one print statement in it.

```
//Here's what the compiler sees:
if (hankees > socks)
    System.out.print("Hankees: ");    //if clause

System.out.println(hankees);          //Statements that
System.out.print("Socks:    ");       //   come after your
System.out.println(socks);            //   if statement
else                                  //An else with no if
{
```

```
    System.out.print("Socks:     ");
    System.out.println(socks);
    System.out.print("Hankees: ");
    System.out.println(hankees);
}
```

Is that as nasty as it ever gets? No, it isn't. When you forget to use braces in an `else` clause, your program compiles. But you're being fooled by an uneventful compilation. When you run the code, things go haywire.

For example, when you run the following code, you get the mumbo-jumbo shown in Figure 9-10.

```
//This is bad code:
if (hankees > socks)
{
    System.out.print("Hankees: ");
    System.out.println(hankees);
    System.out.print("Socks:     ");
    System.out.println(socks);
}
else
    System.out.print("Socks:     ");
    System.out.println(socks);
    System.out.print("Hankees: ");
    System.out.println(hankees);
```

```
C:\JavaPrograms>java WorseTwoTeamsCode
Hankees and Socks scores?  10 7

Hankees: 10
Socks:   7
7
Hankees: 10
```

Once again, the compiler ignores your indentation. So the compiler sees the following messy stuff:

```
//Here's what the compiler sees:
if (hankees > socks)
{
    System.out.print("Hankees: ");
    System.out.println(hankees);
    System.out.print("Socks:     ");
    System.out.println(socks);
}
else
    System.out.print("Socks:     ");   //else clause
```

```
System.out.println(socks);        //Statements that
System.out.print("Hankees: ");    //  come after your
System.out.println(hankees);      //  if statement
```

The last three lines aren't part of your if statement, so the computer executes these lines no matter who wins the game.

Misleading indentation is difficult to diagnose, so indent carefully, and watch those curly braces!

Chapter 10

Which Way Did He Go?

In This Chapter

▶ Untangling complicated conditions

▶ Writing cool conditional code

▶ Intertwining your if statements

*I*t's tax time once again. At the moment, I'm working on Form 12432-89B. Here's what it says:

> If you're married with fewer than three children, and your income is higher than the EIQ (Estimated Income Quota), or if you're single and living in a non-residential area (as defined by Section 10, Part iii of the Uniform Zoning Act), and you're either self-employed as an LLC (Limited Liability Company) or you qualify for veterans benefits, then skip Steps 3 and 4 or 4, 5, and 6, depending on your answers to Questions 2a and 3d.

No wonder I have no time to write! I'm too busy interpreting these tax forms.

Anyway, this chapter deals with the potential complexity of if statements. This chapter has nothing as complex as Form 12432-89B, but if you ever encounter something that complicated, you'll be ready for it.

Forming Bigger and Better Conditions

In Listing 9-2, the code chooses a course of action based on one call to DummiesRandom.getInt. That's fine for the electronic oracle program described in Chapter 9, but what if you're rolling a pair of dice? In Backgammon and other dice games, rolling 3 and 5 isn't the same as rolling 4 and 4, even though the total for both rolls is 8. The next move varies, depending on whether or not you roll doubles. To get the computer to roll two dice, you call DummiesRandom.getInt(6) two times. Then you combine the two rolls into a larger, more complicated if statement.

So to simulate a Backgammon game (and many other, more practical situations) you need to combine conditions.

```
If die1+die2 equals 8 and die1 equals die2, ...
```

You need things like *and* and *or* — things that can wire conditions together. Java has operators to represent these concepts, which are described in Table 10-1 and illustrated in Figure 10-1.

Table 10-1		Logical Operators	
Operator Symbol	*Meaning*	*Example*	*Illustration*
&&	and	4 < age && age < 8	Figure 10-1(a)
||	or	age < 4 || 8 < age	Figure 10-1(b)
!	not	!eachKidGetsTen	Figure 10-1(c)

Figure 10-1: When you satisfy a condition, you're happy.

Combined conditions, like the ones in Table 10-1, can be mighty confusing. That's why I tread carefully when I use such things. Here's a short explanation of each example in the table:

 ✔ 4 < age && age < 8

   The value of the age variable is greater than 4 *and* is less than 8. The numbers 5, 6, 7, 8, 9 . . . are all greater than 4. But among these numbers, only 5, 6, and 7 are less than 8. So only the numbers 5, 6, and 7 satisfy this combined condition.

✔ `age < 4 || 8 < age`

The value of the `age` variable is less than *4 or* is greater than 8. To create the or condition, you use two pipe symbols. On many U.S. English keyboards, you can find the pipe symbol immediately above the Enter key (the same key as the backslash, but shifted).

In this combined condition, the value of the `age` variable is either less than 4 or is greater than 8. So for instance, if a number is less than 4, then the number satisfies the condition. Numbers like 1, 2, and 3 are all less than 4, so these numbers satisfy the combined condition.

Also, if a number is greater than 8, then the number satisfies the combined condition. Numbers like 9, 10, and 11 are all greater than 8, so these numbers satisfy the condition.

✔ `!eachKidGetsTen`

If I weren't experienced with computer programming languages, I'd be confused by the exclamation point. I'd think that `!eachKidGetsTen` means, "Yes, each kid *does* get ten." But that's not what this expression means. This expression says, "The variable `eachKidGetsTen` does *not* have the value `true`." In Java and other programming languages, an exclamation point stands for *negative,* for *no way,* for *not.*

Listing 8-4 has a `boolean` variable named `eachKidGetsTen`. A `boolean` variable's value is either `true` or `false`. Because `!` means *not,* the expressions `eachKidGetsTen` and `!eachKidGetsTen` have opposite values. So when `eachKidGetsTen` is true, `!eachKidGetsTen` is false (and vice versa).

Java's `||` operator is *inclusive.* This means that you get `true` whenever the thing on the left side is `true`, the thing on the right side is `true`, or both things are `true`. For instance, the condition `2<10 || 20<30` is true.

In Java, you can't combine comparisons the way you do in ordinary English. In English, you may say, "We'll have between three and ten people at the dinner table." But in Java, you get an error message if you write `3 <= people <= 10`. To do this comparison, you need to something like `3<=people && people<=10`.

Combining conditions: An example

Here's a handy example of the use of logical operators. A movie theater posts its prices for admission.

Regular price: $9.25

Kids under 12: $5.25

Seniors (65 and older): $5.25

Because the kids' and seniors' prices are the same, you can combine these prices into one category. (That's not always the best programming strategy, but do it anyway for this example.) To find a particular moviegoer's ticket price, you need one or more if statements. There are many ways to structure the conditions, and I chose one of these ways for the code in Listing 10-1.

Listing 10-1   Are You Paying Too Much?

```
class TicketPrice
{
    public static void main(String args[])
    {
        int age;
        double price=0.00;

        System.out.print("How old are you? ");
        age = DummiesIO.getInt();

        if (age >= 12 && age < 65)
            price = 9.25;
        if (age < 12 || age >= 65)
            price = 5.25;

        System.out.print("Please pay $");
        System.out.print(price);
        System.out.print(". ");
        System.out.println("Enjoy the show!");
    }
}
```

Several runs of the TicketPrice program (Listing 10-1) are shown in Figure 10-2. When you turn 12, you start paying full price. You keep paying full price until you become 65. At that point, you pay the reduced price again.

Figure 10-2: Admission prices for *Beginning Programming with Java For Dummies: The Movie.*

```
C:\JavaPrograms>java TicketPrice
How old are you? 11
Please pay $5.25. Enjoy the show!

C:\JavaPrograms>java TicketPrice
How old are you? 12
Please pay $9.25. Enjoy the show!

C:\JavaPrograms>java TicketPrice
How old are you? 35
Please pay $9.25. Enjoy the show!

C:\JavaPrograms>java TicketPrice
How old are you? 64
Please pay $9.25. Enjoy the show!

C:\JavaPrograms>java TicketPrice
How old are you? 65
Please pay $5.25. Enjoy the show!
```

The pivotal part of Listing 10-1 is the lump of `if` statements in the middle, which are illustrated in Figure 10-3:

- ✔ The first `if` statement's condition tests for the regular price group. Anyone who's at least 12 years of age *and* is under 65 belongs in this group.

- ✔ The second `if` statement's condition tests for the fringe ages. A person who's under 12 *or* is 65 or older belongs in this category.

Figure 10-3:
The meanings of the conditions in Listing 10-1.

```
age >= 12 && age < 65
```

```
age < 12 || age >= 65
```

When you form the opposite of an existing condition, you can often follow the pattern in Listing 10-1. The opposite of `>=` is `<`. The opposite of `<` is `>=`. The opposite of `&&` is `||`.

If you change the dollar amounts in Listing 10-1, then you can get into trouble. For instance, with the statement `price = 5.00`, the program displays `Please pay $5.0. Enjoy the show!` This happens because Java doesn't store the two zeros to the right of the decimal point (and Java doesn't know or care that 5.00 is a dollar amount). To fix this kind of thing, see the discussion of `NumberFormat.getCurrencyInstance` in Chapter 18.

When to initialize?

Take a look at Listing 10-1, and notice the `price` variable's initialization.

```
double price=0.00;
```

This line declares the `price` variable and sets the variable's starting value to `0.00`. When I omit this initialization, I get an error message:

```
variable price might not have been initialized
    System.out.print(price);
                  ^
```

What's the deal here? I don't initialize the age variable, but the compiler doesn't complain about that. Why is the compiler fussing over the price variable?

The answer is in the placement of the code's assignment statements. Consider the following two facts:

- ✔ **The statement that assigns a value to** age (age=DummiesIO.getInt()) **is not inside an** if **statement.**

 That assignment statement always gets executed and (as long as nothing extraordinary happens) the variable age is sure to be assigned a value.

- ✔ **Both statements that assign a value to** price (price=9.25 **and** price=5.25) **are inside** if **statements.**

 If you look at Figure 10-3, you see that every age group is covered. No one shows up at the ticket counter with an age that forces both if conditions to be false. So whenever you run the TicketPrice program, either the first or the second price assignment is executed.

 The problem is that the compiler isn't smart enough to check all this. The compiler just sees the structure in Figure 10-4 and becomes scared that the computer won't take either of the true detours.

 If (for some unforeseen reason) both of the if statements' conditions are false, then the variable price doesn't get assigned a value. So without an initialization, price has no value. (More precisely, price has no value that's intentionally given to it in the code.)

 Eventually, the computer reaches the System.out.print(price) statement. It can't display price unless price has a meaningful value. So at that point, the compiler throws up its virtual hands in disgust.

More and more conditions

Last night I had a delicious meal at the neighborhood burger joint. As part of a promotion, I got a discount coupon along with the meal. The coupon is good for $2.00 off the price of a ticket at the local movie theater.

To make use of the coupon in the TicketPrice program, I have to tweak the code in Listing 10-1. The revised code is in Listing 10-2. In Figure 10-5, I take that new code around the block a few times.

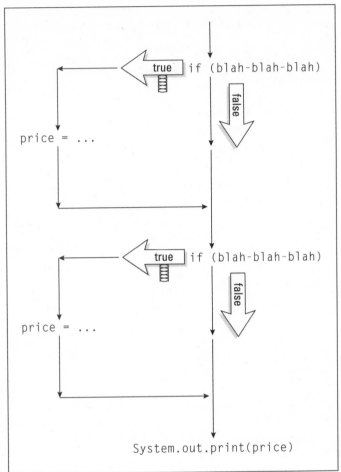

Figure 10-4:
The choices
in Listing
10-1.

Listing 10-2   Do You Have a Coupon?

```
class TicketPriceWithDiscount
{
   public static void main(String args[])
   {
      int age;
      double price=0.00;
      char reply;

      System.out.print("How old are you? ");
      age = DummiesIO.getInt();
```

(continued)

Listing 10-2 *(continued)*

```
        System.out.print("Have a coupon? (Y/N) ");
        reply = DummiesIO.getChar();

        if (age >= 12 && age < 65)
            price = 9.25;
        if (age < 12 || age >= 65)
            price = 5.25;

        if (reply=='Y' || reply=='y')
            price -= 2.00;
        if (reply!='Y' && reply!='y' &&
            reply!='N' && reply!='n')
            System.out.println("Huh?");

        System.out.print("Please pay $");
        System.out.print(price);
        System.out.print(". ");
        System.out.println("Enjoy the show!");
    }
}
```

```
C:\JavaPrograms>java TicketPriceWithDiscount
How old are you? 51
Have a coupon? (Y/N) Y
Please pay $7.25. Enjoy the show!

C:\JavaPrograms>java TicketPriceWithDiscount
How old are you? 51
Have a coupon? (Y/N) y
Please pay $7.25. Enjoy the show!

C:\JavaPrograms>java TicketPriceWithDiscount
How old are you? 51
Have a coupon? (Y/N) N
Please pay $9.25. Enjoy the show!

C:\JavaPrograms>java TicketPriceWithDiscount
How old are you? 51
Have a coupon? (Y/N) X
Huh?
Please pay $9.25. Enjoy the show!
```

Figure 10-5:
Running the
code in
Listing 10-2.

Listing 10-2 has two if statements whose conditions involve characters:

✔ In the first such statement, the computer checks to see if the reply variable stores the letter Y *or* the letter y. If either is the case, then it subtracts 2.00 from the price. (For information on operators like -=, see Chapter 7.)

✔ The second such statement has a hefty condition. The condition tests to see if the reply variable stores any reasonable value at all. If the reply *isn't* Y, *and isn't* y, *and isn't* N, *and isn't* n, then the computer expresses its concern by displaying, "Huh?" (As a paying customer, the word "Huh?" on the automated ticket teller's screen will certainly get your attention.)

When you create a big multipart condition, you always have several ways to think about the condition. For instance, you can rewrite the last condition in Listing 10-2 as if (!(reply=='Y' || reply=='y' || reply=='N' || reply=='n')). *"If it's not the case that* the reply is *either* Y, y, N, *or* n, then display 'Huh?'"* So which way of writing the condition is better — the way I do it in Listing 10-2, or the way I do it in this tip? It depends on your taste. Whatever makes the logic easiest for you to understand is the best way.

Using boolean variables

No matter how good a program is, you can always make it a little bit better. Take the code in Listing 10-2. Does the forest of if statements make you nervous? Do you slow to a crawl when you read each condition? Wouldn't it be nice if you could glance at a condition and make sense of it very quickly?

To some extent, you can. If you're willing to create some additional variables, you can make your code easier to read. Listing 10-3 shows you how.

Listing 10-3   George Boole Would Be Proud

```
class NicePrice
{
    public static void main(String args[])
    {
        int age;
        double price=0.00;
        char reply;
        boolean isKid, isSenior, hasCoupon, hasNoCoupon;

        System.out.print("How old are you? ");
        age = DummiesIO.getInt();

        System.out.print("Have a coupon? (Y/N) ");
        reply = DummiesIO.getChar();

        isKid = age<12;
        isSenior = age>=65;
        hasCoupon = reply=='Y' || reply=='y';
        hasNoCoupon = reply=='N' || reply=='n';

        if (!isKid && !isSenior)
            price = 9.25;
        if (isKid || isSenior)
            price = 5.25;

        if (hasCoupon)
            price -= 2.00;
```

(continued)

Listing 10-3 *(continued)*

```
        if (!hasCoupon && !hasNoCoupon)
            System.out.println("Huh?");

        System.out.print("Please pay $");
        System.out.print(price);
        System.out.print(". ");
        System.out.println("Enjoy the show!");
    }
}
```

Runs of the Listing 10-3 code look like the stuff in Figure 10-5. The only difference between Listings 10-2 and 10-3 is the use of `boolean` variables. In Listing 10-3, you get past all the less than signs and double equal signs before the start of any `if` statements. By the time you encounter the two `if` statements, the conditions can use simple words — words like `isKid`, `isSenior`, and `hasCoupon`. With all these `boolean` variables, expressing each `if` statement's condition is a snap.

You can read more about `boolean` variables in Chapter 8.

Adding a `boolean` variable can make your code more manageable. But some programming languages don't have `boolean` variables, so many programmers prefer to create `if` conditions on the fly. That's why I mix the two techniques (conditions with and without `boolean` variables) in this book.

Mixing different logical operators together

If you read about Listing 10-2, you know that my local movie theater offers discount coupons. The trouble is, I can't use a coupon along with any other discount. I tried to convince the ticket taker that I'm under 12 years of age, but he didn't buy it. When that didn't work, I tried combining the coupon with the senior citizen discount. That didn't work either.

The theater must use some software that checks for people like me. It looks something like the code in Listing 10-4. To watch the code run, take a look at Figure 10-6.

Listing 10-4   No Extra Break for Kids or Seniors

```
class CheckAgeForDiscount
{
    public static void main(String args[])
    {
        int age;
        double price=0.00;
        char reply;
```

```
System.out.print("How old are you? ");
age = DummiesIO.getInt();

System.out.print("Have a coupon? (Y/N) ");
reply = DummiesIO.getChar();

if (age >= 12 && age < 65)
    price = 9.25;
if (age < 12 || age >= 65)
    price = 5.25;

if ((reply=='Y' || reply=='y') &&
    (age >= 12 && age < 65))
    price -= 2.00;

System.out.print("Please pay $");
System.out.print(price);
System.out.print(". ");
System.out.println("Enjoy the show!");
    }
}
```

```
C:\JavaPrograms>java CheckAgeForDiscount
How old are you? 7
Have a coupon? (Y/N) Y
Please pay $5.25. Enjoy the show!

C:\JavaPrograms>java CheckAgeForDiscount
How old are you? 25
Have a coupon? (Y/N) y
Please pay $7.25. Enjoy the show!

C:\JavaPrograms>java CheckAgeForDiscount
How old are you? 25
Have a coupon? (Y/N) n
Please pay $9.25. Enjoy the show!

C:\JavaPrograms>java CheckAgeForDiscount
How old are you? 85
Have a coupon? (Y/N) y
Please pay $5.25. Enjoy the show!

C:\JavaPrograms>java CheckAgeForDiscount
How old are you? 85
Have a coupon? (Y/N) Y
Please pay $5.25. Enjoy the show!
```

Figure 10-6:
Running the
code in
Listing 10-4.

Listing 10-4 is a lot like its predecessors, Listings 10-1 and 10-2. The big difference is the bolded if statement. This if statement tests two things, and each thing has two parts of its own:

1. **Does the customer have a coupon?**

   That is, did the customer reply with either Y *or* with y?

2. **Is the customer in the regular age group?**

   That is, is the customer at least 12 years old *and* younger than 65?

In Listing 10-4, I join items 1 and 2 using the && operator. I do this because both items (item 1 *and* item 2) must be true in order for the customer to qualify for the $2.00 discount, as illustrated in Figure 10-7.

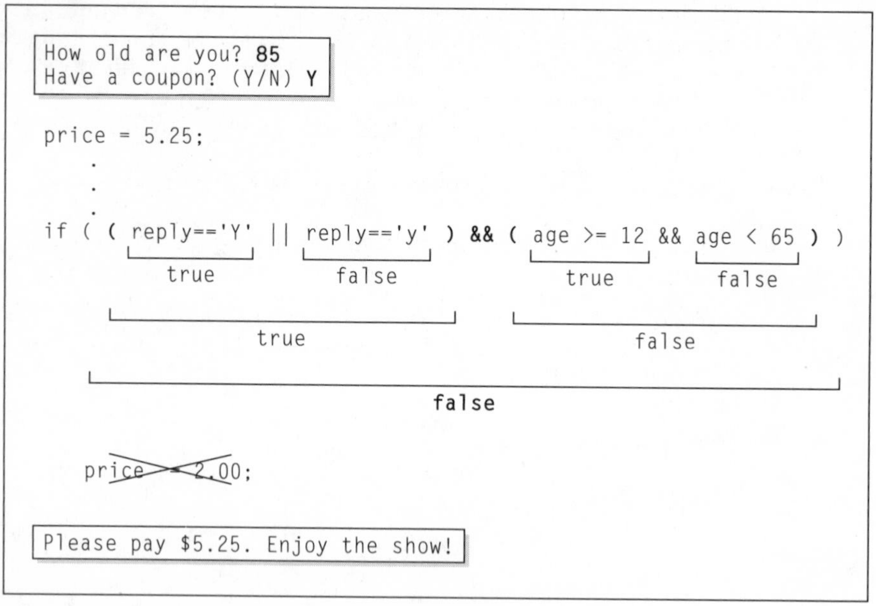

```
How old are you? 85
Have a coupon? (Y/N) Y


price = 5.25;
        .
        .
        .
if ( ( reply=='Y' || reply=='y' ) && ( age >= 12 && age < 65 ) )
           true          false              true          false

              true                            false

                            false

    price -= 2.00;

Please pay $5.25. Enjoy the show!
```

Figure 10-7:
Both the
reply
criterion
and the age
criterion
must be
true.

Using parentheses

Listing 10-4 demonstrates something important about conditions. Sometimes, you need parentheses to make a condition work correctly. Take, for instance, the following incorrect if statement:

```
//This code is incorrect:
if (reply=='Y' || reply=='y' &&
    age >= 12 && age < 65)
    price -= 2.00;
```

Compare this code with the correct code in Listing 10-4. This incorrect code has no parentheses to group reply=='Y' with reply=='y', or to group age >= 12 with age < 65. The result is the bizarre pair of runs in Figure 10-8.

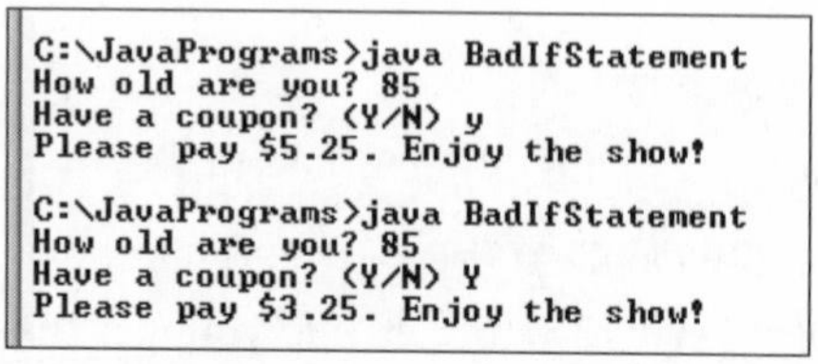

Figure 10-8:
A capital
offense.

```
C:\JavaPrograms>java BadIfStatement
How old are you? 85
Have a coupon? (Y/N) y
Please pay $5.25. Enjoy the show!

C:\JavaPrograms>java BadIfStatement
How old are you? 85
Have a coupon? (Y/N) Y
Please pay $3.25. Enjoy the show!
```

In Figure 10-8, notice how the y and Y inputs yield different ticket prices, even though the age is 85 in both runs. This happens because, without parentheses, any && operator gets evaluated before any || operator. (That's the rule in the Java programming language — evaluate && before ||.) When reply is Y, the condition in the bad if statement takes the following form:

```
reply=='Y' || some-other-stuff-that-doesn't-matter
```

Whenever reply=='Y' is true, the whole condition is automatically true, as illustrated in Figure 10-9.

```
How old are you? 85
Have a coupon? (Y/N) Y

price = 5.25;
        .
        .
        .
if ( reply=='Y' || reply=='y' && age >= 12 && age < 65 )
     └─────────┘    └─────────┘   └──────────┘  └─────────┘
        true          false          true          false
                      └──────────────────────────┘
                                  false
                      └─────────────────────────────────────┘
                                      false
     └──────────────────────────────────────────────────────┘
                                  true

price -= 2.00;

Please pay $3.25. Enjoy the show!
```

Figure 10-9: "True or false" makes "true."

Building a Nest

The year is 1968, and *The Prisoner* is on TV. In the last episode, the show's hero meets his nemesis "Number One." At first Number One wears a spooky happy-face/sad-face mask, and when the mask comes off, there's a monkey mask underneath. To find out what's behind the monkey mask, you have to watch the series on DVD. But in the meantime, notice the layering; a mask within a mask. You can do the same kind of thing with if statements. This section's example shows you how.

But first, take a look at Listing 10-4. In that code, the condition age >= 12 && age < 65 is tested twice. Both times, the computer sends the numbers 12, 65, and the age value through its jumble of circuits, and both times, the computer gets the same answer. This is wasteful, but waste isn't your only concern.

What if you decide to change the age limit for senior tickets? From now on, no one under 100 gets a senior discount. You fish through the code and see the first age >= 12 && age < 65 test. You change 65 to 100, pat yourself on the back, and go home. The problem is, you've changed one of the two age >= 12 && age < 65 tests, but you haven't changed the other. Wouldn't it be better to keep all the age >= 12 && age < 65 testing in just one place?

Listing 10-5 comes to the rescue. In Listing 10-5, I smoosh all my if statements together into one big glob. The code is dense, but it gets the job done nicely.

Listing 10-5   Nested if Statements

```
class AnotherAgeCheck
{
    public static void main(String args[])
    {
        int age;
        double price=0.00;
        char reply;

        System.out.print("How old are you? ");
        age = DummiesIO.getInt();

        System.out.print("Have a coupon? (Y/N) ");
        reply = DummiesIO.getChar();

        if (age >= 12 && age < 65)
        {
            price = 9.25;
            if (reply=='Y' || reply=='y')
                price -= 2.00;
        }
        else
            price = 5.25;

        System.out.print("Please pay $");
        System.out.print(price);
        System.out.print(". ");
        System.out.println("Enjoy the show!");
    }
}
```

Nested if statements

A run of the code in Listing 10-5 looks identical to a run for Listing 10-4. You can see several runs in Figure 10-6. The main idea in Listing 10-5 is to put an if statement inside another if statement. After all, Chapter 9 says that an if statement can take the following form:

```
if (Condition)
    Statement1
else
    Statement2
```

Who says *Statement1* can't be an if statement? For that matter, *Statement2* can also be an if statement. And, yes, you can create an if statement within an if statement within an if statement. There's no predefined limit on the number of if statements that you can have.

```
if (age >= 12 && age < 65)
{
    price = 9.25;
    if (reply=='Y' || reply=='y')
        if (isSpecialFeature)
            price -= 1.00;
        else
            price -= 2.00;
}
else
    price = 5.25;
```

When you put one if statement inside another, you create *nested* if statements. Nested statements aren't difficult to write, as long as you take things slowly, and keep a clear picture of the code's flow in your mind. If it helps, draw yourself a diagram like the one shown in Figure 10-10.

When you nest statements, you must be compulsive about the use of indentation and braces. When code has misleading indentation, then no one (not even the programmer who wrote the code) can figure out how the code works. A nested statement with sloppy indentation is a programmer's nightmare.

As for braces, use them liberally. Sometimes braces are optional. But in general, it's better to use unnecessary braces than to accidentally omit braces that are required. (See Figure 10-11.)

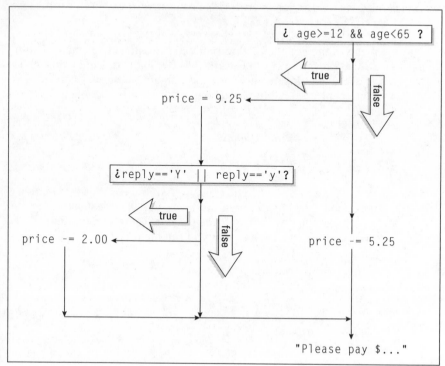

Figure 10-10:
The flow in
Listing 10-5.

```
                                    if (age >= 12 && age < 65)
                                  ⎡ {
Two statements                   |       price = 9.25;
in an if clause;    ←            |       if (reply=='Y' || reply=='y')        One statement
braces required.                 |           price -= 2.00;              ]→ in an if clause;
                                  ⎣ }                                          braces optional.
                          One statement in     else
                          an else clause;  ←⎡      price = 5.25;
                          braces optional.
```

Figure 10-11:
Braces and
nested if
statements.

Cascading if statements

Here's a riddle: You have two baseball teams — the Hankees and the Socks.
You want to display the teams' scores on two separate lines, with the
winner's score coming first. (On the computer screen, the winner's score is
displayed above the loser's score.) What happens when the scores are tied?

Excuse me, but your else is dangling

You can play all kinds of games with nested `if` statements. Most of the time, these games are fun, harmless, and even useful. Once in a while, they get you into trouble. Take, for instance, the code in Listing 10-5. If you omit the `if` statement's curly braces, you get the following (very bad) code:

```
//This is bad code:
if (age >= 12 && age < 65)

    price = 9.25;
    if (reply=='Y' ||
reply=='y')
        price -= 2.00;

else
    price = 5.25;
```

What happens in this bad code when a middle-aged user replies N to having a coupon? If you fall into my clever little trap, you'll answer the question incorrectly. (To answer incorrectly, say, "The price is 9.25.")

The fact is, an `else` becomes very lonely when it doesn't have an `if`. The `else` becomes so lonely that it latches onto the nearest `if` that doesn't already have a steady elsefriend. (As Becky Huehls once said, "No `if` is an island unto its `else`.") In the code shown above, the desperate `else` associates itself with the very nearest `if` — the `if` that checks for the reply's being Y or y. So the indentation in the code is misleading. (And remember, the computer completely ignores your indentation.) The more informative indentation would look like this:

```
if (age >= 12 && age < 65)
    price = 9.25;

if (reply=='Y' || reply=='y')
    price -= 2.00;
else
    price = 5.25;
```

Now, the code is clearer, even if it doesn't do what you want it to do. When a 35-year-old user replies N to having a coupon, the code first assigns 9.25 to `price`. But then, in the second `if` statement, a reply that's neither Y nor y changes the value of `price` to 5.25.

This situation, in which an `else` is forced to roam the streets looking for an available `if`, is called the *dangling else problem*.

Do you give up? The answer is, there's no right answer. What happens depends on the way you write the program. Take a look back at Listing 9-4. When the scores are equal, the condition `hankees > socks` is `false`. So the program's flow of execution drops down to the `else` clause. That clause displays the Socks score first and the Hankees score second. (Refer to Figure 9-7.)

The program doesn't have to work this way. If I take Listing 9-4 and change `hankees > socks` to `hankees >= socks` then, in case of a tie, the Hankees score comes first.

Suppose you want a bit more control. When the scores are equal, you want an `It's a tie` message. To do this, think in terms of a three-pronged fork. You have a prong for a Hankees win, another prong for a Socks win, and a third prong for a tie. You can write this code in several different ways, but one way that makes lots of sense is in Listing 10-6. For three runs of the code in Listing 10-6, see Figure 10-12.

Listing 10-6   In Case of a Tie . . .

```java
class WinLoseOrTie
{
    public static void main(String args[])
    {
        int hankees, socks;

        System.out.print("Hankees and Socks scores?  ");
        hankees = DummiesIO.getInt();
        socks = DummiesIO.getInt();
        System.out.println();

        if (hankees > socks)
        {
            System.out.println("Hankees win...");
            System.out.print("Hankees: ");
            System.out.println(hankees);
            System.out.print("Socks:   ");
            System.out.println(socks);
        }
        else if (socks > hankees)
        {
            System.out.println("Socks win...");
            System.out.print("Socks:   ");
            System.out.println(socks);
            System.out.print("Hankees: ");
            System.out.println(hankees);
        }
        else
        {
            System.out.println("It's a tie...");
            System.out.print("Hankees: ");
            System.out.println(hankees);
            System.out.print("Socks:   ");
            System.out.println(socks);
        }
    }
}
```

Figure 10-12:
Go, team,
go!

```
C:\JavaPrograms>java WinLoseOrTie
Hankees and Socks scores?  9 4

Hankees win...
Hankees: 9
Socks:   4

C:\JavaPrograms>java WinLoseOrTie
Hankees and Socks scores?  3 8

Socks win...
Socks:   8
Hankees: 3

C:\JavaPrograms>java WinLoseOrTie
Hankees and Socks scores?  0 0

It's a tie...
Hankees: 0
Socks:   0
```

Listing 10-6 illustrates a way of thinking about a problem. You have one question with more than two answers. (In this section's baseball problem, the question is "Who wins?" and the answers are "Hankees," "Socks," or "Neither.") The problem begs for an if statement, but an if statement has only two branches — the true branch and the false branch. So you combine alternatives to form *cascading if statements*.

In Listing 10-6, the format for the cascading if statements is

```
if (Condition2)
    Statement1
else if (Condition3)
    Statement2
else
    Statement3
```

In general, you can use else if as many times as you want:

```
if (hankeesWin)
{
    System.out.println("Hankees win...");
    System.out.print("Hankees: ");
    System.out.println(hankees);
    System.out.print("Socks:    ");
    System.out.println(socks);
}
else if (socksWin)
{
    System.out.println("Socks win...");
    System.out.print("Socks:    ");
    System.out.println(socks);
    System.out.print("Hankees: ");
    System.out.println(hankees);
}
else if (isATie)
{
    System.out.println("It's a tie...");
    System.out.print("Hankees: ");
    System.out.println(hankees);
    System.out.print("Socks:    ");
    System.out.println(socks);
}
else if (gameCancelled)
    System.out.println("Sorry, sports fans.");
else
    System.out.println("The game isn't over yet.");
```

Nothing is special about cascading if statements. This isn't a new programming language feature. It's just a new way to think about decisions within your code. Of course, when you think differently, you indent code differently. Here's the way I'd indent Listing 10-6 if I were emphasizing nesting instead of cascading:

```
if (hankees > socks)
{                                                   //----------
   System.out.println("Hankees win...");            //
   System.out.print("Hankees: ");                   //
   System.out.println(hankees);                     //Statement1
   System.out.print("Socks:    ");                  //
   System.out.println(socks);                       //
}                                                   //----------
else
   if (socks > hankees)                             //----------
   {                                                //
      System.out.println("Socks win...");           //
      System.out.print("Socks:    ");               //
      System.out.println(socks);                    //
      System.out.print("Hankees: ");                //Statement2
      System.out.println(hankees);                  //
   }                                                //
   else                                             //
   {                                                //
      System.out.println("It's a tie...");          //
      System.out.print("Hankees: ");                //
      System.out.println(hankees);                  //
      System.out.print("Socks:    ");               //
      System.out.println(socks);                    //
   }                                                //----------
```

I have one big if statement, with another if statement nested inside it. That's what cascading if statements are all about.

An if statement is just one big statement, no matter how many smaller statements you put inside it. In the code shown above, all the text from the if (socks > hankees) line downward is one statement (what I call *Statement2*). This *Statement2* is inside an else clause, but it's the only statement inside that else clause. So *Statement2* doesn't need to be surrounded with curly braces.

Chapter 11

How to Flick a Virtual Switch

*I*magine playing *Let's Make a Deal* with ten different doors. "Choose door number 1, door number 2, door number 3, door number 4. . . . Wait! Let's break for a commercial. When we come back, I'll say the names of the other six doors."

Meet the switch Statement

The code back in Listing 9-2 in Chapter 9 simulates a simple electronic oracle. Ask the program a question, and the program randomly generates a yes or no answer. But, as toys go, the code in Listing 9-2 isn't much fun. The code has only two possible answers. There's no variety. Even the earliest talking dolls could say about ten different sentences.

Say you want to enhance the code of Listing 9-2. The DummiesRandom. getInt() method generates numbers from 1 to 10. So maybe you can display a different sentence for each of the ten numbers. A big pile of if statements should do the trick:

```
if (randomNumber==1)
{
    System.out.println("Yes. Isn't it obvious?");
}
if (randomNumber==2)
{
    System.out.println("No, and don't ask again.");
}
```

```
if (randomNumber==3)
{
    System.out.print("Yessir, yessir!");
    System.out.println(" Three bags full.");
}
if (randomNumber==4)
        .

        .

        .

if (randomNumber<1 || randomNumber>10)
{
    System.out.print("Sorry, the electronic oracle");
    System.out.println(" is closed for repairs.");
}
```

But that approach seems wasteful. Why not create a statement that checks the value of randomNumber just once and then takes an action based on the value that it finds? Fortunately, just such a statement exists: the *switch* statement. Listing 11-1 has an example of a switch statement.

Listing 11-1   An Answer for Every Occasion

```
class TheOldSwitcheroo
{
    public static void main(String args[])
    {
        int randomNumber;

        System.out.print("Type your question, my child:  ");
        DummiesIO.getLine();

        randomNumber = DummiesRandom.getInt();

        switch (randomNumber)
        {
            case 1:
                System.out.println("Yes. Isn't it obvious?");
                break;
            case 2:
                System.out.println("No, and don't ask again.");
                break;
            case 3:
                System.out.print("Yessir, yessir!");
                System.out.println(" Three bags full.");
                break;
            case 4:
                System.out.print("What part of 'no'");
                System.out.println(" don't you understand?");
                break;
            case 5:
```

```
                System.out.println("No chance, Lance.");
                break;
            case 6:
                System.out.println("Sure, whatever.");
                break;
            case 7:
                System.out.print("Yes, but only if");
                System.out.println(" you're nice to me.");
                break;
            case 8:
                System.out.println("Yes (as if I care).");
                break;
            case 9:
                System.out.print("No, not until");
                System.out.println(" Cromwell seizes Dover.");
                break;
            case 10:
                System.out.print("No, not until");
                System.out.println(" Nell squeezes Rover.");
                break;
            default:
                System.out.print("You think you have");
                System.out.print(" problems?");
                System.out.print(" My random number");
                System.out.println(" generator is broken!");
                break;
        }
        System.out.println("Goodbye");
    }
}
```

The cases in a switch statement

Figure 11-1 shows three runs of the program in Listing 11-1. Here's what happens during one of these runs:

✔ The user types a heavy question, and the variable randomNumber gets a value. In the second run of Figure 11-1, this value is 2.

✔ Execution of the code in Listing 11-1 reaches the top of the switch statement, so the computer starts checking this statement's case clauses. The value 2 doesn't match the topmost case clause (the case 1 clause), so the computer moves on to the next case clause.

✔ The value in the next case clause (the number 2) matches the value of the randomNumber variable, so the computer executes the statements in this case 2 clause. These two statements are

```
System.out.println("No, and don't ask again.");
break;
```

The first of the two statements displays `No, and don't ask again` on the screen. The second statement is called a *break* statement. (What a surprise!) When the computer encounters a `break` statement, the computer jumps out of whatever `switch` statement it's in. So in Listing 11-1, the computer skips right past `case 3`, `case 4`, and so on. The computer jumps to the statement just after the end of the `switch` statement.

✔ The computer displays `Goodbye`, because that's what the statement after the `switch` statement tells the computer to do.

Figure 11-1:
Running the
code of
Listing 11-1.

```
C:\JavaPrograms>java TheOldSwitcheroo
Type your question, my child:  Is the Continuum Hypothesis true?
Sure, whatever.
Goodbye

C:\JavaPrograms>java TheOldSwitcheroo
Type your question, my child:  Does P=NP?
No, and don't ask again.
Goodbye

C:\JavaPrograms>java TheOldSwitcheroo
Type your question, my child:  Does Turing machine T halt on input i?
Yes, but only if you're nice to me.
Goodbye
```

The overall idea behind the program in Listing 11-1 is illustrated in Figure 11-2.

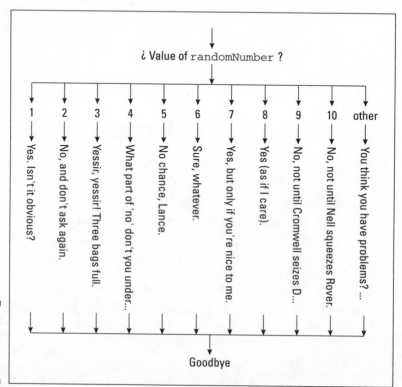

Figure 11-2:
A fork with
eleven
prongs.

¿ Value of `randomNumber` ?

1 — Yes. Isn't it obvious?

2 — No, and don't ask again.

3 — Yessir, yessir! Three bags full.

4 — What part of 'no' don't you under...

5 — No chance, Lance.

6 — Sure, whatever.

7 — Yes, but only if you're nice to me.

8 — Yes (as if I care).

9 — No, not until Cromwell seizes D...

10 — No, not until Nell squeezes Rover.

other — You think you have problems? ...

Goodbye

The default in a switch statement

What if something goes terribly wrong during a run of the Listing 11-1 program? Say the call to DummiesRandom.getInt generates a number that's not in the 1 to 10 range. Then the computer responds by dropping past all the case clauses. Instead of landing on a case clause, the computer jumps to the default clause. In the default clause, the computer displays You think you have problems?..., and then breaks out of the switch statement. After the computer is out of the switch statement, the computer displays Goodbye.

You don't really need to put a break at the very end of a switch statement. In Listing 11-1, the last break (the break that's part of the default clause) is just for the sake of overall tidiness.

Picky details about the switch statement

A switch statement can take the following form:

```
switch (Expression)
{
    case FirstValue:   Statement1
    case SecondValue: Statement2
      // ... more cases...
    default: Statement
}
```

Here are some tidbits about switch statements:

✔ The *Expression* doesn't have to have an int value. It can be char, byte, short, or int. For instance, the following code works nicely:

```
char letterGrade;
letterGrade = DummiesIO.getChar();
switch (letterGrade)
{
    case 'A': System.out.println("Excellent");
            break;
    case 'B': System.out.println("Good");
            break;
    case 'C': System.out.println("Average");
            break;
}
```

✔ The *Expression* doesn't have to be a single variable. It can be any expression of type char, byte, short, or int. For instance, you can simulate the rolling of two dice with the following code:

```
int die1, die2;

die1 = DummiesRandom.getInt(6);
die2 = DummiesRandom.getInt(6);

switch (die1 + die2)
{
    //...etc.
```

✔ The cases in a `switch` statement don't have to be in order. Here's some acceptable code:

```
switch (randomNumber)
{
    case 2:
        System.out.println("No, and don't ask again.");
        break;
    case 1:
        System.out.println("Yes. Isn't it obvious?");
        break;
    case 3:
        System.out.print("Yessir, yessir!");
        System.out.println(" Three bags full.");
        break;
//...etc.
```

This mixing of cases may slow you down when you're trying to read a program, but it's legal nonetheless.

✔ You don't need a `case` for each expected value of the *Expression*. You can leave some expected values to the `default`. Here's an example:

```
switch (randomNumber)
{
    case 1:
        System.out.println("Yes. Isn't it obvious?");
        break;
    case 5:
        System.out.println("No chance, Lance.");
        break;
    case 7:
        System.out.print("Yes, but only if");
        System.out.println(" you're nice to me.");
        break;
    case 10:
        System.out.print("No, not until");
        System.out.println(" Nell squeezes Rover.");
        break;
    default:
        System.out.print("Sorry,");
        System.out.println(" I just can't decide.");
        break;
}
```

✔ The default clause is optional.

```
switch (randomNumber)
{
    case 1:
        System.out.println("Yes. Isn't it obvious?");
        break;
    case 2:
        System.out.println("No, and don't ask again.");
        break;
    case 3:
        System.out.print("I'm too tired.");
        System.out.println(" Go ask somebody else.");
}
System.out.println("Goodbye");
```

If you have no default clause, and a value that's not covered by any of the cases comes up, then the switch statement does nothing. For instance, if randomNumber is 4, then the code shown above displays Goodbye, and nothing else.

✔ In some ways, if statements are more versatile than switch statements. For instance, you can't use a condition in a switch statement's *Expression*:

```
//You can't do this:
switch (age >= 12 && age < 65)
```

You can't use a condition as a case value either:

```
//You can't do this:
switch (age)
{
    case age<=12: //...etc.
```

To break or not to break

In every Java programmer's life, a time comes when he or she forgets to use break statements. At first, the resulting output is confusing, but then the programmer remembers fall-through. The term *fall-through* describes what happens when you end a case without a break statement. What happens is that execution of the code falls right through to the next case in line. Execution keeps falling through until you eventually reach a break statement or the end of the entire switch statement.

If you don't believe me, just look at this switch statement gone bad:

```
//This isn't good code. The programmer forgot some
//  of the break statements:
switch (randomNumber)
{
```

```
    case 1:
        System.out.println("Yes. Isn't it obvious?");
    case 2:
        System.out.println("No, and don't ask again.");
    case 3:
        System.out.print("Yessir, yessir!");
        System.out.println(" Three bags full.");
    case 4:
        System.out.print("What part of 'no'");
        System.out.println(" don't you understand?");
        break;
    case 5:
        System.out.println("No chance, Lance.");
    case 6:
        System.out.println("Sure, whatever.");
    case 7:
        System.out.print("Yes, but only if");
        System.out.println(" you're nice to me.");
    case 8:
        System.out.println("Yes (as if I care).");
    case 9:
        System.out.print("No, not until");
        System.out.println(" Cromwell seizes Dover.");
    case 10:
        System.out.print("No, not until");
        System.out.println(" Nell squeezes Rover.");
    default:
        System.out.print("You think you have");
        System.out.print(" problems?");
        System.out.print(" My random number");
        System.out.println(" generator is broken!");
}
System.out.println("Goodbye");
```

I've put two runs of this code in Figure 11-3. In the first run, the
randomNumber is 7. The program executes cases 7 through 10, and the
default. In the second run, the randomNumber is 3. The program executes
cases 3 and 4. Then, because case 4 has a break statement, the program
jumps out of the switch and displays Goodbye.

```
C:\JavaPrograms>java BadBreaks
Type your question, my child:  Do good things happen to good people?
Yes, but only if you're nice to me.
Yes (as if I care).
No, not until Cromwell seizes Dover.
No, not until Nell squeezes Rover.
You think you have problems? My random number generator is broken!
Goodbye

C:\JavaPrograms>java BadBreaks
Type your question, my child:  Is your switch statement missing some breaks?
Yessir, yessir! Three bags full.
What part of 'no' don't you understand?
Goodbye
```

Using Fall-through to Your Advantage

Often, when you're using a switch statement, you don't want fall-through, so you pepper break statements throughout the switch. But, sometimes, fall-through is just the thing you need.

Take the number of days in a month. Is there a simple rule for this? Months containing the letter "r" have 31 days? Months in which "i" comes before "e" except after "c" have 30 days?

You can fiddle with if conditions all you want. But to handle all the possibilities, I prefer a switch statement. Listing 11-2 demonstrates the idea.

Listing 11-2   Finding the Number of Days in a Month

```
class DaysInEachMonth
{
    public static void main(String args[])
    {
        int month, numberOfDays=0;
        boolean isLeapYear;

        System.out.print("Which month? ");
        month = DummiesIO.getInt();

        switch(month)
        {
            case 1:
            case 3:
            case 5:
            case 7:
            case 8:
            case 10:
            case 12:
                numberOfDays=31;
                break;
            case 4:
            case 6:
            case 9:
            case 11:
                numberOfDays=30;
                break;
            case 2:
                System.out.print("Leap year (true/false)? ");
                isLeapYear = DummiesIO.getBoolean();
                if (isLeapYear)
                    numberOfDays=29;
```

(continued)

Listing 11-2 *(continued)*

```
                else
                    numberOfDays=28;
        }

        System.out.print(numberOfDays);
        System.out.println(" days");
    }
}
```

Figure 11-4 shows several runs of the program in Listing 11-2. For month number 6, the computer jumps to `case 6`. There are no statements inside the `case 6` clause, so that part of the program's run is pretty boring.

```
C:\JavaPrograms>java DaysInEachMonth
Which month? 1
31 days

C:\JavaPrograms>java DaysInEachMonth
Which month? 6
30 days

C:\JavaPrograms>java DaysInEachMonth
Which month? 2
Leap year (true/false)? false
28 days

C:\JavaPrograms>java DaysInEachMonth
Which month? 2
Leap year (true/false)? true
29 days
```

Figure 11-4:
How many
days until
the next big
deadline?

But with no `break` in the `case 6` clause, the computer marches right along to `case 9`. Once again, the computer finds no statements and no `break`, so the computer ventures to the next case, which is `case 11`. At that point, the computer hits pay dirt. The computer assigns 30 to `numberOfDays`, and breaks out of the entire `switch` statement. (See Figure 11-5.)

February is the best month of all. For one thing, the February case in Listing 11-2 contains a call to my `DummiesIO.getBoolean` method. The method expects me to type either `true` or `false`. The code uses whatever word I type to assign a value to a `boolean` variable. (In Listing 11-2, I assign `true` or `false` to the `isLeapYear` variable.)

February also contains its own `if` statement. In Chapter 10, I nest `if` statements within other `if` statements. But in February, I nest an `if` statement within a `switch` statement. That's cool.

```
switch(month)
{        ⑥
   case 1:
   case 3:
   case 5:
   case 7:
   case 8:
   case 10:
   case 12:
       numberOfDays=31;
       break;
   case 4:
   case 6:
   case 9:
   case 11:
       numberOfDays=30;
       break;
   case 2:
       System.out.print("Leap year (true/false)? ");
       isLeapYear = DummiesIO.getBoolean();
       if (isLeapYear)
           numberOfDays=29;
       else
           numberOfDays=28;
}
System.out.print(numberOfDays);
System.out.printIn(" days");
```

Figure 11-5:
Follow the
bouncing
ball.

Using a Conditional Operator

Java has a neat feature that I can't resist writing about. Using this feature, you can think about alternatives in a very natural way.

And what do I mean by "a natural way?" If I think out loud as I imitate the if statement near the end of Listing 11-2, I come up with this:

```
//The thinking in Listing 11-2:
What should I do next?
If this is a leap year,
    I'll make the numberOfDays be 29;
Otherwise,
    I'll make the numberOfDays be 28.
```

I'm wandering into an if statement without a clue about what I'm doing next. That seems silly. It's February, and everybody knows what you do in February. You ask how many days the month has.

In my opinion, the code in Listing 11-2 doesn't reflect the most natural way to think about February. So here's a more natural way:

```
//A more natural way to think about the problem:
The value of numberOfDays is...
    Wait! Is this a leap year?
        If yes, 29
        If no, 28
```

In this second, more natural way of thinking, I know from the start that I'm picking a number of days. So by the time I reach a fork in the road (Is this a leap year?), the only remaining task is to choose between 29 and 28.

I can make the choice with finesse:

```
case 2:
    System.out.print("Leap year (true/false)? ");
    isLeapYear = DummiesIO.getBoolean();
    numberOfDays = isLeapYear ? 29 : 28;
}
```

The ? : combination is called a *conditional operator*. In Figure 11-6, I show you how my natural thinking about February can morph into the conditional operator's format.

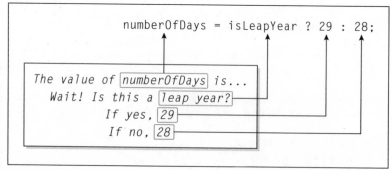

Figure 11-6: From your mind to the computer's code.

Taken as a whole, isLeapYear ? 29 : 28 is an expression with a value. And what value does this expression have? Well, the value of isLeapYear ? 29 : 28 is either 29 or 28. It depends on whether isLeapYear is or isn't true. That's how the conditional operator works:

- ✔ If the stuff before the question mark is `true`, then the whole expression's value is whatever comes between the question mark and the colon.
- ✔ If the stuff before the question mark is `false`, then the whole expression's value is whatever comes after the colon.

Figure 11-7 gives you goofy way to visualize these ideas.

So the conditional operator's overall effect is as if the computer is executing

```
numberOfDays = 29;
```

or

```
numberOfDays = 28;
```

One way or another, `numberOfDays` gets a value, and the code solves the problem with style.

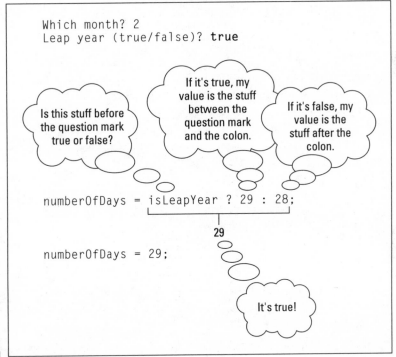

Figure 11-7: Have you ever seen an expression talking to itself?

Chapter 12

Around and Around It Goes

Chapter 8 has code to reverse the letters in a four-letter word that the user enters. In case you jumped over Chapter 8 or you just don't want to flip back, here's a quick recap of the code:

```
c1 = DummiesIO.getChar();
c2 = DummiesIO.getChar();
c3 = DummiesIO.getChar();
c4 = DummiesIO.getChar();

System.out.print(c4);
System.out.print(c3);
System.out.print(c2);
System.out.print(c1);
```

The code is just dandy for words with exactly four letters, but how do you reverse a five letter word? As the code stands, you have to add two new statements:

```
c1 = DummiesIO.getChar();
c2 = DummiesIO.getChar();
c3 = DummiesIO.getChar();
c4 = DummiesIO.getChar();
c5 = DummiesIO.getChar();

System.out.print(c5);
System.out.print(c4);
System.out.print(c3);
System.out.print(c2);
System.out.print(c1);
```

What a drag! You add statements to a program whenever the size of a word changes! You remove statements when the input shrinks! That can't be the best way to solve the problem. Maybe you can command a computer to add statements automatically. (But then again, maybe you can't.)

As luck would have it, you can do something that's even better. You can write a statement once, and tell the computer to execute the statement many times. How many times? You can tell the computer to execute a statement as many times as it needs to be executed.

That's the big idea. The rest of this chapter has the details.

Repeating Instructions Over and Over Again (Java while Statements)

Here's a simple dice game: Keep rolling two dice until you roll 7 or 11. Listing 12-1 has a program that simulates the action in the game, and Figure 12-1 shows two runs of the program.

Listing 12-1   Roll 7 or 11

```
class SimpleDiceGame
{
    public static void main(String args[])
    {
        int die1=0, die2=0;

        while(die1+die2 != 7  &&  die1+die2 != 11)
        {
            die1 = DummiesRandom.getInt(6);
            die2 = DummiesRandom.getInt(6);

            System.out.print(die1);
            System.out.print(" ");
            System.out.println(die2);
        }

        System.out.print("Rolled ");
        System.out.println(die1+die2);
    }
}
```

At the core of Listing 12-1 is a thing called a *while statement* (also known as a *while loop*). Rephrased in English, the `while` statement in Listing 12-1 would say

```
while the sum of the two dice isn't 7 and isn't 11
keep doing all the stuff in curly braces:
{



}
```

The stuff in curly braces (the stuff that is repeated over and over again) is the code that gets two new random numbers and displays those random numbers' values. The statements in curly braces are repeated as long as die1+die2 != 7 && die1+die2 != 11 keeps being true.

Each repetition of the statements in the loop is called an *iteration* of the loop. In Figure 12-1, the first run has two iterations, and the second run has ten iterations.

Figure 12-1:
Momma
needs a
new pair of
shoes.

```
C:\JavaPrograms>java SimpleDiceGame
6 2
2 5
Rolled 7

C:\JavaPrograms>java SimpleDiceGame
3 1
1 2
4 5
5 5
1 2
2 2
1 5
2 1
3 3
5 6
Rolled 11
```

When die1+die2 != 7 && die1+die2 != 11 is no longer true (that is, when the sum is either 7 or 11), then the repeating of statements stops dead in its tracks. The computer marches on to the statements that come after the loop.

Following the action in a loop

To trace the action of the code in Listing 12-1, I'll borrow numbers from the first run in Figure 12-1:

✔ At the start, the values of die1 and die2 are both 0.

✔ The computer gets to the top of the while statement, and checks to see if die1+die2 != 7 && die1+die2 != 11 is true. (See Figure 12-2.) The condition is true so the computer takes the true path in Figure 12-3.

The computer performs an iteration of the loop. During this iteration, the computer gets new values for die1 and die2, and prints those values on the screen. In the first run of Figure 12-1, the new values are 6 and 2.

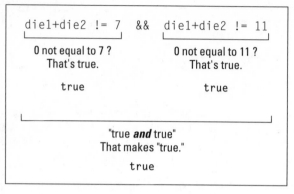

Figure 12-2:
Two wrongs
don't make
a right, but
two trues
make a true.

✔ The computer returns to the top of the `while` statement, and checks to see if `die1+die2 != 7 && die1+die2 != 11` is still true. The condition is true so the computer takes the `true` path in Figure 12-3.

The computer performs another iteration of the loop. During this iteration, the computer gets new values for `die1` and `die2`, and prints those values on the screen. In Figure 12-1, the new values are 2 and 5.

✔ The computer returns to the top of the `while` statement, and checks to see if `die1+die2 != 7 && die1+die2 != 11` is still true. Lo and behold! This condition has become false! (See Figure 12-4.) The computer takes the `false` path in Figure 12-3.

The computer leaps to the statements after the loop. The computer displays `Rolled 7`, and ends its run of the program.

No early bailout

In Listing 12-1, when the computer finds `die1+die2 != 7 && die1+die2 != 11` to be true, the computer marches on and executes all five statements inside the loop's curly braces. The computer executes

```
die1 = DummiesRandom.getInt(6);
die2 = DummiesRandom.getInt(6);
```

Maybe (just maybe), the new values of `die1` and `die2` add up to 7. Even so, the computer doesn't jump out in mid-loop. The computer finishes the iteration, and executes

```
System.out.print(die1);
System.out.print(" ");
System.out.println(die2);
```

one more time. The computer performs the test again (to see if `die1+die2 != 7 && die1+die2 != 11` is still true) only after it fully executes all five statements in the loop.

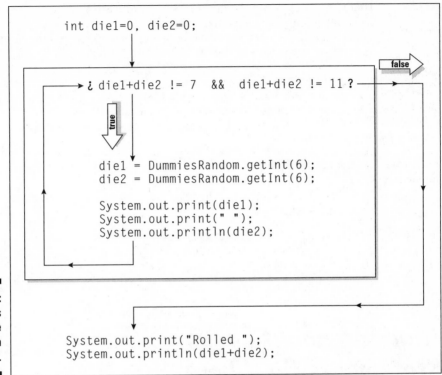

Figure 12-3:
Paths
through the
code in
Listing 12-1.

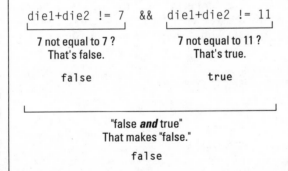

Figure 12-4:
Look!
I rolled a
seven!

Brace yourself

Here's a format for the `while` statement:

```
while (Condition)
    Statement
```

That's nice, but notice the curly brace underneath the word `while` in Listing 12-1. Taken together, everything from that open curly brace to the close curly brace directly below it constitutes one big, compound statement. It's the *Statement* in the format above.

Almost everything that's true about an `if` statement's curly braces is also true about a loop's curly braces. (See Chapter 9.) In particular, you don't need curly braces as long as, without the braces, the loop contains only one statement. For instance, the following `while` statement is legal:

```
while(roll != 7  &&  roll != 11)
    roll = DummiesRandom.getInt(12);
```

Of course, it never hurts to add extra curly braces, so the following `while` statement is also legal:

```
while(roll != 7  &&  roll != 11)
{
    roll = DummiesRandom.getInt(12);
}
```

Thinking about Loops (What Statements Go Where)

Here's a simplified version of the card game Twenty-One: You keep taking cards until the total is 21 or higher. Then, if the total is 21, you win. If the total is higher, you lose. (By the way, each face card counts as a 10.) To play this game, you want a program whose runs look like the runs in Figure 12-5.

```
C:\JavaPrograms>java PlayTwentyOne
Card      Total
8         8
8         16
2         18
6         24
You lose :-(
C:\JavaPrograms>java PlayTwentyOne
Card      Total
5         5
2         7
8         15
2         17
4         21
You win :->
```

Figure 12-5:
You win sum; you lose sum.

In most sections of this book, I put a program's listing before the description of the program's features. But this section is different. This section deals with strategies for composing code. So in this section, I start by brainstorming about strategies.

Finding some pieces

How do you write a program that plays a simplified version of Twenty-One?
I start by fishing for clues in the game's rules, spelled out in this section's
first paragraph. The big fishing expedition is illustrated in Figure 12-6.

With the reasoning in Figure 12-6, I need a loop and an `if` statement:

```
while (total < 21)
{
    //do stuff
}

if (total == 21)
    //You win
else
    //You lose
```

What else do I need to make this program work? Look at the sample output in
Figure 12-5. I need a heading with the words `Card` and `Total`. That's a call to
`System.out.println`:

```
System.out.println("Card      Total");
```

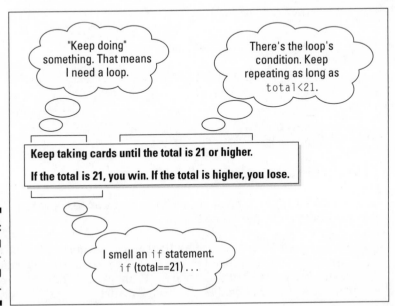

Figure 12-6:
Thinking
about a pro-
gramming
problem.

I also need several lines of output — each containing two numbers. For instance, in Figure 12-5, the line 2 18 displays the values of two variables. One variable stores the most recently picked card; the other variable stores the total of all cards picked so far:

```
System.out.print(card);
System.out.print("        ");
System.out.println(total);
```

Now I have four chunks of code, but I haven't decided how they all fit together. Well, you can go right ahead and call me crazy. But at this point in the process, I imagine those four chunks of code circling around one another, like part of a dream sequence in a low-budget movie. As you may imagine, I'm not very good at illustrating circling code in dream sequences. Even so, I handed my idea to the art department at Wiley Publishing, and they came up with the picture in Figure 12-7.

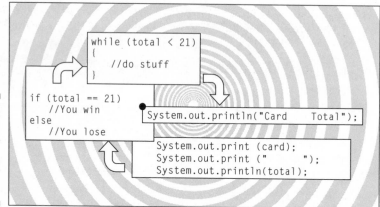

Figure 12-7: ... and where they stop, nobody knows.

Assembling the pieces

Where should I put each piece of code? The best way to approach the problem is to ask how many times each piece of code should be executed:

✔ **The program displays** card **and** total **values more than once.** For instance, in the first run of Figure 12-5, the program displays these values five times (first 8 8, then 8 16, and so on). To get this repeated display, I put the code that creates the display inside the loop:

```
while (total < 21)
{
    System.out.print(card);
    System.out.print("        ");
    System.out.println(total);
}
```

✔ **The program displays the** Card Total **heading only once per run.** This display comes before any of the repeated number displays, so I put the heading code before the loop:

```
System.out.println("Card    Total");

while (total < 21)
{
    System.out.print(card);
    System.out.print("        ");
    System.out.println(total);
}
```

✔ **The program displays** You win **or** You lose **only once per run.** This message display comes after the repeated number displays. So I put the win/lose code after the loop:

```
//Preliminary draft code - NOT ready for prime time:
System.out.println("Card    Total");

while (total < 21)
{
    System.out.print(card);
    System.out.print("        ");
    System.out.println(total);
}

if (total==21)
    System.out.println("You win :-)");
else
    System.out.println("You lose :-(");
```

Getting values for variables

I almost have a working program. But if I take the code that I've developed for a mental test run, I face a few problems. To see what I mean, picture yourself in the computer's shoes for a minute. (Well, a computer doesn't have shoes. Picture yourself in the computer's boots.)

You start at the top of the code shown previously (the code that starts with the Preliminary draft comment). In the code's first statement, you display the words Card Total. So far, so good. But then you encounter the while loop, and test the condition total < 21. Well, is total less than 21, or isn't it? Honestly, I'm tempted to make up an answer, because I'm embarrassed about not knowing what the total variable's value is. (I'm sure the computer is embarrassed too.)

The variable total must have a known value before the computer reaches the top of the while loop. Because a player starts with no cards at all, the initial total value should be 0. That settles it. I declare int total=0 at the top of the program.

But what about my friend, the card variable? Should I set card to zero also? No. There's no zero-valued card in a deck (at least, not when I'm playing fair). Besides, card should get a new value several times during the program's run.

Wait! In the previous sentence, the phrase *several times* tickles a neuron in my brain. It stimulates the *inside a loop* reflex. So I place an assignment to the card variable inside my while loop:

```
//This is a DRAFT - still NOT ready for prime time:
int card, total=0;

System.out.println("Card     Total");

while (total < 21)
{
    card = DummiesRandom.getInt();

    System.out.print(card);
    System.out.print("        ");
    System.out.println(total);
}

if (total==21)
    System.out.println("You win :-)");
else
    System.out.println("You lose :-(");
```

The code still has an error, and I can probably find the error with more computer role-playing. But instead, I get daring. I run this beta code to see what happens. Figure 12-8 shows part of a run.

```
C:\JavaPrograms>java WorkInProgress21
Card    Total
9       0
8       0
3       0
3       0
6       0
3       0
6       0
8       0
10       0
6       0
2       0
10       0
9       0
```

Figure 12-8:
An incorrect run.

Unfortunately, the run in Figure 12-8 doesn't stop on its own. This kind of processing is called an *infinite loop*. The loop runs and runs until someone trips over the computer's extension cord.

With most systems' command prompts (including those on Unix, Linux, and Microsoft Windows systems), holding down the Ctrl key while pressing the C key stops the execution of a runaway program. To just pause a program's execution, press Ctrl+S. To resume execution, press Ctrl+Q.

From infinity to affinity

For some problems, an infinite loop is normal and desirable. Take, for instance, a real-time mission critical application — air traffic control, or the monitoring of a heart-lung machine. In these situations, a program should run and run and run.

But a game of Twenty-One should end pretty quickly. In Figure 12-8, the game doesn't end because the `total` never reaches 21 or higher. In fact, the `total` is always zero. The problem is that my code has no statement to change the `total` variable's value. I should add each card's value to the `total`:

```
total += card;
```

Again, I ask myself where this statement belongs in the code. How many times should the computer execute this assignment statement? Once at the start of the program? Once at the end of the run? Repeatedly?

The computer should repeatedly add a card's value to the running total. In fact, the computer should add to the total each time a card gets drawn. So the assignment statement above should be inside the `while` loop, right alongside the statement that gets a new `card` value:

```
card = DummiesRandom.getInt();
total += card;
```

With this revelation, I'm ready to see the complete program. The code is in Listing 12-2, and two runs of the code are shown in Figure 12-5.

Listing 12-2   A Simplified Version of the Game Twenty-One

```
class PlayTwentyOne
{
    public static void main(String args[])
    {
        int card, total=0;
```

(continued)

Escapism

You can use a neat trick to make a program's output line up correctly. In Figure 12-5, the numbers 8 8, then 8 16 (and so on) are displayed. I want these numbers to be right under the heading words Card and Total. Normally, you can get perfect vertical columns by pressing the tab key, but a computer program creates the output in Figure 12-5. How can you get a computer program to press the tab key?

In Java, there's a way. You can put \t inside double quote marks.

```
System.out.println("Card\tTotal");
System.out.print(card);
System.out.print("\t");
System.out.println(total);
```

In the first statement, the computer displays Card, then jumps to the next tab stop on the screen, and then displays Total. In the next three statements, the computer displays a card

number (like the number 8), then jumps to the next tab stop (directly under the word Total), and then displays a total value (like the number 16). It's easier to picture this than to read about it. So to help you picture it in your mind, I've pictured it in my book. Please see the following figure.

The \t combination of characters is an example of an *escape sequence*. Another of Java's escape sequences, the combination \n, moves the cursor to a new line. In other words, System.out.print("Hello\n") does the same thing as System.out.println ("Hello").

Note: Most systems' command prompt windows have tab stops at fixed eight-space intervals. Unlike the tabs in your favorite word processing program, the command prompt window's tab stops cannot be moved.

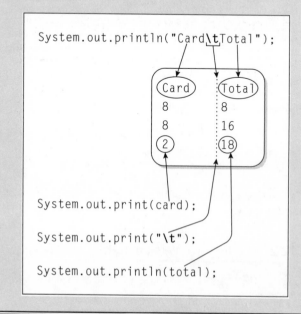

Listing 12-2 *(continued)*

```
System.out.println("Card     Total");

while (total < 21)
{
    card = DummiesRandom.getInt();
    total += card;

    System.out.print(card);
    System.out.print("           ");
    System.out.println(total);
}

if (total==21)
    System.out.println("You win :-)");
else
    System.out.println("You lose :-(");
    }
}
```

If you've read this whole section, then you're probably exhausted. Creating a loop can be a lot of work. Fortunately, the more you practice, the easier it becomes.

Thinking About Loops (Priming)

I remember when I was a young boy. We lived on Front Street in Philadelphia, near where the El train turned onto Kensington Avenue. Come early morning, I'd have to go outside and get water from the well. I'd pump several times before any water would come out. Ma and Pa called it "priming the pump."

These days I don't prime pumps. I prime `while` loops. Take the case of a busy network administrator. She needs a program that extracts a user name from an e-mail address. For instance, the program reads

```
John@BurdBrain.com
```

and writes

```
John
```

How does the program do it? Like other examples in the chapter, this problem involves repetition:

```
Repeatedly do the following:
   Read a character.
   Write the character.
```

The program then stops the repetition when it finds the @ sign. I take a stab at writing this program. My first attempt doesn't work, but it's a darn good start. It's in Listing 12-3.

Listing 12-3   Trying to Get a User Name from an E-mail Address

```java
//This code does NOT work, but I'm not discouraged.
class FirstAttempt
{
    public static void main(String args[])
    {
        char symbol = ' ';

        while (symbol != '@')
        {
            symbol = DummiesIO.getChar();
            System.out.print(symbol);
        }

        System.out.println();
    }
}
```

When you run the code in Listing 12-3, you get the output shown in Figure 12-9. The user types one character after another — the letter J, then o, then h, and so on. At first, the program in Listing 12-3 does nothing. (The computer doesn't send any of the user's input to the program until the user presses Enter.) After the user types a whole e-mail address and presses Enter, the program gets its first character (the J in John).

Unfortunately, the program's output isn't what you expect. Instead of just the user name John, you get the user name and the @ sign.

Figure 12-9:
Oops! Got
the @ sign
too.

```
C:\JavaPrograms>java FirstAttempt
John@BurdBrain.com
John@
```

To find out why this happens, follow the computer's actions as it reads the input John@BurdBrain.com:

```
Set symbol to ' ' (a blank space).

Is that blank space the same as an @ sign?
No, so perform a loop iteration.
    Get the letter 'J'.
    Print the letter 'J'.

Is that 'J' the same as an @ sign?
No, so perform a loop iteration.
    Get the letter 'o'.
    Print the letter 'o'.

Is that 'o' the same as an @ sign?
No, so perform a loop iteration.
    Get the letter 'h'.
    Print the letter 'h'.

Is that 'h' the same as an @ sign?
No, so perform a loop iteration.
    Get the letter 'n'.
    Print the letter 'n'.

Is that 'n' the same as an @ sign?   //Here's the problem.
No, so perform a loop iteration.
    Get the @ sign.
    Print the @ sign.                //Oops!

Is that @ sign the same as an @ sign?
Yes, so stop iterating.
```

Near the end of the program's run, the computer compares the letter n with the @ sign. Because n isn't an @ sign, the computer dives right into the loop:

- The first statement in the loop reads an @ sign from the keyboard.

- The second statement in the loop doesn't check to see if it's time to stop printing. Instead, that second statement just marches ahead and displays the @ sign.

After you've displayed the @ sign, there's no going back. You can't change your mind and undisplay the @ sign. So the code in Listing 12-3 doesn't quite work.

Working on the problem

You learn from your mistakes. The problem with Listing 12-3 is that, between reading and writing a character, the program doesn't check for an @ sign. Instead of doing "Test, Get, Print," it should do "Get, Test, Print." That is, instead of doing this:

```
Is that 'o' the same as an @ sign?
No, so perform a loop iteration.
    Get the letter 'h'.
    Print the letter 'h'.

Is that 'h' the same as an @ sign?
No, so perform a loop iteration.
    Get the letter 'n'.
    Print the letter 'n'.

Is that 'n' the same as an @ sign?    //Here's the problem.
No, so perform a loop iteration.
    Get the @ sign.
    Print the @ sign.                 //Oops!
```

the program should do this:

```
    Get the letter 'o'.
Is that 'o' the same as an @ sign?
No, so perform a loop iteration.
    Print the letter 'o'.

    Get the letter 'n'.
Is that 'n' the same as an @ sign?
No, so perform a loop iteration.
    Print the letter 'n'.

    Get the @ sign.
Is that @ sign the same as an @ sign?
Yes, so stop iterating.
```

This cycle is shown in Figure 12-10.

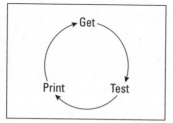

Figure 12-10:
What the
program
needs to do.

You can try to imitate the following informal pattern:

```
    Get a character.
Is that character the same as an @ sign?
If not, perform a loop iteration.
    Print the character.
```

The problem is, you can't create a `while` loop that looks like this:

```
//This is not correct code:
{
    symbol = DummiesIO.getChar();
while (symbol != '@')
    System.out.print(symbol);
}
```

You can't sandwich a `while` statement's condition between two of the statements that you intend to repeat. So what can you do? You need to follow the flow in Figure 12-11. Because every `while` loop starts with a test, that's where you jump into the circle: first Test, then Print, and finally Get.

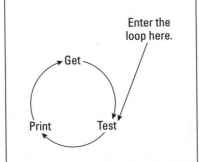

Figure 12-11:
Jumping
into a loop.

Listing 12-4 shows the embodiment of this "test, then print, then get" strategy.

Listing 12-4   Nice Try, But . . .

```
//This code almost works, but there's one tiny error:
class SecondAttempt
{
    public static void main(String args[])
    {
        char symbol = ' ';

        while (symbol != '@')
        {
            System.out.print(symbol);
            symbol = DummiesIO.getChar();
        }

        System.out.println();
    }
}
```

A run of the Listing 12-4 code is shown in Figure 12-12. The code is almost correct, but I still have a slight problem. Notice the blank space before the user's input. The program races prematurely into the loop. The first time the computer executes the statements

```
System.out.print(symbol);
symbol = DummiesIO.getChar();
```

the computer displays an unwanted blank space. Then the computer gets the J in John. In some applications, an extra blank space is no big deal. But in other applications, extra output can be disastrous.

Figure 12-12:
The computer displays an extra blank space.

```
C:\JavaPrograms>java SecondAttempt
 John@BurdBrain.com
John
```

Fixing the problem

Disastrous or not, an unwanted blank space is the symptom of a logical flaw. The program shouldn't display results before it has any meaningful results to display. The solution to this problem is called . . . (drum roll, please) . . . *priming the loop.* You pump the getChar method once to get some values flowing. Listing 12-5 shows you how to do it.

Listing 12-5   How to Prime a Pump

```
//This code works correctly!
class GetUserName
{
    public static void main(String args[])
    {
        char symbol;

        symbol = DummiesIO.getChar();

        while (symbol != '@')
        {
            System.out.print(symbol);
            symbol = DummiesIO.getChar();
        }

        System.out.println();
    }
}
```

Listing 12-5 follows the strategy shown in Figure 12-13. First you get a character (the letter J in John, for instance), then you enter the loop. After you're in the loop, you test the letter against the @ sign, and print the letter if it's appropriate to do so. Figure 12-14 shows a beautiful run of the GetUserName program.

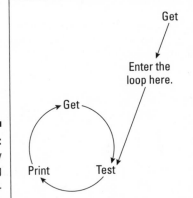

Figure 12-13:
The strategy in Listing 12-5.

Figure 12-14:
A run of the code in Listing 12-5.

```
C:\JavaPrograms>java GetUserName
John@BurdBrain.com
John
```

The priming of loops in an important programming technique. But it's not the end of the story. In Chapters 14, 15, and 16, you can read about some other useful looping tricks.

Chapter 13

Piles of Files (Dealing with Information Overload)

In This Chapter

▶ Using data on your hard drive

▶ Writing code to access the hard drive

▶ Troubleshooting input/output behavior

Consider these scenarios:

✔ You're a business owner with hundreds of invoices. To avoid boxes full of paper, you store invoice data in a file on your hard drive. You need customized code to sort and classify the invoices.

✔ You're an astronomer with data from scans of the night sky. When you're ready to analyze a chunk of data, you load the chunk onto your computer's hard drive.

✔ You're the author of a popular self-help book. Last year's fad was called the Self Mirroring Method. This year's craze is the Make Your Cake System. You can't modify your manuscript without converting to the publisher's new specifications. The trouble is, there's no existing software to make the task bearable.

Each situation calls for a new computer program, and each program reads from a large data file. On top of all that, each program creates a brand new file containing bright, shiny results.

In previous chapters, the examples get input from the keyboard and send output to the screen. That's fine for small tasks, but you can't have the computer prompt you for each bit of night sky data. For big problems, you need lots of data, and the best place to store the data is on a computer's hard drive.

Running a Disk-Oriented Program

To deal with volumes of data, you need tools for reading from (and writing to) disk files. At the mere mention of disk files, some peoples' hearts start to palpitate with fear. After all, a disk file is elusive and invisible. It's stored somewhere inside your computer, with some magic magnetic process.

The truth is, getting data from a disk is very much like getting data from the keyboard. And printing data to a disk is like printing data to the computer screen.

Consider the scenario when you run the code in the previous chapters. You type some stuff on the keyboard. The program takes this stuff, and spits out some stuff of its own. The program sends this new stuff to the screen. In effect, the flow of data goes from the keyboard, to the computer's innards, and on to the screen, as shown in Figure 13-1.

Of course, the goal in this chapter is the scenario in Figure 13-2. There's a file containing data on your hard drive. The program takes data from the disk file and spits out some brand new data. The program then sends the new data to another file on the hard drive. In effect, the flow of data goes from a disk file, to the computer's innards, and on to another disk file.

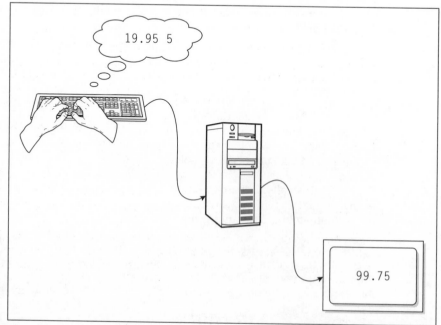

Figure 13-1:
Using the keyboard and screen.

Figure 13-2:
Using disk
files.

The two scenarios in Figures 13-1 and 13-2 are very similar. In fact, it helps to remember these fundamental points:

✓ **The stuff in a disk file is no different from the stuff that you type on a keyboard.**

If a keyboard-reading program expects you to type 19.95 5, then the corresponding disk-reading program expects a file containing those same characters, 19.95 5. If a keyboard-reading program expects you to press Enter and type more characters, then the corresponding disk-reading program expects more characters on the next line in the file.

✓ **The stuff in a disk file is no different from the stuff that you see on the screen.**

If a screen-printing program displays the number 99.75, then the corresponding disk-writing program writes the number 99.75 to a file. If a screen-printing program moves the cursor to the next line, then the corresponding disk-writing program creates a new line in the file.

If you have trouble imagining what you have in a disk file, just imagine the text that you would type on the keyboard, or the text that you would see on the computer screen. That same text can appear in a file on your disk.

A sample program

Listing 13-1 contains a keyboard/screen program. The program multiplies unit price by quantity to get a total price. A run of the code is shown in Figure 13-3.

Listing 13-1   Using the Keyboard and the Screen

```java
class ComputeTotal
{
    public static void main(String args[])
    {
        double unitPrice, quantity, total;

        unitPrice = DummiesIO.getDouble();
        quantity = DummiesIO.getInt();

        total = unitPrice*quantity;

        System.out.println(total);
    }
}
```

Figure 13-3:
Read from
the
keyboard;
write to the
screen.

```
C:\JavaPrograms>java ComputeTotal
19.95 5
99.75
```

The goal is to write a program like the one in Listing 13-1. But instead of talking to your keyboard and screen, this new program talks to your hard drive. The new program reads unit price and quantity from your hard drive, and writes the total back to your hard drive.

DummiesIO versus real life

The material in this chapter relies heavily on features of my DummiesIO code, which is both a blessing and a curse. It's a blessing because DummiesIO is easy to use. It's a curse because the standard Java input/output programs are much more complicated than DummiesIO.

That's okay. When you write your own programs, you can still use my DummiesIO code. Just copy DummiesIO.java to whatever directory contains your own Java program. (If you press on beyond the material in this book and you start using *named Java packages,* then you'll need some additional tricks. Visit www.BurdBrain. com and download my com.BurdBrain.io package. The package comes with some documentation to help you get going.)

In a heavy-duty corporate setting, you should eventually wean yourself away from DummiesIO and switch to Java's standard input/output code. Even when you do, the concepts that you've discovered by using DummiesIO will serve you well.

Fortunately, my DummiesIO code makes it very easy to interact with a hard drive. A nice example is in Listing 13-2.

Listing 13-2   Using Input and Output Files

```
class ReadAndWrite
{
    public static void main(String args[])
    {
        double unitPrice, quantity, total;

        unitPrice = DummiesIO.getDouble("rawData.txt");
        quantity = DummiesIO.getInt("rawData.txt");

        total = unitPrice*quantity;

        DummiesIO.println("cookedData.txt", total);
    }
}
```

Running the sample program

Testing the code in Listing 13-2 is a three-step process. Here are the steps:

1. Put the file rawData.txt **in your** JavaPrograms **directory.**

Open a text editor (Windows Notepad, for instance). Start a brand new document, and type 19.95 5 in the document, as shown in Figure 13-4. Save the file in your JavaPrograms directory, and name the file rawData.txt.

Figure 13-4:
Editing an
input file.

What I call your JavaPrograms directory isn't necessarily a folder named JavaPrograms. For more information, see Chapter 3.

2. Compile and run the code in Listing 13-2.

I do this in Figure 13-5, but I'm the first to admit it — Figure 13-5 is duller than dirt. First I type the javac command to compile the code. I get back another command prompt. Then I type the java command to run the code. And what do I get? I get another command prompt.

Figure 13-5:
Compiling
and running
the code in
Listing 13-2.

```
C:\JavaPrograms>javac ReadAndWrite.java
C:\JavaPrograms>java ReadAndWrite
C:\JavaPrograms>_
```

After issuing the `java` command, the total lack of any noticeable action gives some people the willies. The truth is, a program like the one in Listing 13-2 does all of its work behind the scenes. The program has no statements that read from the keyboard and has no statements that print to the screen. So if you have a very loud hard drive, you may hear a little chirping sound when you issue the `java` command, but you won't type any program input, and you won't see any program output.

You composed and saved the program's input in Step 1. So what do you do to see the program's output?

3. **View the contents of the** `cookedData.txt` **file.**

There are at least two ways to see the program's output. You can open the `cookedData.txt` file with a text editor, or you can display the file in your command prompt window:

A. If you open the file with a text editor, you see something like the stuff shown in Figure 13-6. The `cookedData.txt` file contains the value of the variable `total`.

Figure 13-6:
Viewing an
output file.

```
cookedData.txt - Notepad
File   Edit   Format   Help
99.75
```

B. To display the file in your command prompt window, first make your `JavaPrograms` directory the working directory. (To do this, you use the `cd` command. For details, see Chapter 3.)

After arriving at the `JavaPrograms` directory, issue a command that's specific to your operating system. In Windows, use the `type` command:

```
type cookedData.txt
```

In Unix or Linux, use the `cat` command:

```
cat cookedData.txt
```

For this section's example, you work with three different files — the input file (rawData.txt), the Java program file (ReadAndWrite.java), and the output file (cookedData.txt). In this situation, my advice is, "Don't close any editor windows." Save the rawData.txt file, but leave the editor window open in case you want to change the file's contents. Later, after you've run the program, you want to examine the resulting cookedData.txt file. To do this, open a brand new editor window. With all your windows open, you can go back and forth easily between the input file, the program file, and the output file.

Troubleshooting problems with disk files

If the steps above give you any trouble, your most likely place to see that trouble is in Step 2. During that step, you run the code in Listing 13-2, and the computer executes DummiesIO.getDouble("rawData.txt").

If the Java Virtual Machine can't find the rawData.txt file, then your screen erupts with a message like the one shown in Figure 13-7. This wake-up call can be very frustrating. In many cases, you know darn well that there's a rawData.txt file on your hard drive. The stupid computer simply can't find it.

Figure 13-7: The computer can't find your file.

```
C:\JavaPrograms>java ReadAndWrite
java.io.FileNotFoundException: rawData.txt (The system cannot find the file
specified)
        at java.io.FileInputStream.open(Native Method)
        at java.io.FileInputStream.<init>(Unknown Source)
        at java.io.FileInputStream.<init>(Unknown Source)
        at DummiesIO.getFileForReading(DummiesIO.java:148)
        at DummiesIO.openOrUseExisting(DummiesIO.java:28)
        at DummiesIO.getNonblankToken(DummiesIO.java:89)
        at DummiesIO.getDouble(DummiesIO.java:212)
        at ReadAndWrite.main(ReadAndWrite.java:7)
```

There's no quick, sure-fire way to fix this problem. But you should always check the following things first:

✔ **Check again for a file named** rawData.txt.

Open an Explorer window and look for a file with that name. Or go to your command prompt window and list the files in your JavaPrograms directory. In Windows, you list files using the dir command. In Unix or Linux, you use the ls command. (For a look at the Windows dir command, refer to Figures 3-3 and 3-5 in Chapter 3.)

The filenames displayed in Windows Explorer can be misleading. You may see the name rawData even though the file's real name is rawData.txt. To fix this problem once and for all, read the sidebar in Chapter 3 about those pesky filename extensions.

✔ **Check the spelling of the file's name.**

Make sure that the name in your program is exactly the same as the name of the file on your hard drive. Check every occurrence of the file's name in your program. Just one misplaced letter can keep the computer from finding a file. In Unix and Linux, the difference between uppercase and lowercase can baffle the computer.

✔ **Check that the file is in the correct directory.**

Sure, you have a file named rawData.txt. But, to find the file, don't expect the computer to search everywhere on your hard drive.

As a general rule, you should have rawData.txt and the Listing 13-2 code in the same directory on your hard drive. But file locations can be tricky. If you use an integrated development environment, or an unusual setup of any kind, then the normal rules may not apply to you.

So here's a trick you can use: Compile and run this stripped-down version of the code in Listing 13-2:

```
class JustWrite
{
    public static void main(String args[])
    {
        DummiesIO.println("cookedData.txt", 99.75);
    }
}
```

This program has no need for a stinking rawData.txt file. If you run this code and get no error messages, then search your hard drive for this program's output (the cookedData.txt file). Note the name of the directory that contains the cookedData.txt file. When you put rawData.txt in this same directory, then any problem you had running the Listing 13-2 code should go away.

✔ **Check the rawData.txt file's content.**

It never hurts to peek inside the rawData.txt file, and make sure that the file contains the numbers 19.95 5. To do this, choose option A or option B in Step 3 of the step list in the preceding section, "Running the sample program."

Writing a Disk-Oriented Program

Listing 13-2 is very much like Listing 13-1. In fact, you can go from Listing 13-1 to Listing 13-2 with some simple find-and-replace editing. Table 13-1 shows you how.

Table 13-1	Modifying Code for File Input and Output
Find all occurrences of	*Replace each occurrence with*
DummiesIO.getDouble()	DummiesIO.getDouble("rawData.txt")
DummiesIO.getInt()	DummiesIO.getInt("rawData.txt")
System.out.println (total)	DummiesIO.println ("cookedData.txt", total)

Reading from a file

If you don't like the blind obedience that it takes to use Table 13-1, you can grasp the underlying ideas.

All the DummiesIO.get methods can read from existing disk files. Just put the name of a file inside the method call's parentheses. For instance, to read a double value from a file named salaries.dat, use code of the following kind:

```
double employeeSalary;
employeeSalary = DummiesIO.getDouble("salaries.dat");
```

To read an int value from a file named hitCount, and then display the int value, you can do something like this:

```
System.out.println(DummiesIO.getInt("hitCount"));
```

Notice how I read from a file named hitCount, not hitCount.txt or hitCount.dat. Anything that you put after the dot is called a *filename extension*, and for a file full of numbers and other data, the filename extension is optional. Sure, a Java program must be called *something*.java, but a data file can be named mydata.txt, mydata.reallymine.allmine, or just mydata. As long as the name in your DummiesIO method call is the same as the filename on your computer's hard drive, everything is okay. (If you do Windows, make sure that Notepad doesn't automatically append the .txt extension without your knowing about it. See the section about what could possibly go wrong in Chapter 3.)

Writing to a file

My DummiesIO code has its own print and println methods. In most cases, you put two things inside the method call's parentheses:

✔ The name of a file

✔ A value that you send to the file

Here are some examples:

✔ During a run of the code in Listing 13-2, the variable `total` stores the number 99.75. To deposit 99.75 into the `cookedData.txt` file, you execute

```
DummiesIO.println("cookedData.txt", total);
```

✔ In another version of the program, you may decide not to use a `total` variable. To write 99.75 to the `cookedData.txt` file, you can call

```
DummiesIO.println("cookedData.txt", unitPrice*quantity);
```

✔ To display `OK` on the screen, you can make the following method call:

```
System.out.print("OK");
```

To write `OK` to a file named `approval.txt`, you can make the following method call:

```
DummiesIO.print("approval.txt", "OK");
```

When you call my `DummiesIO.print` method, you put two values between the parentheses. Even when both values are quoted, the two values serve very different purposes. The first value (before the comma) is the name of a file. The second value is the data to be deposited into the file. The misleading call `DummiesIO.print("OK", "approval.txt")` would put the characters `approval.txt` into a new file named `OK`. A line like `DummiesIO.print("OK")` wouldn't work at all. (The compiler would give you an error message.)

✔ You may decide to write `OK` as two separate characters. To write to the screen, you can make the following calls:

```
System.out.print('O');
System.out.print('K');
```

And to write `OK` to the `approval.txt` file, you make these calls:

```
DummiesIO.print("approval.txt", 'O');
DummiesIO.print("approval.txt", 'K');
```

✔ Like their counterparts for `System.out`, the methods `DummiesIO.print` and `DummiesIO.println` differ in their end-of-line behaviors. For instance, you want to display the following text on the screen:

```
Hankees  Socks
7        3
```

To do this, you can make the following method calls:

```
System.out.print("Hankees  ");
System.out.println("Socks");
System.out.print(7);
```

```
System.out.print("          ");
System.out.println(3);
```

To plant the same text into a file named `scores.dat`, you can make these method calls:

```
DummiesIO.print("scores.dat", "Hankees  ");
DummiesIO.println("scores.dat", "Socks");
DummiesIO.print("scores.dat", 7);
DummiesIO.print("scores.dat", "          ");
DummiesIO.println("scores.dat", 3);
```

Name that file

What if a file that contains data is not in your `JavaPrograms` directory? If that's the case, when you call a `DummiesIO` method, the file's name must include folder names. For instance, imagine that your operating system is Windows, and that a file named `totals` is in a folder named `advertisements`. (See the following figure.) Then, to get data from the `totals` file, you include the folder name, the filename and (to be on the safe side) the drive letter:

```
DummiesIO.getInt("c:\\
    advertisements\\totals"))
```

Notice how I use double backslashes. To find out why, look at the sidebar entitled "Escapism" in Chapter 12. The string `"\totals"` with a single backslash stands for a tab, followed by `otals`. But in this example, the file's name is `totals`, not `otals`. With a single backslash,

the name `...advertisements\totals"` would not work correctly.

Inside quotation marks, you use the double backslash to indicate what would usually be a single backslash. So the string `"c:\\advertisements\\totals"` stands for `c:\advertisements\totals`. That's good, because `c:\advertisements\totals` is the way you normally refer to a file in Windows.

Of course, if you use Unix or Linux, then you're in luck. This double backslash nonsense doesn't apply to you. Just call

```
DummiesIO.getInt("/home/bburd/
    advertisements/totals")
```

or something similar that reflects your system's directory structure.

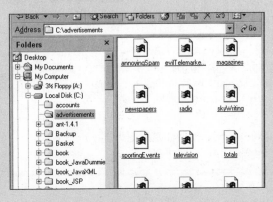

When you make up a new data filename, you don't have to use a particular three-letter extension. In fact, you don't have to use an extension at all. Out of habit, I normally use .txt or .dat, but I could also use .text, .data, .flatworm, or I could skip the extension entirely.

Writing, Rewriting, and Re-rewriting

Given my mischievous ways, I tried a little experiment. I asked myself what would happen if I ran the same file-writing program twice. I created a tiny program — the program in Listing 13-3. Then I conducted the session shown in Figure 13-8.

Using industrial strength input and output

In real life, most input/output programs are more complicated than my DummiesIO code. For one thing, most input/output programs have separate methods for connecting to an existing file, or for creating a brand new file. These extra methods don't read any data from a file, and they don't write any data to a file. These methods just open connections to files in preparation for eventual reading or writing. For instance, with the standard Java API code, you have to execute statements of the following kind:

```
fileIn = new
    FileInputStream
    ("rawData.txt");
streamIn = new
    InputStreamReader(fileIn);
bufferIn = new
    BufferedReader(streamIn);
```

You have to do this before you can read anything from the rawData.txt file. Other methods (methods that also do no reading or writing) close the connection when you're finished using a file.

There's another big difference between real life and DummiesIO. With standard Java input code, you get a line of characters from the rawData.txt file by making a call of the following kind:

```
bufferIn.readLine()
```

This call to readLine makes no visible reference to rawData.txt. But the preceding chain of assignments makes the variable bufferIn stand for the rawData.txt file. With standard input code, you use a variable like bufferIn whenever you read from or write to a file. With DummiesIO, you use an actual filename instead.

Look once more at Listing 13-2, and notice how the name rawData.txt appears in both DummiesIO.get calls. In a longer program that uses DummiesIO, a file's name may appear fifteen, twenty, or even a hundred times. That represents a potential pitfall: If you misspell the filename just once, then you won't find out about it until you run the program. So, when you use my DummiesIO code, type each file's name carefully. Use copy and paste whenever you can to avoid typos.

Listing 13-3   A Little Experiment

```
class WriteOK
{
   public static void main(String args[])
   {
      DummiesIO.print  ("approval.txt", 'O');
      DummiesIO.println("approval.txt", 'K');
   }
}
```

Figure 13-8:
Testing the
waters.

```
C:\JavaPrograms>type approval.txt
The system cannot find the file specified.

C:\JavaPrograms>java WriteOK

C:\JavaPrograms>type approval.txt
OK

C:\JavaPrograms>java WriteOK

C:\JavaPrograms>type approval.txt
OK
```

Here's the sequence of events in Figure 13-8:

✔ **I display whatever is in the file** approval.txt.

At this point in the experiment, I don't yet have a file named approval.txt, so the computer can't find the file. That's okay. Every experiment has to start somewhere.

✔ **I run the code in Listing 13-3 and try again to display** approval.txt **file's contents.**

This time around, my hard drive has an approval.txt file. The file contains OK — the output of the code in Listing 13-3. Apparently, the first method call in Listing 13-3 does two things:

   • The call creates a new file named approval.txt.

   • The call plops the letter O into the approval.txt file.

      In contrast, the second method call in Listing 13-3 does only one thing:

   • The call adds the letter K to the approval.txt file.

That's the way my DummiesIO code works. The first print or println call creates a file. Successive print and println calls add to the existing file.

✔ **In Figure 13-8, I run the code from Listing 13-3 a second time. Then I display** approval.txt **file's contents.**

At this point, I could imagine seeing OKOK in the approval.txt file. But that's not what I see. After running the code twice, the approval.txt file contains just one OK. Here's why:

- The first method call in Listing 13-3 deletes my existing approval.txt file. The call creates a new, empty approval.txt file.

- After creating a new approval.txt file, the first method call drops the letter O into the new file.

- The second method call adds the letter K to the same approval.txt file.

So that's the story. Each time you run the program, the first print or println call trashes whatever approval.txt file is already on the hard drive. Subsequent calls in the same run add data to a newly created approval.txt file.

Chapter 14

Creating Loops within Loops

. . . .

. . . .

If you're an editor at Wiley Publishing, please don't read the next few paragraphs. In the next few paragraphs, I give away an important trade secret (something you really don't want me to do).

I'm about to describe a surefire process for writing a best-selling *For Dummies* book. Here's the process:

Write several words to create a sentence. Do this several times to create a paragraph.

```
Repeat the following to form a paragraph:
   Repeat the following to form a sentence:
      Write a word.
```

Repeat the above instructions several times to make a section. Make several sections, and then make several chapters.

```
Repeat the following to form a best-selling For Dummies book:
   Repeat the following to form a chapter:
      Repeat the following to form a section:
         Repeat the following to form a paragraph:
            Repeat the following to form a sentence:
               Write a word.
```

This process involves a loop within a loop within a loop within a loop within a loop. It's like a verbal M.C. Escher print. Is it useful, or is it frivolous?

Well, in the world of computer programming, this kind of thing happens all the time. Most five-layered loops are hidden behind method calls, but two-layered loops within loops are everyday occurrences. So this chapter tells you how to compose a loop within a loop. It's very useful stuff.

By the way, if you're a Wiley Publishing editor, you can start reading again from this point onward.

Paying Your Old Code a Little Visit

The program in Listing 12-5 extracts a user name from an e-mail address. For instance, the program reads

```
John@BurdBrain.com
```

from the keyboard, and writes

```
John
```

to the screen. Let me tell you . . . in this book, I have some pretty lame excuses for writing programs, but this simple e-mail example tops the list! Why would you want to type something on the keyboard, only to have the computer display part of what you typed? There must be a better use for code of this kind.

Sure enough, there is. The BurdBrain.com network administrator has a list of ten thousand employees' e-mail addresses. More precisely, the administrator's hard drive has a file named `email.txt`. This file contains ten thousand e-mail addresses, with one address on each line, as shown in Figure 14-1.

Figure 14-1:
A list of
e-mail
addresses.

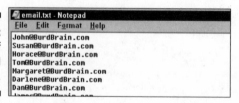

```
email.txt - Notepad
File  Edit  Format  Help
John@BurdBrain.com
Susan@BurdBrain.com
Horace@BurdBrain.com
Tom@BurdBrain.com
Margaret@BurdBrain.com
Darlene@BurdBrain.com
Dan@BurdBrain.com
James@BurdBrain.com
```

The company's e-mail software has an interesting feature. To send e-mail within the company, you don't need to type an entire e-mail address. For instance, to send e-mail to John, you can type the user name `John` instead of `John@BurdBrain.com`. (This `@BurdBrain.com` part is called the *host name*.)

So the company's network administrator wants to distill the content of the `email.txt` file. She wants a new file, `usernames.txt`, that contains user names with no host names, as shown in Figure 14-2.

Figure 14-2:
User names
extracted
from the list
of e-mail
addresses.

Reworking some existing code

To solve the administrator's problem, you need to modify the code in Listing 12-5. The new version gets an e-mail address from a disk file and writes a user name to another disk file. The new version is in Listing 14-1.

Listing 14-1   From One File to Another

```
class ListOneUsername
{
   public static void main(String args[])
   {
      char symbol;

      symbol = DummiesIO.getChar("email.txt");

      while (symbol != '@')
      {
         DummiesIO.print("usernames.txt", symbol);
         symbol = DummiesIO.getChar("email.txt");
      }

      DummiesIO.println("usernames.txt");
   }
}
```

Listing 14-1 does almost the same thing as its forerunner in Listing 12-5. The only difference is that the code in Listing 14-1 doesn't interact with the user. Instead, the code in Listing 14-1 interacts with disk files.

Running your code

Here's how you run the code in Listing 14-1:

1. **Put the file** `email.txt` **in your** `JavaPrograms` **directory.**

   Use Windows Notepad (or some other text editor) to create `email.txt`. In the `email.txt` file, put just one e-mail address. Any address will do, as long as the address contains an @ sign.

2. **Compile and run the code in Listing 14-1.**

   When you run the code, you see no output on the screen. All you see is another command prompt.

3. **View the contents of the** `usernames.txt` **file.**

   If your `email.txt` file contains `John@BurdBrain.com`, then the `usernames.txt` file contains `John`.

For more details on any of these steps, see the discussion that comes immediately after Listing 13-2 in Chapter 13.

Creating Useful Code

The previous section describes a network administrator's problem — creating a file filled with user names from a file filled with e-mail addresses. The code in Listing 14-1 solves part of the problem — it extracts just one e-mail address. That's a good start, but to get just one user name, you don't need a computer program. A pencil and paper does the trick.

So don't keep the network administrator waiting any longer. In this section, you develop a program that processes dozens, hundreds, and even thousands of e-mail addresses from a file on your hard drive.

First you need a strategy to create the program. Take the statements in Listing 14-1 and run them over and over again. Better yet, have the statements run themselves over and over again. Fortunately, you already know how to do something over and over again: You use a loop. (See Chapter 12 for the basics on loops.)

So here's the strategy: Take the statements in Listing 14-1 and enclose them in a larger loop:

```
while (not at the end of the email.txt file)
{
    Execute the statements in Listing 14-1
}
```

Looking back at the code in Listing 14-1, you see that the statements in that code have a `while` loop of their own. So this strategy involves putting one loop inside another loop:

```
while (not at the end of the email.txt file)
{
    //Blah-blah
    while (symbol != '@')
    {
        //Blah-blah-blah
    }
    //Blah-blah-blah-blah
}
```

Because one loop is inside the other, they're called *nested loops*. The old loop (the `symbol != '@'` loop) is the *inner loop*. The new loop (the end-of-file loop) is called the *outer loop*.

Checking for the end of a file

Now all you need is a way to test the loop's condition. How do you know when you're at the end of the `email.txt` file?

Most input/output programs have mechanisms to solve this problem, and my `DummiesIO` program is no exception. My code has a method named `DummiesIO.endOfFile`. The method answers `true` or `false` to the following question:

> Has the program read everything there is to read in the `email.txt` file?

If the program's `getChar` calls have gobbled up all the characters in the `email.txt` file, then the value of `DummiesIO.endOfFile("email.txt")` is `true`. So to keep looping while you're not at the end of the `email.txt` file, you do the following:

```
while (!DummiesIO.endOfFile("email.txt"))
{
    Execute the statements in Listing 14-1
}
```

The first realization of this strategy is in Listing 14-2.

Listing 14-2   The Mechanical Combining of Two Loops

```
//This code does NOT work (but you learn from your mistakes).
class FirstEffort
{
    public static void main(String args[])
    {
        char symbol;
```

(continued)

Listing 14-2 *(continued)*

```
        while (!DummiesIO.endOfFile("email.txt"))
        {
            symbol = DummiesIO.getChar("email.txt");

            while (symbol != '@')
            {
                DummiesIO.print("usernames.txt", symbol);
                symbol = DummiesIO.getChar("email.txt");
            }

            DummiesIO.println("usernames.txt");
        }
    }
}
```

When you run the code in Listing 14-2, you get the disappointing response shown in Figure 14-3.

Figure 14-3:
You goofed.

```
C:\JavaPrograms>java FirstEffort
No more data in the file.
java.io.EOFException
        at DummiesIO.getCharFromToken(DummiesIO.java:121)
        at DummiesIO.getChar(DummiesIO.java:254)
        at FirstEffort.main(FirstEffort.java:15)
```

How it feels to be a computer

What's wrong with the code in Listing 14-2? To find out, I role-play the computer. "If I were a computer, what would I do when I execute the code in Listing 14-2?"

The first several things that I'd do are pictured in Figure 14-4. I would read the J in John, then write the J in John, and then read the letter o (also in John).

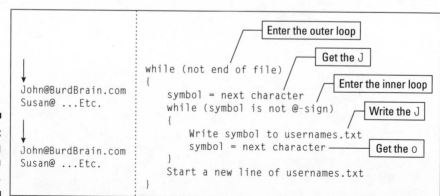

Figure 14-4:
Role-playing the code in Listing 14-2.

After a few trips through the inner loop, I'd get the @ sign in John@BurdBrain. com, as shown in Figure 14-5.

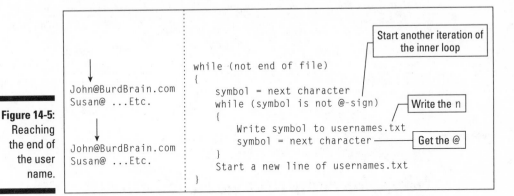

Figure 14-5: Reaching the end of the user name.

Finding this @ sign would jump me out of the inner loop and back to the top of the outer loop, as shown in Figure 14-6.

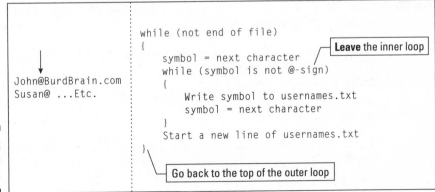

Figure 14-6: Leaving the inner loop.

I'd get the B in BurdBrain, and sail back into the inner loop. But then (horror of horrors!) I'd write that B to the usernames.txt file. (See Figure 14-7.)

There's the error! You don't want to write host names to the usernames.txt file. When the computer found the @ sign, it should have skipped past the rest of John's e-mail address.

At this point, you have a choice. You can jump straight to the corrected code in Listing 14-3, or you can read on to find out about the No more data message in Figure 14-3.

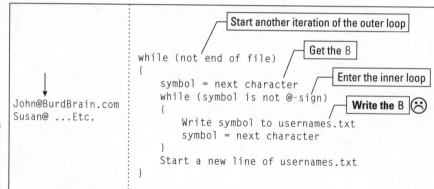

Figure 14-7:
The error of
my ways.

Why the computer accidentally pushes past the end of the file

Ah! You decided to read on to see why Figure 14-3 has that nasty No more data message.

Once again, I role-play the computer. I've completed the steps in Figure 14-7. I shouldn't process BurdBrain.com with the inner loop. But unfortunately, I do.

I keep running and processing more e-mail addresses. When I get to the end of the last e-mail address, I grab the m in BurdBrain.com and go back to test for an @ sign, as shown in Figure 14-8.

```
                              while (not end of file)
                              {
                                  symbol = next character
                                  while (symbol is not @-sign)
   ... @BurdBrain.com              {
   James@BurdBrain.com                 Write symbol to usernames.txt
                                       symbol = next character ——————[ Get the m ]
                                  }
                                  Start a new line of usernames.txt
                              }
                                                     [ Go back to the top of the inner loop ]
```

Figure 14-8:
The
journey's
last leg.

Now I'm in trouble. This last m certainly isn't an @ sign. So I jump into the inner loop, and try to get yet another character. (See Figure 14-9.) The email.txt file has no more characters, so I send an error message to the computer screen. (The error message is back in Figure 14-3.)

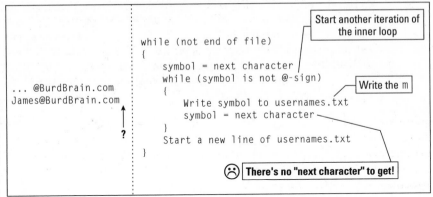

Figure 14-9:
Trying to
read past
the end of
the file.

Solving the problem

Listing 14-3 has the solution to the problem described with Figures 14-1 and
14-2. The code in this listing is almost identical to the code in Listing 14-2.
The only difference is the added call to DummiesIO.getLine. When the computer reaches an @ sign, this getLine call gobbles up the rest of the input
line. (In other words, the getLine call gobbles up the rest of the e-mail
address. The idea works because each e-mail address is on its own separate
line.) After chewing and swallowing @BurdBrain.com, the computer moves
gracefully to the next line of input.

Listing 14-3 That's Much Better!

```
//This code is correct!!
class ListAllUsernames
{
    public static void main(String args[])
    {
        char symbol;

        while (!DummiesIO.endOfFile("email.txt"))
        {
            symbol = DummiesIO.getChar("email.txt");

            while (symbol != '@')
            {
                DummiesIO.print("usernames.txt", symbol);
                symbol = DummiesIO.getChar("email.txt");
            }

            DummiesIO.getLine("email.txt");
            DummiesIO.println("usernames.txt");
        }
    }
}
```

To run the code in Listing 14-3, you need an `email.txt` file — a file like the one shown in Figure 14-1. You can use Windows Notepad (or some other text editor) to create the file. In the `email.txt` file, type several e-mail addresses. Any addresses will do, as long as each address contains an @ sign and each address is on its own separate line. Save the `email.txt` file in your `JavaPrograms` directory. For more details, see the steps that come immediately after Listing 13-2 in Chapter 13.

With Listing 14-3, you've reached an important milestone. You've analyzed a delicate programming problem and found a complete, working solution. The tools you used included thinking about strategies and role-playing the computer. As time goes on, you can use these tools to solve bigger and better problems.

Chapter 15

The Old Runaround

. . . .

. . . .

I remember it distinctly — the sense of dread I would feel on the way to Aunt Edna's house. She was a kind old woman, and her intentions were good. But visits to her house were always so agonizing.

First we'd sit in the living room and talk about other relatives. That was okay, as long as I understood what people were talking about. Sometimes, the gossip would be about adult topics, and I'd become very bored.

After all the family chatter, my father would help Aunt Edna with her bills. That was fun to watch, because Aunt Edna had a genetically inherited family ailment. Like me and many of my ancestors, Aunt Edna couldn't keep track of paperwork to save her life. It was as if the paper had allergens that made Aunt Edna's skin crawl. After ten minutes of useful bill paying, my father would find a mistake, an improper tally or something else in the ledger that needed attention. He'd ask Aunt Edna about it, and she'd shrug her shoulders. He'd become agitated trying to track down the problem, while Aunt Edna rolled her eyes and smiled with ignorant satisfaction. It was great entertainment.

Then, when the bill paying was done, we'd sit down to eat dinner. That's when I would remember why I dreaded these visits. Dinner was unbearable. Aunt Edna believed in Fletcherism — a health movement whose followers chewed each mouthful of food one hundred times. The more devoted followers used a chart, with a different number for the mastication of each kind of food. The minimal number of chews for any food was 32 — one chomp for each tooth in your mouth. People who did this said they were "Fletcherizing."

Mom and Dad thought the whole Fletcher business was silly, but they respected Aunt Edna and felt that people her age should be humored, not defied. As for me, I thought I'd explode from the monotony. Each meal lasted forever. Each mouthful was an ordeal. I can still remember my mantra — the words I'd say to myself without meaning to do so:

```
I've chewed 0 times so far.
Have I chewed 100 times yet? If not, then
    Chew!
    Add 1 to the number of times that I've chewed.
    Go back to "Have I chewed" to find out if I'm done yet.
```

Repeating Statements a Certain Number Times (Java for Statements)

Life is filled with examples of counting loops. And computer programming mirrors life (. . . or is it the other way around?). When you tell a computer what to do, you're often telling the computer to print three lines, process ten accounts, dial a million phone numbers, or whatever. Because counting loops are so common in programming, the people who create programming languages have developed statements just for loops of this kind. In Java, the statement that repeats something a certain number of times is called a *for* statement. An example of a `for` statement is in Listing 15-1.

Listing 15-1   Horace Fletcher's Revenge

```
class AuntEdnaSettlesForTen
{
    public static void main(String args[])
    {
        for (int count=0; count<10; count++)
        {
            System.out.print("I've chewed ");
            System.out.print(count);
            System.out.println(" time(s).");
        }

        System.out.println ("10 times! Hooray!");
        System.out.println("I can swallow!");
    }
}
```

Figure 15-1 shows you what you get when you run the program of Listing 15-1:

- ✔ The `for` statement in Listing 15-1 starts by setting the `count` variable equal to 0.

- ✔ Then the `for` statement tests to make sure that `count` is less than 10 (which it certainly is).

✔ Then the `for` statement dives ahead and executes the printing statements between the curly braces. At this early stage of the game, the computer prints `I've chewed 0 time(s)`.

✔ Then the `for` statement executes `count++` — that last thing inside the `for` statement's parentheses. This last action adds 1 to the value of `count`.

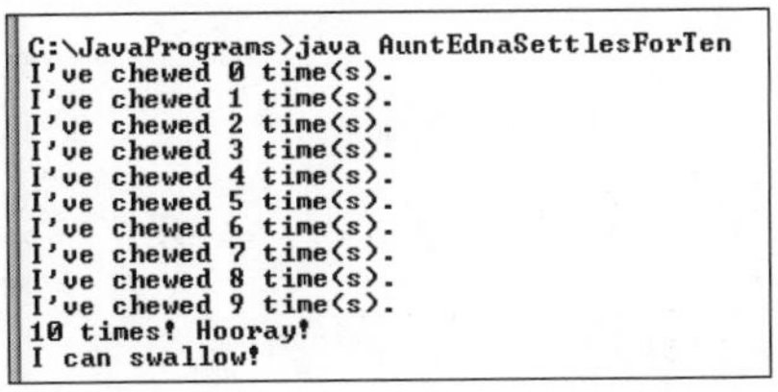

Figure 15-1:
Chewing ten
times.

```
C:\JavaPrograms>java AuntEdnaSettlesForTen
I've chewed 0 time(s).
I've chewed 1 time(s).
I've chewed 2 time(s).
I've chewed 3 time(s).
I've chewed 4 time(s).
I've chewed 5 time(s).
I've chewed 6 time(s).
I've chewed 7 time(s).
I've chewed 8 time(s).
I've chewed 9 time(s).
10 times! Hooray!
I can swallow!
```

This ends the first iteration of the `for` statement in Listing 15-1. Of course, there's more to this loop than just one iteration:

✔ With `count` now equal to 1, the `for` statement checks again to make sure that `count` is less than 10. (Yes, 1 is smaller than 10.)

✔ Because the test turns out okay, the `for` statement marches back into the curly braced statements and prints `I've chewed 1 time(s)` on the screen.

✔ Then the `for` statement executes that last `count++` inside its parentheses. The statement adds 1 to the value of `count`, increasing the value of `count` to 2.

And so on. This whole thing keeps being repeated over and over again until, after ten iterations, the value of `count` finally reaches 10. When this happens, the check for `count` being less than 10 fails, and the loop's execution ends. The computer jumps to whatever statement comes immediately after the `for` statement. In Listing 15-1, the computer prints `10 times! Hooray! I can swallow!` The whole process is illustrated in Figure 15-2.

The anatomy of a for statement

A typical `for` statement looks like this:

```
for (Initialization ; Condition ; Update)
   Statement
```

After the word `for`, you put three things in parentheses: an *Initialization*, a *Condition*, and an *Update*.

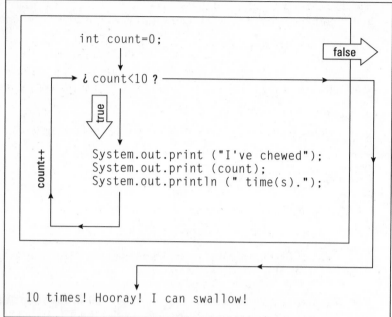

Figure 15-2:
The action
of the for
loop in
Listing 15-1.

Each of the three items in parentheses plays its own distinct role:

- ✔ **Initialization:** The initialization is executed once, when the run of your program first reaches the for statement.

- ✔ **Condition:** The condition is tested several times (at the start of each iteration).

- ✔ **Update:** The update is also evaluated several times (at the end of each iteration).

If it helps, think of the loop as if its text is shifted all around:

```
//This is NOT real code
int count=0
for count<10
{
    System.out.print("I've chewed ");
    System.out.print(count);
    System.out.println(" time(s).");
    count++;
}
```

You can't write a real for statement this way. (The compiler would throw code like this right into the garbage can.) Even so, this is the order in which the parts of the for statement are executed.

Braces (again)

In a `for` loop, the situation with curly braces mirrors the situation in `while` loops:

- ✔ **With several actions inside the loop, curly braces are required.**

  For an example, see Listing 15-1.

- ✔ **With one action inside the loop, curly braces are optional.**

  For instance, the following `for` statement is okay:

```
for (int count=0; count<10; count++)
   System.out.println(count);
```

But the following `for` statement is okay too:

```
for (int count=0; count<10; count++)
{
   System.out.println(count);
}
```

The first line of a `for` statement (the word `for` followed by stuff in parentheses) is not a complete statement. So you almost never put a semicolon at the end of this line. If you make a mistake and end this line with a semicolon, you usually put the computer into an endless, do-nothing loop. The computer's cursor just sits there and blinks until you forcibly stop the program's run.

Initializing a for loop

Look at the first line of the `for` loop in Listing 15-1, and notice the declaration `int count=0`. That's something new. When you create a `for` loop, you can declare a variable (like `count`) as part of the loop initialization.

If you declare a variable in the initialization of a `for` loop, then you can't use that variable outside the loop. For instance, in Listing 15-1, try putting `System.out.println(count)` after the end of the loop:

```
//This code does not compile.
for (int count=0; count<10; count++)
{
   System.out.print("I've chewed ");
   System.out.print(count);
   System.out.println(" time(s).");
}

System.out.print(count);   //The count variable doesn't
                           // exist here.
```

With this extra reference to the count variable, the compiler gives you an error message. You can see the message in Figure 15-3. If you're not experienced with for statements, the message may surprise you. "Whadaya mean 'cannot resolve symbol'? There's a count variable just four lines above that statement." Ah, yes. But the count variable is declared in the for loop's initialization. Outside the for loop, that count variable doesn't exist.

Figure 15-3:
What count variable? I don't see a count variable.

```
C:\JavaPrograms>javac BadForLoop.java
BadForLoop.java:12: cannot resolve symbol
symbol  : variable count
location: class BadForLoop
        System.out.print(count);
                         ^
1 error
```

To use a variable outside of a for statement, you have to declare that variable outside the for statement. You can even do this with the for statement's counting variable. Listing 15-2 has an example.

Listing 15-2   Using a Variable Declared Outside of a for Loop

```java
class AuntEdnaDoesItAgain
{
    public static void main(String args[])
    {
        int count;

        for (count=0; count<10; count++)
        {
            System.out.print("I've chewed ");
            System.out.print(count);
            System.out.println(" time(s).");
        }

        System.out.print(count);
        System.out.println (" times! Hooray!");
        System.out.println("I can swallow!");
    }
}
```

A run of the code in Listing 15-2 looks exactly like the run for Listing 15-1. The run is pictured in Figure 15-1. Unlike its predecessor, Listing 15-2 enjoys the luxury of using the count variable to display the number 10. It can do this because, in Listing 15-2, the count variable belongs to the entire main method, and not to the for loop alone.

Versatile looping statements

If you were stuck on a desert island with only one kind of loop, what kind would you want to have? The answer is, you can get along with any kind of loop. The choice between a `while` loop and a `for` loop is about the code's style and efficiency. It's not about necessity.

Anything that you can do with a `for` loop, you can do with a `while` loop as well. Take, for instance, the `for` loop in Listing 15-1. Here's how you can achieve the same effect with a `while` loop:

```
int count=0;
while (count<10)
{
    System.out.print("I've
    chewed ");
    System.out.print(count);
    System.out.println("
    time(s).");
    count++;
}
```

In the `while` loop, you have explicit statements to declare, initialize, and increment the `count` variable.

The same kind of trick works in reverse. Anything that you can do with a `while` loop, you can do with a `for` loop as well. But turning certain `while` loops into `for` loops seems strained and unnatural. Consider a `while` loop from Listing 12-2:

```
while (total < 21)
{
    card =
    DummiesRandom.getInt();
    total += card;
    System.out.print(card);
    System.out.print("       ");
    System.out.println(total);
}
```

Turning this loop into a `for` loop means wasting most of the stuff inside the `for` loop's parentheses:

```
for ( ; total<21 ; )
{
    card =
    DummiesRandom.getInt();
    total += card;
    System.out.print(card);
    System.out.print("       ");
    System.out.println(total);
}
```

The `for` loop above has a condition, but it has no initialization and no update. That's okay. Without an initialization, nothing special happens when the computer first enters the `for` loop. And without an update, nothing special happens at the end of each iteration. It's strange, but it works.

Notice the words `for (count=0` in Listing 15-2. Because `count` is declared above the `for` statement, you don't declare `count` again in the `for` statement's initialization. I tried declaring `count` twice, as in the following code:

```
//This does NOT work:
int count;

for (int count=0; count<10; count++)
{
    ...etc.
```

and the compiler told me to clean up my act:

```
count is already defined in main(java.lang.String[])
        for (int count=0; count<10; count++)
             ^
```

Using Nested for Loops

Because you're reading *Beginning Programming with Java For Dummies,* I assume that you manage a big hotel. The next chapter tells you everything you need to know about hotel management. But before you begin reading that chapter, you can get a little preview in this section.

I happen to know that your hotel has nine floors, and each floor of your hotel has twenty rooms. On this sunny afternoon, someone hands you a diskette containing a file full of numbers. You copy this hotelData file to your JavaPrograms directory, and then open the file with a text editor. You see the stuff shown in Figure 15-4.

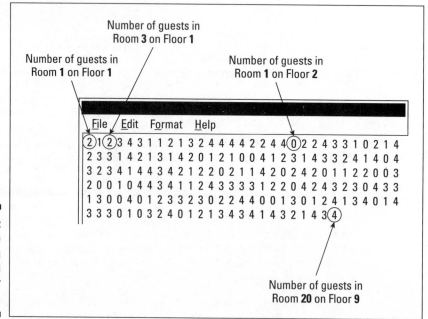

Figure 15-4:
A file
containing
hotel
occupancy
data.

This file gives the number of guests in each room. For instance, at the start of the file, you see 2 1 2. This means that, on the first floor, Room 1 has 2 guests, Room 2 has 1 guest, and Room 3 has 2 guests. After reading twenty of these numbers, you see 0 2 2. So, on the second floor, Room 1 has 0 guests, Room 2 has 2 guests, and Room 3 has 2 guests. The story continues until the last number in the file. According to that number, Room 20 on the ninth floor has 4 guests.

You'd like a more orderly display of these numbers — a display of the kind in Figure 15-5. So you whip out your keyboard to write a quick Java program.

Figure 15-5:
A readable
display of
the data in
Figure 15-4.

```
C:\JavaPrograms>java DisplayHotelData
Floor 1:   2 1 2 3 4 3 1 1 2 1 3 2 4 4 4 4 2 2 4 4
Floor 2:   0 2 2 4 3 3 1 0 2 1 4 2 3 3 1 4 2 1 3 1
Floor 3:   4 2 0 1 2 1 0 0 4 1 2 3 1 4 3 3 2 4 1 4
Floor 4:   0 4 3 2 3 4 1 4 4 3 4 2 1 2 2 0 2 1 1 4
Floor 5:   2 0 2 4 2 0 1 1 2 2 0 0 3 2 0 1 0 4 4
Floor 6:   3 4 1 1 2 4 3 3 3 1 2 2 0 4 2 4 3 2 3
Floor 7:   0 4 3 3 1 3 0 0 4 0 1 2 3 3 2 3 0 2 2 4
Floor 8:   4 0 0 1 3 0 1 2 4 1 3 4 0 1 4 3 3 3 0 1
Floor 9:   0 3 2 4 0 1 2 1 3 4 3 4 1 4 3 2 1 4 3 4
```

As in some earlier examples, you decide which statements go where by asking yourself how many times each statement should be executed. For starters, the display in Figure 15-5 has nine lines, and each line has 20 numbers:

```
for (each of 9 floors)
    for (each of 20 rooms on a floor)
        get a number from the file and
        display the number on the screen.
```

So your program has a for loop within a for loop — a pair of nested for loops.

Next, you notice how each line begins in Figure 15-5. Each line contains the word Floor, followed by the floor number. Because this Floor display occurs only nine times in Figure 15-5, the statements to print this display belong in the *for each of 9 floors* loop (and not in the *for each of 20 rooms* loop). The statements should be before the *for each of 20 rooms* loop, because this Floor display comes once before each line's twenty number display:

```
for (each of 9 floors)
    display "Floor" and the floor number,
    for (each of 20 rooms on a floor)
        get a number from the file and
        display the number on the screen.
```

You're almost ready to write the code. But there's one detail that's easy to forget. (Well, it's a detail that I always forget.) After displaying 20 numbers, the program advances to a new line. This new-line action happens only nine times during the run of the program, and it always happens *after* the program displays 20 numbers:

```
for (each of 9 floors)
    display "Floor" and the floor number,
    for (each of 20 rooms on a floor)
        get a number from the file and
        display the number on the screen,
    Go to the next line.
```

That does it. That's all you need. The code to create the display of Figure 15-5 is in Listing 15-3.

Listing 15-3   Hey! Is This a For-by-For?

```
class DisplayHotelData
{
    public static void main(String args[])
    {
        for (int floor=1; floor<=9; floor++)
        {
            System.out.print("Floor ");
            System.out.print(floor);
            System.out.print(":   ");

            for (int roomNum=1; roomNum<=20; roomNum++)
            {
                System.out.print(DummiesIO.getInt("hotelData"));
                System.out.print(' ');
            }

            System.out.println();
        }
    }
}
```

The code in Listing 15-3 has the variable floor going from 1 to 9, and has the variable roomNum going from 1 to 20. Because the roomNum loop is inside the floor loop, the writing of twenty numbers happens 9 times. That's good. It's exactly what I want.

Repeating Until You Get What You Need (Java do Statements)

I introduce Java's while loop in Chapter 12. When you create a while loop, you write the loop's condition first. After the condition, you write the code that gets repeatedly executed.

```
while (Condition)
    Code that gets repeatedly executed
```

This way of writing a `while` statement is no accident. The look of the statement emphasizes an important point — that the computer always checks the condition before executing any of the repeated code.

If the loop's condition is never true, then the stuff inside the loop is never executed — not even once. In fact, you can easily cook up a `while` loop whose statements are never executed (although I can't think of a reason why you would ever want to do it):

```
//This code doesn't print anything:
int twoPlusTwo=2+2;
while (twoPlusTwo==5)
{
    System.out.println("Are you kidding?");
    System.out.println("2+2 doesn't equal 5.");
    System.out.print  ("Everyone knows that");
    System.out.println(" 2+2 equals 3.");
}
```

In spite of this silly `twoPlusTwo` example, the `while` statement turns out to be the most useful of Java's looping constructs. In particular, the `while` loop is good for situations in which you must look before you leap. For example: "While money is in my account, write a mortgage check every month." When you first encounter this statement, if your account has a zero balance, you don't want to write a mortgage check — not even one check.

But at times (not many), you want to leap before you look. Take, for instance, the situation in which you're asking the user for a response. Maybe the user's response makes sense, but maybe it doesn't. Maybe the user's finger slipped, or perhaps the user didn't understand the question. In many situations, it's important to correctly interpret the user's response. If the user's response doesn't make sense, you must ask again.

Consider a program that deletes several files. Before deleting anything, the program asks for confirmation from the user. If the user types Y, then delete; if the user types N, then don't delete. Of course, deleting files is serious stuff. Mistaking a bad keystroke for a "yes" answer can delete the company's records. (And mistaking a bad keystroke for a "no" answer can preserve the company's incriminating evidence.) So if there's any doubt about the user's response, the program should ask the user to respond again.

Pause a moment to think about the flow of actions — what should and shouldn't happen when the computer executes the loop. A loop of this kind doesn't need to check anything before getting the user's first response.

Indeed, before the user gives the first response, the loop has nothing to check. The loop shouldn't start with "as long as the user's response is invalid, get another response from the user." Instead, the loop should just leap ahead, get a response from the user, and then check the response to see if it made sense. The code to do all this is in Listing 15-4.

Listing 15-4   Repeat Before You Delete

```
/*
 * DISCLAIMER: Neither the author nor Wiley Publishing, Inc.,
 * nor anyone else even remotely connected with the
 * creation of this book, assumes any responsibility
 * for any damage of any kind due to the use of this code,
 * or the use of any work derived from this code, including
 * any work created partially or in full by the reader.
 *
 * Sign here:_____
 */
class IHopeYouKnowWhatYoureDoing
{
    public static void main(String args[]) throws Exception
    {
        char reply;

        do
        {
            System.out.print("Reply with Y or N...");
            System.out.print("  Delete all .keep files? ");
            reply = DummiesIO.getChar();
        }
        while (reply!='Y' && reply!='N');

        if (reply=='Y')
            Runtime.getRuntime().exec("cmd /c del *.keep");
    }
}
```

The code in Listing 15-4 works on all the industrial-strength versions of Microsoft Windows, including Windows NT, 2000, and XP. To get the same effect in Windows 95, 98, or Me, you have to change the last line of code as follows:

```
Runtime.getRuntime().exec("start command /c del *.keep");
```

To work the same magic in Unix or Linux, you can use the following command:

```
Runtime.getRuntime().exec
    (new String[] {"/bin/sh", "-c", "rm -f *.keep"});
```

One way or another, the call to Runtime.getRuntime...*yada-yada* deletes all files whose names end with .keep.

In Listing 15-4, the call to `Runtime.getRuntime().exec` enables the Java program to execute an operating system command. This `Runtime` business can be tricky to use, so don't fret over the details. Just take my word for it — the call to `Runtime.getRuntime().exec` in Listing 15-4 deletes files. Listing 15-4 uses another feature of Java that's not covered in this book. The header of the listing's `main` method has an extra piece of text called a *throws clause*. I need the throws clause because, inside the `main` method, I call this particular API method named `exec`. Some method calls simply force you to use a throws clause. (I'll leave it at that. For more details, read *Java 2 For Dummies*.)

Using Java's do statement

A run of the Listing 15-4 program is shown in Figure 15-6. Before deleting a bunch of files, the program asks the user if it's okay to do the deletion. If the user gives one of the two expected answers (Y or N) then the program proceeds according to the user's wishes. But if the user enters any other letter (or any digit, punctuation symbol, or whatever), then the program asks the user for another response.

```
C:\TEMP>dir *.keep
 Volume in drive C has no label.
 Volume Serial Number is 2222-2222

 Directory of C:\TEMP

01/23/2003  05:51p            1,103,345 doNotDelete.keep
01/23/2003  05:49p              919,700 importantData.keep
01/23/2003  05:51p            1,266,545 irreplaceable.keep
01/23/2003  05:52p                    9 smallButImportant.keep
               4 File(s)      3,289,599 bytes
               0 Dir(s)   2,302,197,760 bytes free

C:\TEMP>java IHopeYouKnowWhatYoureDoing
Reply with Y or N...  Delete all .keep files? U
Reply with Y or N...  Delete all .keep files? 8
Reply with Y or N...  Delete all .keep files? y
Reply with Y or N...  Delete all .keep files? n
Reply with Y or N...  Delete all .keep files? Y

C:\TEMP>dir *.keep
 Volume in drive C has no label.
 Volume Serial Number is 2222-2222

 Directory of C:\TEMP

File Not Found

C:\TEMP>_
```

Figure 15-6: No! Don't do it!

In Figure 15-6, the user hems and haws for a while, first with the letter U, then the digit 8, and then with lowercase letters. Finally, the user enters Y, and the program deletes all the `.keep` files. If you compare the two directory listings (before and after the run of the program), you'll see that the program trashes all files with names ending in `.keep`.

To write the program in Listing 15-4, you need a loop — a loop that repeatedly asks the user if the `.keep` files should be deleted. The loop continues to ask until the user gives a meaningful response. The loop tests its condition at the end of each iteration, after each of the user's responses.

That's why the program in Listing 15-4 has a *do* loop (also known as a *do . . . while* loop). With a do loop, the program jumps right in, executes some statements, and then checks a condition. If the condition is true, then the program goes back to the top of the loop for another go-around. If the condition is false, then the computer leaves the loop (and jumps to whatever code comes immediately after the loop). The action of the loop in Listing 15-4 is illustrated in Figure 15-7.

A closer look at the do statement

The format of a do loop is

```
do
    Statement
while (Condition)
```

Writing the *Condition* at the end of the loop reminds me that the computer executes the *Statement* inside the loop first. After the computer executes the *Statement*, the computer goes on to check the *Condition*. If the *Condition* is true, the computer goes back for another iteration of the *Statement*.

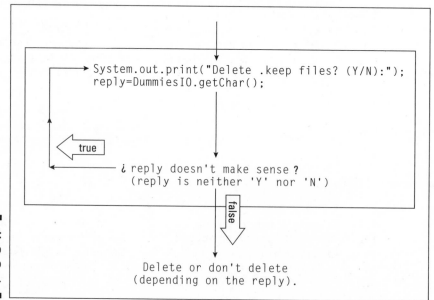

Figure 15-7:
Here we go
loop, do
loop.

And what about the curly braces between the words do and while? If you know the story with if statements, while statements, and for statements, then the story with do statements is boring (and repetitious!) The curly braces in a do statement are optional when there's only one action inside the loop. For instance, the do statement in Listing 15-4 has curly braces, but a taciturn program (one that insists on a reply of Y or N, but never prompts the user) can "do" without curly braces:

```
do
    reply = DummiesIO.getChar();
while (reply!='Y' && reply!='N');
```

With a do loop, the computer always executes the statements inside the loop at least once:

```
//This code prints something:
int twoPlusTwo=2+2;
do
{
    System.out.println("Are you kidding?");
    System.out.println("2+2 doesn't equal 5.");
    System.out.print  ("Everyone knows that");
    System.out.println(" 2+2 equals 3.");
}
while (twoPlusTwo==5);
```

This code displays Are you kidding? 2+2 doesn't equal 5 . . . *and so on*, and then tests the condition twoPlusTwo==5. Because twoPlusTwo==5 is false, the computer doesn't go back for another iteration. Instead, the computer jumps to whatever code comes immediately after the loop.

Part IV
Using Program Units

The 5th Wave   By Rich Tennant

THAT IT! TARZAN TAKE NO MORE! KEEP GET BAD MESSAGE! WHAT MEAN?! TARZAN TRY EVERYTHING! MAKE TARZAN MAD LIKE CHEETAH! WANT PUT ROLODEX THROUGH SCREEN!

SYNTAX ERROR!

In this part . . .

Way back in the Elvis Era, people thought that computer programs should be big lists of instructions. Then, during the Groovy Sixties, people decided to modularize their programs. A typical program consisted of several methods (like the `main` methods in this book's examples). Finally, during the Weighty Eighties, programmers grouped methods and other things into units called *objects*.

Far from being the flavor of the month, Object-Oriented Programming has become the backbone of modern computing. This part of the book tells you all about it.

Chapter 16

Using Loops and Arrays

This chapter has seven illustrations. For these illustrations, the people at Wiley Publishing insist on following numbering: Figure 16-1, Figure 16-2, Figure 16-3, Figure 16-4, Figure 16-5, Figure 16-6, and Figure 16-7. But I like a different kind of numbering. I'd like to number the illustrations figure[0], figure[1], figure[2], figure[3], figure[4], figure[5], and figure[6]. Read on in this chapter, and you'll find out why.

Some for Loops in Action

The Java Motel, with its ten comfortable rooms, sits in a quiet place off the main highway. Aside from a small, separate office, the motel is just one long row of ground floor rooms. Each room is easily accessible from the spacious front parking lot.

Oddly enough, the motel's rooms are numbered 0 through 9. I could say that the numbering is a fluke — something to do with the builder's original design plan. But the truth is, starting with 0 makes the examples in this chapter easier to write.

You, as the Java Motel's manager, store occupancy data in a file on your computer's hard drive. The file has one entry for each room in the motel. For instance, in Figure 16-1, Room 0 has one guest, Room 1 has four guests, Room 2 is empty, and so on.

Figure 16-1:
Occupancy
data for the
Java Motel.

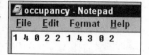

You want a report showing the number of guests in each room. Because you know how many rooms you have, this problem begs for a `for` loop. The code to solve this problem is in Listing 16-1, and a run of the code is shown in Figure 16-2.

Listing 16-1   A Program to Generate an Occupancy Report

```
public class ShowOccupancy
{
    public static void main(String args[])
    {
        System.out.println("Room\tGuests");

        for(int roomNum=0; roomNum<10; roomNum++)
        {
            System.out.print(roomNum);
            System.out.print("\t");
            System.out.println(DummiesIO.getInt("occupancy"));
        }
    }
}
```

```
C:\JavaPrograms>java ShowOccupancy
Room    Guests
0       1
1       4
2       0
3       2
4       2
5       1
6       4
7       3
8       0
9       2
```

Figure 16-2:
Running the
code in
Listing 16-1.

Listing 16-1 uses a `for` loop — a loop of the kind described in Chapter 15. As the `roomNum` variable's value marches from 0 to 9, the program displays one number after another from the `occupancy` file.

To read more about getting numbers from a disk file like my `occupancy` file, see Chapter 13.

Deciding on a loop's limit at runtime

On occasion, you may want a more succinct report than the one in Figure 16-2. "Don't give me a long list of rooms," you say. "Just give me the number of guests in Room 3." To get such a report, you need a slightly smarter program. The program is in Listing 16-2, with runs of the program shown in Figure 16-3.

Listing 16-2   Report on One Room Only, Please

```
public class ShowOneRoomOccupancy
{
    public static void main(String args[])
    {
        int whichRoom;

        System.out.print("Which room? ");
        whichRoom = DummiesIO.getInt();

        for(int roomNum=0; roomNum<whichRoom; roomNum++)
            DummiesIO.getInt("occupancy");

        System.out.print("Room ");
        System.out.print(whichRoom);
        System.out.print(" has ");
        System.out.print(DummiesIO.getInt("occupancy"));
        System.out.println(" guests.");
    }
}
```

```
C:\JavaPrograms>java ShowOneRoomOccupancy
Which room? 3
Room 3 has 2 guest(s).

C:\JavaPrograms>java ShowOneRoomOccupancy
Which room? 5
Room 5 has 1 guest(s).

C:\JavaPrograms>java ShowOneRoomOccupancy
Which room? 8
Room 8 has 0 guest(s).

C:\JavaPrograms>java ShowOneRoomOccupancy
Which room? 10
Room 10 has No more data in the file.
java.io.EOFException
        at DummiesIO.getNonblankToken(DummiesIO.java:105)
        at DummiesIO.getInt(DummiesIO.java:238)
        at ShowOneRoomOccupancy.main(ShowOneRoomOccupancy.java:16)
```

Figure 16-3:
A few
one-room
reports.

If Listing 16-2 has a moral, it's that the number of for loop iterations can vary from one run to another. The loop in Listing 16-2 runs on and on as long as the counting variable roomNum is less than a room number specified by the user. When the roomNum is the same as the number specified by the user (that is, when roomNum is the same as whichRoom), the computer jumps out of the loop. Then the computer grabs one more int value from the occupancy file and displays that value on the screen.

As you stare at the runs in Figure 16-3, it's important to remember the unusual numbering of rooms. Room 3 has two guests because Room 3 is the *fourth* room in the occupancy file of Figure 16-1. That's because the motel's rooms are numbered 0 through 9.

Using all kinds of conditions in a for loop

Look at the run in Figure 16-3, and notice the program's awful behavior when the user mistakenly asks about a nonexistent room. The motel has no Room 10. If you ask for the number of guests in Room 10, the program tries to read more numbers than the occupancy file contains. This unfortunate attempt causes an end-of-file error.

Listing 16-3 fixes the end-of-file problem.

Listing 16-3   A More Refined Version of the One-Room Code

```
public class BetterShowOneRoom
{
    public static void main(String args[])
    {
        int whichRoom;

        System.out.print("Which room? ");
        whichRoom = DummiesIO.getInt();

        for(int roomNum=0; roomNum<whichRoom &&
            !DummiesIO.endOfFile("occupancy"); roomNum++)
        {
            DummiesIO.getInt("occupancy");
        }

        if (!DummiesIO.endOfFile("occupancy"))
        {
            System.out.print("Room ");
            System.out.print(whichRoom);
            System.out.print(" has ");
            System.out.print(DummiesIO.getInt("occupancy"));
            System.out.println(" guest(s).");
        }
    }
}
```

The code in Listing 16-3 isn't earth shattering. To get this code, you take the code in Listing 16-2 and add a few tests for the end of the occupancy file. You perform the DummiesIO.endOfFile test before each call to getInt. That way, if the call to getInt is doomed to failure, you catch the potential failure before it happens. A few test runs of the code in Listing 16-3 are shown in Figure 16-4.

```
C:\JavaPrograms>java BetterShowOneRoom
Which room? 0
Room 0 has 1 guest(s).

C:\JavaPrograms>java BetterShowOneRoom
Which room? 6
Room 6 has 4 guest(s).

C:\JavaPrograms>java BetterShowOneRoom
Which room? 2
Room 2 has 0 guest(s).

C:\JavaPrograms>java BetterShowOneRoom
Which room? 10

C:\JavaPrograms>
```

Figure 16-4:
The bad
room
number 10
gets no
response.

For information on my `DummiesIO.endOfFile` method, see Chapter 14.

Listing 16-3 has a big fat condition to keep the `for` loop going:

```
for(int roomNum=0; roomNum<whichRoom &&
    !DummiesIO.endOfFile("occupancy"); roomNum++)
```

Many `for` loop conditions are simple "less than" tests, but there's no rule saying that all `for` loop conditions have to be so simple. In fact, any expression can be a `for` loop's condition, as long as the expression has value `true` or `false`. The condition in Listing 16-3 combines a "less than" with a call to my `DummiesIO.endOfFile` method.

Reader, Meet Arrays; Arrays, Meet the Reader

A weary traveler steps up to the Java Motel's front desk. "I'd like a room," says the traveler. So the desk clerk runs a report like the one in Figure 16-2. Noticing the first vacant room in the list, the clerk suggests Room 2. "I'll take it," says the traveler.

It's so hard to get good help these days. How many times have you told the clerk to fill the higher numbered rooms first? The lower numbered rooms are older, and they are badly in need of repair. For instance, Room 3 has an indoor pool. (The pipes leak, so the carpet is soaking wet.) Room 2 has no heat (not in wintertime, anyway). Room 1 has serious electrical problems (so, for that room, you always get payment in advance). Besides, Room 8 is vacant, and you charge more for the higher numbered rooms.

Here's where a subtle change in presentation can make a big difference. You need a program that lists vacant rooms in reverse order. That way, Room 8 catches the clerk's eye before Room 2 does.

Think about strategies for a program that displays data in reverse. With the input from Figure 16-1, the program's output should look like the display shown in Figure 16-5.

```
C:\JavaPrograms>java VacanciesInReverse
Room 8 is vacant.
Room 2 is vacant.
```

Here's the first (bad) idea for a programming strategy:

```
Get the last value in the occupancy file.
If the value is 0, print the room number.

Get the next-to-last value in the occupancy file.
If the value is 0, print the room number.

...And so on.
```

With some fancy input/output programs, this may be a workable strategy. But no matter what input/output program you use, jumping directly to the end or to the middle of a file is a big pain in the boot. It's especially bad if you plan to jump repeatedly. So go back to the drawing board and think of something better.

Here's an idea! Read all the values in the occupancy file and store each value in a variable of its own. Then you step through the variables in reverse order, displaying a room number when it's appropriate to do so.

This idea works, but the code is so ugly that I refuse to dignify it by calling it a "Listing." No, this is just a "see the following code" kind of thing. So please, see the following ugly code:

```
//Ugh! I can't stand this ugly code!
guestsIn0 = DummiesIO.getInt("occupancy");
guestsIn1 = DummiesIO.getInt("occupancy");
guestsIn2 = DummiesIO.getInt("occupancy");
guestsIn3 = DummiesIO.getInt("occupancy");
guestsIn4 = DummiesIO.getInt("occupancy");
guestsIn5 = DummiesIO.getInt("occupancy");
guestsIn6 = DummiesIO.getInt("occupancy");
guestsIn7 = DummiesIO.getInt("occupancy");
```

```
guestsIn8 = DummiesIO.getInt("occupancy");
guestsIn9 = DummiesIO.getInt("occupancy");

if (guestsIn9 == 0)
    System.out.println(9);
if (guestsIn8 == 0)
    System.out.println(8);
if (guestsIn7 == 0)
    System.out.println(7);
if (guestsIn6 == 0)

// ... And so on.
```

What you're lacking is a uniform way of naming ten variables. That is, it would be nice to write

```
//Nice idea, but this is not real Java code:

for (int roomNum=0; roomNum<10; roomNum++)  //Read forwards
    guestsInroomNum = DummiesIO.getInt("occupancy");

for (int roomNum=9; roomNum>=0; roomNum--)  //Write backwards
    if (guestsInroomNum == 0)
        System.out.println(roomNum);
```

Well, there is a way to write loops of this kind. All you need is some square brackets. When you add square brackets to the idea shown in the preceding code, you get what's called an array. An *array* is a row of values, like the row of rooms in a one-floor motel. To picture the array, just picture the Java Motel:

✔ First, picture the rooms, lined up next to one another.

✔ Next, picture the same rooms with their front walls missing. Inside each room you can see a certain number of guests.

✔ If you can, forget that the two guests in Room 9 are putting piles of bills into a big briefcase. Ignore the fact that the guest in Room 5 hasn't moved away from the TV set in a day and a half. Instead of all these details, just see numbers. In each room, see a number representing the count of guests in that room. (If freeform visualization isn't your strong point, then take a look at Figure 16-6.)

In the lingo of Java programming, the entire row of rooms is called an *array*. Each room in the array is called a *component* of the array (also known as an array *element*). Each component has two numbers associated with it:

✔ **Index:** In the case of the Java Motel array, the index is the room number (a number from 0 to 9).

✔ **Value:** In the Java Motel array, the value is the number of guests in a given room (a number stored in a component of the array).

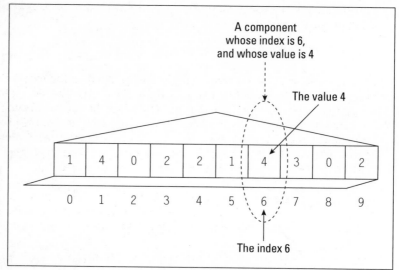

Figure 16-6:
An abstract
snapshot of
rooms in the
Java Motel.

Using an array saves you from having to declare ten separate variables: guestsIn0, guestsIn1, guestsIn2, and so on. To declare an array with ten values in it, you can write two fairly short lines of code:

```
int guestsIn[];
guestsIn = new int[10];
```

You can even squish these two lines into one longer line:

```
int guestsIn[] = new int[10];
```

In either of these code snippets, notice the use of the number 10. This number tells the computer to make the guestsIn array have ten components. Each component of the array has a name of its own. The starting component is named guestsIn[0], the next is named guestsIn[1], and so on. The last of the ten components is named guestsIn[9].

In creating an array, you always specify the number of components. The array's indices always start with 0 and end with the number that's one less than the total number of components. For instance, if your array has ten components (and you declare the array with new int[10]), then the array's indices go from 0 to 9.

Storing values in an array

After you've created an array, you can put values into the array's components. For instance, the guests in Room 6 are fed up with all those mint candies that you put on people's beds. So they check out and Room 6 becomes vacant.

You should put the value 0 into the 6 component. You can do it with this assignment statement:

```
guestsIn[6]=0;
```

On one weekday, business is awful. No one's staying at the motel. But then you get a lucky break. A big bus pulls up to the motel. The side of the bus has a sign that says "Loners' Convention." Out of the bus come 25 people, each walking to the motel's small office, none paying attention to the others who were on the bus. Each person wants a private room. Only 10 of them can stay at the Java Motel, but that's okay, because you can send the other 15 loners down the road to the old C-Side Resort and Motor Lodge.

Anyway, to register 10 of the loners into the Java Motel, you put one guest in each of your 10 rooms. Having created an array, you can take advantage of the array's indexing and write a `for` loop, like this:

```
for (int roomNum=0; roomNum<10; roomNum++)
    guestsIn[roomNum] = 1;
```

This loop takes the place of ten assignment statements, because the computer executes the statement `guestsIn[roomNum] = 1` ten times. The first time around, the value of `roomNum` is 0, so in effect, the computer executes

```
guestsIn[0] = 1;
```

In the next loop iteration, the value of `roomNum` is 1, so the computer executes the equivalent of the following statement:

```
guestsIn[1] = 1;
```

During the next iteration, the computer behaves as if it's executing

```
guestsIn[2] = 1;
```

And so on. When `roomNum` gets to be 9, the computer executes the equivalent of the following statement:

```
guestsIn[9] = 1;
```

Notice how the loop's counter goes from 0 to 9. Compare this with Figure 16-6, and remember that the indices of an array go from 0 to one less than the number of components in the array. Looping with room numbers from 0 to 9 covers all the rooms in the Java Motel.

When you work with an array, and you step through the array's components using a `for` loop, you normally start the loop's counter variable at 0. To form the condition that tests for another iteration, you often write an expression like `roomNum<arraySize`, where *arraySize* is the number of components in the array.

Creating a report

The code to create the report in Figure 16-5 is shown in Listing 16-4. This new program uses the idea in the world's ugliest code (the code from several pages back with variables guestsIn0, guestsIn1, and so on). But instead of having ten separate variables, Listing 16-4 uses an array.

Listing 16-4   Traveling through Data Both Forwards and Backwards

```
class VacanciesInReverse
{
   public static void main(String args[])
   {
      int guestsIn[];
      guestsIn = new int[10];

      for (int roomNum=0; roomNum<10; roomNum++)
         guestsIn[roomNum] = DummiesIO.getInt("occupancy");

      for (int roomNum=9; roomNum>=0; roomNum--)
         if (guestsIn[roomNum] == 0)
         {
            System.out.print("Room ");
            System.out.print(roomNum);
            System.out.println(" is vacant.");
         }
   }
}
```

Notice the stuff in parentheses in the VacanciesInReverse program's second for loop. It's easy to get these things wrong. You're aiming for a loop that checks Room 9, then Room 8, and so on.

```
if (guestsIn[9] == 0)
   System.out.print(roomNum);
if (guestsIn[8] == 0)
   System.out.print(roomNum);
if (guestsIn[7] == 0)
   System.out.print(roomNum);

...And so on, until you get to...

if (guestsIn[0] == 0)
   System.out.print(roomNum);
```

Some observations about the code:

✔ The loop's counter must start at 9:

```
for (int roomNum=9; roomNum>=0; roomNum--)
```

✔ Each time through the loop, the counter goes *down* by one:

```
for (int roomNum=9; roomNum>=0; roomNum--)
```

✔ The loop keeps going as long as the counter is *greater than or equal to* 0:

```
for (int roomNum=9; roomNum>=0; roomNum--)
```

Think through each of these three items, and you'll write a perfect `for` loop.

Working with Arrays

Earlier in this chapter, a busload of loners showed up at your motel. When they finally left, you were glad to get rid them, even if it meant having all your rooms empty for a while. But now, another bus pulls into the parking lot. This bus has a sign that says "Gregarian Club." Out of the bus come 50 people, each more gregarious than the next. Now everybody in your parking lot is clamoring to meet everyone else. While they meet and greet, they're all frolicking toward the front desk, singing the club's theme song. (Oh no! It's the Gregarian Chant!)

The first five Gregarians all want Room 7. It's a tight squeeze, but you were never big on fire codes anyway. Next comes a group of three with a yen for Room 0. (They're computer programmers, and they think the room number is cute.) Then there's a pack of four Gregarians who want Room 3. (The in-room pool sounds attractive to them.)

With all this traffic, you better switch on your computer. You start a program that enables you to enter new occupancy data. The program has five parts:

✔ **Create an array, and then put 0 in each of the array's components.**

When the Loners' Club members left, the motel was suddenly empty. (Heck, even before the Loners' Club members left, the motel seemed empty.) To declare an array and fill the array with zeros, you execute code of the following kind:

```
int guestsIn[];
guestsIn = new int[10];

for (int roomNum=0; roomNum<10; roomNum++)
    guestsIn[roomNum] = 0;
```

✔ **Get a room number, and then get the number of guests who will be staying in that room.**

With DummiesIO, reading numbers typed by the user is pretty humdrum stuff. Do a little prompting and a little getting, and you're all set:

```
System.out.print("Room number: ");
whichRoom = DummiesIO.getInt();
System.out.print("How many guests? ");
numGuests = DummiesIO.getInt();
```

✔ **Use the room number and the number of guests to change a value in the array.**

Earlier in this chapter, to put one guest in Room 2, you executed

```
guestsIn[2] = 1;
```

So now, you have two variables — numGuests and whichRoom. Maybe numGuests is 5, and whichRoom is 7. To put numGuests in whichRoom (that is, to put 5 guests in Room 7), you can execute

```
guestsIn[whichRoom] = numGuests;
```

That's the crucial step in the design of your new program.

✔ **Ask the user if the program should keep going.**

Are there more guests to put in rooms? To find out, execute this code:

```
    System.out.print("Do another? ");
}
while (DummiesIO.getChar()=='Y');
```

✔ **Display the number of guests in each room.**

No problem! You already did this. You can steal the code (almost verbatim) from Listing 16-1:

```
System.out.println("Room\tGuests");
for(int roomNum=0; roomNum<10; roomNum++)
{
    System.out.print(roomNum);
    System.out.print("\t");
    System.out.println(guestsIn[roomNum]);
}
```

The only difference between this latest code snippet and the stuff in Listing 16-1 is that this new code uses the guestsIn array. The first time through this loop, the code does

```
System.out.println(guestsIn[0]);
```

displaying the number of guests in Room 0. The next time through the loop, the code does

```
System.out.println(guestsIn[1]);
```

displaying the number of guests in Room 1. The last time through the loop, the code does

```
System.out.println(guestsIn[9]);
```

That's perfect.

The complete program (with these five pieces put together) is in Listing 16-5. A run of the program is shown in Figure 16-7.

Listing 16-5   Storing Occupancy Data in an Array

```
class AddGuests
{
    public static void main(String args[])
    {
        int whichRoom, numGuests;
        int guestsIn[];
        guestsIn = new int[10];

        for (int roomNum=0; roomNum<10; roomNum++)
            guestsIn[roomNum] = 0;

        do
        {
            System.out.print("Room number: ");
            whichRoom = DummiesIO.getInt();
            System.out.print("How many guests? ");
            numGuests = DummiesIO.getInt();
            guestsIn[whichRoom] = numGuests;

            System.out.println();
            System.out.print("Do another? ");
        }
        while (DummiesIO.getChar()=='Y');

        System.out.println();
        System.out.println("Room\tGuests");
        for(int roomNum=0; roomNum<10; roomNum++)
        {
            System.out.print(roomNum);
            System.out.print("\t");
            System.out.println(guestsIn[roomNum]);
        }
    }
}
```

```
C:\JavaPrograms>java AddGuests
Room number: 7
How many guests? 5

Do another? Y
Room number: 0
How many guests? 3

Do another? Y
Room number: 3
How many guests? 4

Do another? N

Room    Guests
0       3
1       0
2       0
3       4
4       0
5       0
6       0
7       5
8       0
9       0
```

Figure 16-7:
Running the
code in
Listing 16-5.

Hey! The program in Listing 16-5 is pretty big! It may be the biggest program so far in this book. But *big* doesn't necessarily mean *difficult.* If each piece of the program makes sense, you can create each piece on its own, and then put all the pieces together. Voilà! The code is manageable.

Chapter 17

Programming with Objects and Classes

. . . .

In This Chapter

▶ Creating classes

▶ Making objects from classes

▶ Joining the exclusive "I understand classes and objects" society

. . . .

Chapters 6, 7, and 8 introduce Java's primitive types — things like `int`, `double`, `char`, and `boolean`. That's great, but how often does a real-world problem deal exclusively with such simple values? Consider an exchange between a merchant and a customer. The customer makes a purchase, which can involve item names, model numbers, credit card info, sales tax rates, and lots of other stuff.

In older computer programming languages, you treat an entire purchase like a big pile of unbundled laundry. Imagine a mound of socks, shirts, and other pieces of clothing. You have no basket, so you grab as much as you can handle. As you walk to the washer, you drop a few things — a sock here and a washcloth there. This is like the older way of storing the values in a purchase. In older languages, there's no purchase. There are only `double` values, `char` values, and other loose items. You put the purchase amount in one variable, the customer's name in another, and the sales tax data somewhere else. But that's awful. You tend to drop things on your way to the compiler. With small errors in a program, you can easily drop an amount here and a customer's name there.

So with laundry and computer programming, you're better off if you have a basket. The newer programming languages, like Java, allow you to combine values and make new, more useful kinds of values. For example, in Java you can combine `double` values, `boolean` values, and other kinds of values to create something that you call a `Purchase`. Because your purchase info is all in one big bundle, it's easier to keep track of the purchase's pieces. That's the start of an important computer programming concept — the notion of *object-oriented programming*.

Creating a Class

I start with a "traditional" example. The program in Listing 17-1 processes simple purchase data. Two runs of the program are shown in Figure 17-1.

Listing 17-1   Doing It the Old-Fashioned Way

```
class ProcessData
{
    public static void main(String args[])
    {
        double amount;
        boolean taxable;
        double total;

        System.out.print("Amount: ");
        amount = DummiesIO.getDouble();
        System.out.print("Taxable? (true/false) ");
        taxable = DummiesIO.getBoolean();

        if (taxable)
            total = amount*1.05;
        else
            total = amount;

        System.out.print("Total: ");
        System.out.println(total);
    }
}
```

Figure 17-1:
Processing
a customer's
purchase.

```
C:\JavaPrograms>java ProcessData
Amount: 20.00
Taxable? (true/false) false
Total: 20.0

C:\JavaPrograms>java ProcessData
Amount: 20.00
Taxable? (true/false) true
Total: 21.0
```

If the output in Figure 17-1 looks funny, it's because I do nothing in the code to control the number of digits beyond the decimal point. So in the output, the value $20.00 looks like 20.0. That's okay. I show you how to fix the problem in Chapter 18.

Reference types and Java classes

The code in Listing 17-1 involves a few simple values — amount, taxable, and total. So here's the main point of this chapter: By combining several simple values, you can get a single, more useful value. That's the way it works. You take some of Java's primitive types, whip them together to make a primitive type stew, and what do you get? You get a more useful type called a *reference type*. Listing 17-2 has an example.

Listing 17-2   What It Means to Be a Purchase

```
class Purchase
{
    double amount;
    boolean taxable;
    double total;
}
```

The code in Listing 17-2 has no `main` method, so you can compile the code, but you can't run it. Figure 17-2 shows you the story. When you `javac` the file in Listing 17-2, you get back another command prompt. So far, so good. But try to `java` the code in Listing 17-2, and the computer balks. Because Listing 17-2 has no `main` method, there's no place to start the executing. (In fact, the code in Listing 17-2 has no statements at all. There's nothing to execute.)

Figure 17-2:
The code in
Listing 17-2
has no main
method.

```
C:\JavaPrograms>javac Purchase.java

C:\JavaPrograms>java Purchase
Exception in thread "main" java.lang.NoSuchMethodError: main

C:\JavaPrograms>_
```

Using a newly defined class

To do something useful with the code in Listing 17-2, you need a `main` method. You can put the `main` method in a separate file. Listing 17-3 shows you such a file.

Listing 17-3   Making Use of Your Purchase Class

```
class ProcessPurchase
{
    public static void main(String args[])
    {
        Purchase onePurchase = new Purchase();

        System.out.print("Amount: ");
        onePurchase.amount = DummiesIO.getDouble();
        System.out.print("Taxable? (true/false) ");
        onePurchase.taxable = DummiesIO.getBoolean();
```

(continued)

Listing 17-3 *(continued)*

```
        if (onePurchase.taxable)
            onePurchase.total = onePurchase.amount*1.05;
        else
            onePurchase.total = onePurchase.amount;

        System.out.print("Total: ");
        System.out.println(onePurchase.total);

    }
}
```

The best way to understand the code in Listing 17-3 is to compare it, line by line, with the code in Listing 17-1. In fact, there's a mechanical formula for turning the code in Listing 17-1 into the code in Listing 17-3. Table 17-1 describes the formula.

Table 17-1	Converting Your Code to Use a Class
In Listing 17-1	*In Listing 17-3*
double amount; boolean taxable; double total;	Purchase onePurchase = new Purchase();
amount	onePurchase.amount
taxable	onePurchase.taxable
total	onePurchase.total

The two programs (in Listings 17-1 and 17-3) do essentially the same thing, but one uses primitive variables, and the other leans on the Purchase code from Listing 17-2. Both programs have runs like the ones shown back in Figure 17-1.

Running code that straddles two separate files

Here's how you create and run the combined code in Listings 17-2 and 17-3:

1. **Put the code from Listing 17-2 in your** JavaPrograms **directory.**

   Either type the code with a text editor, or copy the code after downloading it from www.BurdBrain.com or www.dummies.com/extras. Either way, name the file Purchase.java.

2. **Put the code from Listing 17-3 in your** `JavaPrograms` **directory.**

   Type it yourself, or copy it from `www.BurdBrain.com` or `www.dummies.com/extras`. Name it `ProcessPurchase.java`.

3. **Compile** `ProcessPurchase.java`.

   If you use the command prompt window, type

   ```
   javac ProcessPurchase.java
   ```

   With this single `javac` command, the computer compiles both `ProcessPurchase.java` and `Purchase.java`. That's because the Java compiler is smart. When you type this `javac` command, the compiler starts compiling the code in Listing 17-3. Partway into Listing 17-3, the compiler sees the line

   ```
   Purchase onePurchase = new Purchase();
   ```

   At this point, the compiler says "Hey! What does `Purchase` mean?" So the compiler goes looking for a file named `Purchase.class` or `Purchase.java`. When the compiler finds `Purchase.java` (the file that you create in Step 1), the compiler performs its magic on `Purchase.java`. (It compiles `Purchase.java`, creating the `Purchase.class` file). So that's how it works — you can compile two `.java` files with just one `javac` command.

   You can make up any file name for the code in Listing 17-2, as long as you call it *SomethingOrOther*`.java`. But, if you don't name it `Purchase.java`, then in Step 3, the compiler won't be able to find the `Purchase` code. To compile all the code, you'll have to type **javac *SomethingOrOther*.java** first, and then type **javac ProcessPurchase.java** separately.

4. **Run the code in Listing 17-3.**

   If you use a command prompt window, type

   ```
   java ProcessPurchase
   ```

   This command runs the code in Listing 17-3, which in turn uses variables from the code in Listing 17-2.

You cannot apply the `java` command to a piece of code that has no `main` method. That's why, in Step 4 in the preceding list, you type `java ProcessPurchase`, and not `java Purchase`. If you type `java Purchase`, you get an error message like the one shown in Figure 17-2.

Why bother?

On the surface, the code in Listing 17-3 is longer, more complicated, and harder to read. But think about a big pile of laundry. It may take time to find a basket, and to shovel socks into the basket. But when you have clothes in the basket, the clothes are much easier to carry. It's the same way with the code in Listing 17-3. When you have your data in a `Purchase` basket, it's much easier to do complicated things with purchases.

From Classes Come Objects

The code in Listing 17-2 defines a class. A *class* is a design plan; it describes the way in which you intend to combine and use pieces of data. For instance, the code in Listing 17-2 announces your intention to combine `double`, `boolean`, and `double` values to make new `Purchase` values.

Classes are central to all Java programming. But Java is called an object-oriented language. Java isn't called a class-oriented language. In fact, no one uses the term class-oriented language. Why not?

Well, you can't put your arms around a class. A class isn't real. A class without an object is like a day without chocolate. If you're sitting in a room right now, then glance at all the chairs in the room. How many chairs are in the room? Two? Five? Twenty? In a room with five chairs, you have five chair objects. Each chair (each object) is something real, something you can use, something you can sit on.

A language like Java has classes and objects. So what's the difference between a class and an object?

- ✔ An object is a thing.
- ✔ A class is a design plan for things of that kind.

For example, how would you describe what a chair is? Well, a chair has a seat, a back, and legs. In Java, you may write the stuff in Listing 17-4.

Listing 17-4   What It Means to Be a Chair

```
//This is real Java code, but this code cannot be compiled
//  on its own:

class Chair
{
    FlatHorizonalPanel seat;
    FlatVerticalPanel back;
    LongSkinnyVerticalRods legs;
}
```

The code above is a design plan for chairs. The code tells you that each chair has three things. The code names the things (`seat`, `back`, and `legs`), and tells you a little bit about each thing. (For instance, a seat is a `Flat`

HorizontalPanel.) In the same way, the code in Listing 17-2 tells you that each purchase has three things. The code names the things (amount, taxable, and total), and tells you the primitive type of each thing.

So imagine some grand factory at the edge of the universe. While you sleep each night, this factory stamps out tangible objects — objects that you'll encounter during the next waking day. Tomorrow you'll go for an interview at the Sloshy Shoes Company. So tonight, the factory builds chairs for the company's offices. The factory builds chair objects, as shown in Figure 17-3, from the almost-real code in Listing 17-4.

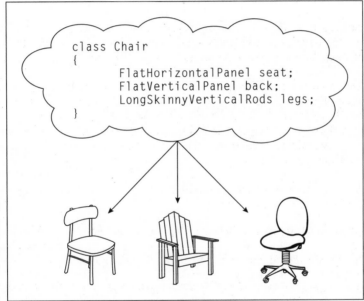

Figure 17-3: Chairs objects from the Chair class.

In Listing 17-3, the line

```
Purchase onePurchase = new Purchase();
```

behaves like that grand factory at the edge of the universe. Instead of creating chair objects, that line in Listing 17-3 creates a purchase object, as shown in Figure 17-4. That Listing 17-3 line is a declaration with an initialization. Just as the line

```
int count=0;
```

declares the count variable and sets count to 0, the line in Listing 17-3 declares the onePurchase variable, and makes onePurchase point to a brand new object. That new object contains three parts: an amount part, a taxable part, and a total part.

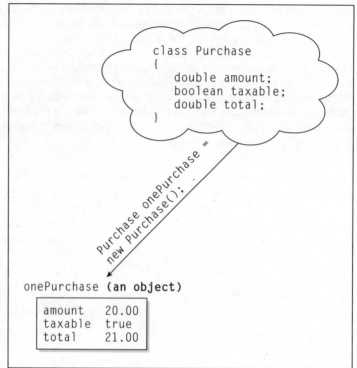

class Purchase
{
    double amount;
    boolean taxable;
    double total;
}

Purchase onePurchase = new Purchase();

onePurchase (an object)

amount   20.00
taxable   true
total   21.00

Figure 17-4:
An object
created
from the
Purchase
class.

If you want to be picky, there's a difference between the stuff in Figure 17-4 and the action of the big bold statement in Listing 17-3. Figure 17-4 shows an object with the values 20.00, true, and 21.00 stored in it. The statement in Listing 17-3 creates a new object, but it doesn't fill the object with useful values. Getting values comes later in Listing 17-3.

Understanding (or ignoring) the subtleties

Sometimes, when you refer to a particular object, you want to emphasize which class the object came from. Well, subtle differences in emphasis call for big differences in terminology. So here's how Java programmers use the terminology:

✔ The bold line in Listing 17-3 creates a new *object*.

✔ The bold line in Listing 17-3 creates a new *instance of the* Purchase *class*.

The words *object* and *instance* are almost synonymous, but Java programmers never say "object of the Purchase class" (or if they do, they feel funny).

By the way, if you mess up this terminology and say something like "object of the Purchase class," then no one jumps down your throat. Everyone understands what you mean, and life goes on as usual. In fact, I often use a phrase like "Purchase object" to describe an instance of the Purchase class. The difference between object and instance isn't terribly important. But it's very important to remember that the words object and instance have the same meaning. (Okay! They have *nearly* the same meaning.)

Making reference to an object's parts

After you've created an object, you use dots to refer to the object's parts. For example, in Listing 17-3, I put a value into the onePurchase object's amount part with the following code:

```
onePurchase.amount = DummiesIO.getDouble();
```

Later in Listing 17-3, I get the amount part's value with the following code:

```
onePurchase.total = onePurchase.amount*1.05;
```

This dot business may look cumbersome, but it really helps programmers when they're trying to organize the code. In Listing 17-1, each variable is a separate entity. But in Listing 17-3, each use of the word amount is inextricably linked to the notion of a purchase. That's good.

Creating several objects

After you've created a Purchase class, you can create as many purchase objects as you want. For instance, in Listing 17-5, I create three purchase objects.

Listing 17-5   Processing Purchases

```
class ProcessPurchasesss
{
    public static void main(String args[])
    {
        Purchase aPurchase;
```

(continued)

Listing 17-5 *(continued)*

```
        for (int count=0; count<3; count++)
        {
            aPurchase = new Purchase();

            System.out.print("Amount: ");
            aPurchase.amount = DummiesIO.getDouble();
            System.out.print("Taxable? (true/false) ");
            aPurchase.taxable = DummiesIO.getBoolean();

            if (aPurchase.taxable)
                aPurchase.total = aPurchase.amount*1.05;
            else
                aPurchase.total = aPurchase.amount;

            System.out.print("Total: ");
            System.out.println(aPurchase.total);
            System.out.println();
        }

    }
}
```

Figure 17-5 has a run of the code in Listing 17-5, and Figure 17-6 illustrates the concept.

Figure 17-5:
Running
the code in
Listing 17-5.

```
C:\JavaPrograms>java ProcessPurchasesss
Amount: 20.00
Taxable? (true/false) true
Total: 21.0

Amount: 20.00
Taxable? (true/false) false
Total: 20.0

Amount: 95.00
Taxable? (true/false) true
Total: 99.75
```

Listing 17-5 has only one variable that refers to purchase objects. (The variable's name is aPurchase.) The program has three purchase objects because the assignment statement

```
aPurchase = new Purchase();
```

is executed three times (once for each iteration of the for loop). Just as you can separate an int variable's assignment from the variable's declaration

```
int count;
count = 0;
```

you can also separate a Purchase variable's assignment from the variable's declaration:

```
Purchase aPurchase;

for (int count=0; count<3; count++)
{
    aPurchase = new Purchase();
```

In fact, after you've created the code in Listing 17-2, the word Purchase stands for a brand new type — a reference type. Java has eight built-in primitive types, and has as many reference types as people can define during your lifetime. In Listing 17-2, I define the Purchase reference type, and you can define reference types too.

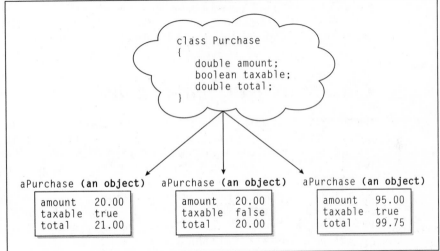

Figure 17-6:
From one
class come
three
objects.

Table 17-2 has a brief comparison of primitive types and reference types.

Table 17-2	Java Types	
	Primitive Type	*Reference Type*
How it's created	Built into the language	Defined as a Java class
How many are there	Eight	Indefinitely many
Sample variable declaration	`int count;`	`Purchase aPurchase;`
Sample assignment	`count=0;`	`aPurchase = new Purchase();`
Assigning a value to one of its parts	(Not applicable)	`aPurchase.amount = 20.00;`

Another Way to Think About Classes

When you start learning object-oriented programming, you may think this class idea is a big hoax. Some geeks in Silicon Valley had nothing better to do, so they went to a bar and made up some confusing gibberish about classes. They don't know what it means, but they have fun watching people struggle to understand it.

Well, that's not what classes are all about. Classes are serious stuff. What's more, classes are useful. Many reputable studies have shown that classes and object-oriented programming save time and money.

Even so, the notion of a class can be very elusive. Even experienced programmers — the ones who are new to object-oriented programming — have trouble understanding how an object differs from a class.

Classes, objects, and tables

Because classes can be so mysterious, I'll expand your understanding with another analogy. Figure 17-7 has a table of three purchases. The table's title consists of one word (the word "Purchase") and the table has three column headings — the words "amount," "taxable," and "total." Well, the code in Listing 17-2 has the same stuff — Purchase, amount, taxable, and total. So in Figure 17-7, think of the top part of the table (the title and column headings) as a class. Like the code in Listing 17-2, this top part of the table tells us what it means to be a Purchase. (It means having an amount value, a taxable value, and a total value.)

Purchase		
amount	taxable	total
20.00	true	21.00
20.00	false	20.00
95.00	true	99.75

```
class Purchase
{
    double amount;
    boolean taxable;
    double total;
}
```

Figure 17-7:
A table of purchases.

A class is like the top part of a table. And what about an object? Well, an object is like a row of a table. For example, with the code in Listing 17-5 and the input in Figure 17-5, I create three objects (three instances of the Purchase class). The first object has amount value 20.00, taxable value true, and total value 21.00. In the table, the first row has these three values — 20.00, true, and 21.00, as shown in Figure 17-8.

Figure 17-8:
A purchase
corresponds
to a row of
the table.

	Purchase	
amount	taxable	total
20.00	true	21.00
20.00	false	20.00
95.00	true	99.75

```
aPurchase = new Purchase();
    ...
aPurchase.amount = DummiesIO.getDouble();
aPurchase.taxable = DummiesIO.getBoolean();
    ...
aPurchase.total = aPurchase.amount*1.05;
```

Some questions and answers

Here's the world's briefest object-oriented programming FAQ:

✔ **Can I have an object without having a class?**

No, you can't. In Java, every object is an instance of a class.

✔ **Can I have a class without having an object?**

Yes, you can. In fact, almost every program in this book creates a class without an object. Take Listing 17-5, for example. The code in Listing 17-5 defines a class named ProcessPurchasesss. And nowhere in Listing 17-5 (or anywhere else) do I create an instance of the Process Purchasesss class. I have a class with no objects. That's just fine. It's business as usual.

✔ **After I've created a class and its instances, can I add more instances to the class?**

Yes, you can. In Listing 17-5, I create one instance, then another, and then a third. If I went one additional time around the for loop, I'd have a fourth instance, and I'd put a fourth row in the table of Figure 17-8. With no objects, three objects, four objects, or more objects, I still have the same old Purchase class.

✔ **Can an object come from more than one class?**

Bite your tongue! Maybe other object-oriented languages allow this nasty class cross-breeding, but in Java, it's strictly forbidden. That's one of the things that distinguishes Java from some of the languages that preceded it. Java is cleaner, more uniform, and easier to understand.

Chapter 18

Using Methods from a Java Class

I hope you didn't read Chapter 17, because I tell a big lie in the beginning of the chapter. Actually, it's not a lie. It's an exaggeration.

Actually, it's not an exaggeration. It's a careful choice of wording. In Chapter 17, I write that the gathering of data into a class is the start of object-oriented programming. Well, that's true. Except that many programming languages had data-gathering features before object-oriented programming became popular. Pascal had *records*. C had *structs*.

To be painfully precise, the grouping of data into usable blobs is only a pre-requisite to object-oriented programming. You're not really doing object-oriented programming until you combine both data and methods in your classes.

This chapter starts the "methods" ball rolling, and Chapter 19 rounds out the picture.

The String Class

The String class is declared in the Java API. This means that, somewhere in the stuff you download from java.sun.com is a file named String.java. If you hunt down this String.java file and peek at the file's code, you find some very familiar-looking stuff:

```
class String
{
    ...And so on.
```

In your own code, you can use this String class without ever seeing what's inside the String.java file. That's one of the great things about object-oriented programming.

A simple example

A String is bunch of characters. It's like having several char values in a row. You can declare a variable to be of type String and store several letters in the variable. Listing 18-1 has a tiny example.

Listing 18-1   I'm Repeating Myself Again (Again)

```
class JazzyEchoLine
{
    public static void main(String args[])
    {
        String lineIn;
        lineIn = DummiesIO.getLine();
        System.out.println(lineIn);
    }
}
```

A run of Listing 18-1 is shown in Figure 18-1. This run bears an uncanny resemblance to runs of Listing 5-1 from Chapter 5. That's because Listing 18-1 is a reprise of the effort in Listing 5-1.

Figure 18-1:
Running
the code in
Listing 18-1.

```
C:\JavaPrograms>java JazzyEchoLine
Do as I write, not as I do.
Do as I write, not as I do.
```

The new idea in Listing 18-1 is the use of a String. In Listing 5-1, I have no variable to store the user's input. But in Listing 18-1, I create the lineIn variable. This variable stores a bunch of letters, like the letters Do as I write, not as I do.

Putting String variables to good use

The program in Listing 18-1 takes the user's input and echoes it back on the screen. This is a wonderful program, but (like many college administrators that I know) it doesn't seem to be particularly useful.

So take a look at a more useful application of Java's String type. A nice one is in Listing 18-2.

Listing 18-2   Putting a Name in a String Variable

```
class ProcessMoreData
{
    public static void main(String args[])
    {
        String fullName;
        double amount;
        boolean taxable;
        double total;

        System.out.print("Customer's full name: ");
        fullName = DummiesIO.getLine();
        System.out.print("Amount: ");
        amount = DummiesIO.getDouble();
        System.out.print("Taxable? (true/false) ");
        taxable = DummiesIO.getBoolean();

        if (taxable)
            total = amount*1.05;
        else
            total = amount;

        System.out.println();
        System.out.print("The total for ");
        System.out.print(fullName);
        System.out.print(" is ");
        System.out.print(total);
        System.out.println(".");
    }
}
```

A run of the code in Listing 18-2 is shown in Figure 18-2. The code stores Barry A. Burd in a variable called fullName, and displays the fullName variable's content as part of the output. To make this program work, you have to store Barry A. Burd somewhere. After all, the program follows a certain outline:

```
Get a name.
Get some other stuff.
Compute the total.
Display the name (along with some other stuff).
```

If you don't have the program store the name somewhere then, by the time it's done getting other stuff and computing the total, it forgets the name (so the program can't display the name).

Figure 18-2:
Making a
purchase.

```
C:\JavaPrograms>java ProcessMoreData
Customer's full name: Barry A. Burd
Amount: 20.00
Taxable? (true/false) true

The total for Barry A. Burd is 21.0.
```

Reading and writing strings

To read a String value from the keyboard, you can call either DummiesIO.
getString or DummiesIO.getLine:

   ✔ **The method** getString **reads up to the next blank space.**

   For instance, with the input Barry A. Burd, the statements

   ```
   String firstName = DummiesIO.getString();
   String middleInit = DummiesIO.getString();
   String lastName = DummiesIO.getString();
   ```

   assign Barry to firstName, A. to middleInit, and Burd to lastName.

   ✔ **The method** getLine **reads up to the end of the current line.**

   For example, with input Barry A. Burd, the statement

   ```
   String fullName = DummiesIO.getLine();
   ```

   assigns Barry A. Burd to the variable fullName. (Hey, being an author
   has some hidden perks.)

To display a String value, you can call one of your old friends,
System.out.print or System.out.println. In fact, most of the programs
in this book display String values. In Listing 18-2, a statement like

```
System.out.print("Customer's full name: ");
```

displays the String value "Customer's full name: ".

Chapter 4 introduces a bunch of characters, enclosed in double quote marks:

```
"Chocolate, royalties, sleep"
```

In Chapter 4, I call this a *literal* of some kind. (It's a literal because, unlike a
variable, it looks just like the stuff that it represents.) Well, in this chapter,
I can continue the story about Java's literals:

   ✔ In Listing 18-2, amount and total are double variables, and 1.05 is
   a double literal.

   ✔ In Listing 18-2, fullName is a String variable, and things like
   "Customer's full name: " are String literals.

In a Java program, you surround the letters in a `String` literal with double quote marks.

You can use my `DummiesIO` program to write `String` values to a disk file. For details, see Chapter 13.

Using an Object's Methods

If you're not too concerned about classes and reference types, then the use of the type `String` in Listing 18-2 is no big deal. Almost everything you can do with a primitive type seems to work with the `String` type as well. But there's danger around the next curve. Take a look at the code in Listing 18-3, and the run of the code shown in Figure 18-3.

Listing 18-3   A Faulty Password Checker

```
//This code does not work:
class TryToCheckPassword
{
    public static void main(String args[])
    {
        String password="swordfish";
        String userInput;

        System.out.print("What's the password? ");
        userInput = DummiesIO.getString();

        if (password==userInput)
            System.out.println("You're okay!");
        else
            System.out.println("You're a menace.");
    }
}
```

Figure 18-3:
But I typed the correct password!

```
C:\JavaPrograms>java TryToCheckPassword
What's the password? swordfish
You're a menace.
```

Here are the facts as they appear in this example:

✔ According to the code in Listing 18-3, the value of `password` is `"swordfish"`.

✔ In Figure 18-3, in response to the program's prompt, the user types swordfish. So in the code, the value of userInput is "swordfish".

✔ The if statement checks the condition password==userInput. Because both variables have the value "swordfish", the condition *should* be true, but. . . .

✔ The condition is *not* true, because the program's output is You're a menace.

What's going on here? I try beefing up the code to see if I can find any clues. An enhanced version of the password-checking program is in Listing 18-4, with a run of the new version shown in Figure 18-4.

Listing 18-4   An Attempt to Debug the Code in Listing 18-3

```
class DebugCheckPassword
{
    public static void main(String args[])
    {
        String password="swordfish";
        String userInput;

        System.out.print("What's the password? ");
        userInput = DummiesIO.getString();

        System.out.println();
        System.out.print("You typed            ");
        System.out.println(userInput);
        System.out.print("But the password is ");
        System.out.println(password);
        System.out.println();

        if (password==userInput)
            System.out.println("You're okay!");
        else
            System.out.println("You're a menace.");
    }
}
```

Figure 18-4:
This looks
even worse.

```
C:\JavaPrograms>java DebugCheckPassword
What's the password? swordfish

You typed            swordfish
But the password is swordfish

You're a menace.
```

Ouch! I'm stumped this time. The run in Figure 18-4 shows that both the `userInput` and `password` variables have value `swordfish`. So why doesn't the program accept the user's input?

Well, when you compare two things with a double equal sign, reference types and primitive types don't behave the same way. Take, for example, `int` **versus** `String`:

✔ You can compare two `int` values with a double equal sign. When you do, things work exactly as you would expect. For example, the condition in the following code is true:

```
int apples=7;
int oranges=7;

if (apples == oranges)
    System.out.println("They're equal.");
```

✔ When you compare two `String` values with the double equal sign, things don't work the way you expect. The computer doesn't check to see if the two `String` values contain the same letters. Instead, the computer checks some esoteric property of the way variables are stored in memory.

For your purposes, the term *reference type* is just a fancy name for a class. Because `String` is defined to be a class in the Java API, I call `String` a reference type. This terminology highlights the parallel between primitive types (such as `int`) and classes (that is, reference types, such as `String`).

Comparing strings

In the preceding bullets, the difference between `int` and `String` is mighty interesting. But if the double equal sign doesn't work for `String` values, how do you check to see if Joe User enters the correct password? You do it with the code in Listing 18-5.

Listing 18-5   Calling an Object's Method

```
//This program works!
class CheckPassword
{
    public static void main(String args[])
    {
        String password="swordfish";
        String userInput;

        System.out.print("What's the password? ");
        userInput = DummiesIO.getString();
```

(continued)

Listing 18-5 *(continued)*

```
    if (password.equals(userInput))
        System.out.println("You're okay!");
    else
        System.out.println("You're a menace.");
    }
}
```

A run of the new password-checking code is shown in Figure 18-5 and, let me tell you, it's a big relief! The code in Listing 18-5 actually works! When the user types `swordfish`, the `if` statement's condition is true.

Figure 18-5:
At last,
Joe User
can log in.

```
C:\JavaPrograms>java CheckPassword
What's the password? swordfish
You're okay!
```

The truth about classes and methods

The magic in Listing 18-5 is the use of a method named `equals`. I have two ways to explain the `equals` method — a simple way, and a more detailed way. First, here's the simple way: The `equals` method compares the characters in one string with the characters in another. If the characters are the same, then the condition inside the `if` statement is true. That's all there is to it.

Don't use a double equal sign to compare two `String` objects. Instead, use one of the objects' `equals` methods.

For a more detailed understanding of the `equals` method, flip back to Chapter 17 and take a look at Figures 17-7 and 17-8. Those figures illustrate the similarities between classes, objects, and the parts of a table. In the figures, each row represents a purchase, and each column represents a feature that purchases possess.

You can observe the same similarities for any class, including Java's `String` class. In fact, what Figure 17-7 does for purchases, Figure 18-6 does for strings.

	String	
value	**count**	**equals**
swordfish	9	**(A method to compare** swordfish **with any string)**
catfish	7	**(A method to compare** catfish **with any string)**

Figure 18-6: Viewing the String class and String objects as parts of a table.

The stuff shown in Figure 18-6 is much simpler than the real String class story. But Figure 18-6 makes a good point. Like the purchases in Figure 17-7, each string has its own features. For instance, each string has a value (the actual characters stored in the string) and each string has a count (the number of characters stored in the string). You can't really write the following line of code:

```
//This code does NOT work:
System.out.println(password.count);
```

but that's because the stuff in Figure 18-6 omits a few subtle details.

Anyway, each row in Figure 18-6 has three items — a value, a count, and an equals method. So each row of the table contains more than just data. Each row contains an equals method, a way of doing something useful with the data. It's as if each object (each instance of the String class) has three things:

- ✔ A bunch of characters (the object's value)
- ✔ A number (the object's count)
- ✔ A way of being compared with other strings (the object's equals method)

That's the essence of object-oriented programming. Each string has its own personal copy of the equals method. For example, in Listing 18-5, the password string has its own equals method. When you call the password string's equals method and put the userInput string in the method's parentheses, the method compares the two strings to see if those strings contain the same characters.

The userInput string in Listing 18-5 has an equals method too. I could use the userInput string's equals method to compare this string with the password string. But I don't. In fact, in Listing 18-5, I don't use the user Input string's equals method at all. (To compare the userInput with the password, I had to use either the password string's equals method or the userInput string's equals method. So I made an arbitrary choice: I chose the password string's method.)

Calling an object's methods

Calling a string's equals method is like getting a purchase's total. With both equals and total, you use your old friend, the dot. For example, in Listing 17-3, you write

```
System.out.println(onePurchase.total);
```

and in Listing 18-5, you write

```
if (password.equals(userInput))
```

A dot works the same way for an object's variables and its methods. In either case, a dot takes the object and picks out one of the object's parts. It works whether that part is a piece of data (as in onePurchase.total) or a method (as in password.equals).

Combining and using data

At this point in the chapter, I can finally say, "I told you so." Here's a quotation from Chapter 17:

> A class is a design plan. The class describes the way in which you intend to *combine* and *use* pieces of data.

A class can define the way you *use* data. How do you use a password and a user's input? You check to see if they're the same. That's why Java's String class defines an equals method.

An object can be more than just a bunch of data. With object-oriented programming, each object possesses copies of methods for using that object.

Static Methods

You have a fistful of checks. Each check has a number, an amount, and a payee. You print checks like these with your very own laser printer. To print the checks, you use a Java class. Each object made from the Check class has three variables (number, amount, and payee). And each object has one method (a print method). You can see all this in Figure 18-7.

	Check		
number	amount	payee	print
1705	$25.09	The Butcher	(method to cut the check)
1699	$31.27	The Baker	(method to cut the check)
1702	$12.35	The Candlestick Maker	(method to cut the check)

Figure 18-7: The Check class and some check objects.

sort

You'd like to print the checks in numerical order. So you need a method to *sort* the checks. If the checks in Figure 18-7 were sorted, the check with number 1699 would come first, and the check with number 1705 would come last.

The big question is, should each check have its own sort method? Does the check with number 1699 need to sort itself? And the answer is no. Some methods just shouldn't belong to the objects in a class.

So where do such methods belong? How can you have a sort method without creating a separate sort for each check?

Here's the answer. You make the sort method be *static*. Anything that's static belongs to a whole class, not to any particular instance of the class. If the sort method is static, then the entire Check class has just one copy of the sort method. This copy stays with the entire Check class. No matter how many instances of the Check class you create — three, ten, or none — you have just one sort method.

For an illustration of this concept, look back at Figure 18-7. The whole class has just one sort method. So the sort method is static. No matter how you call the sort method, that method uses the same values to do its work.

Of course, each individual check (each object, each row of the table in Figure 18-7) still has its own `number`, its own `amount`, its own `payee`, and it's own `print` method. When you `print` the first check, you get one amount, and when you `print` the second check get another. Because there's a `number`, an `amount`, a `payee`, and a `print` method for each object, I call these things *non-static*. I call them non-static, because . . . well . . . because they're not static.

Calling static and non-static methods

In this book, my first use of the word `static` is way back in Listing 4-1. I use `static` as part of every `main` method (and this book's listings have lots of `main` methods). In Java, your `main` method has to be static. That's just the way it goes.

To call a static method, you use a class's name along with a dot. This is just slightly different from the way you call a non-static method:

- ✔ **To call an ordinary (non-static) method, you follow an object with a dot.**

  For instance, a program to process the checks in Figure 18-7 may contain code of the following kind:

  ```
  Check firstCheck;
  firstCheck.number = 1705;
  firstCheck.amount = 25.09;
  firstCheck.payee = "The Butcher";
  firstCheck.print();
  ```

- ✔ **To call a class's static method, you follow the class name with a dot.**

  For instance, to sort the checks in Figure 18-7, you may call

  ```
  Check.sort();
  ```

An example

The code in Listing 18-5 introduces a non-static method named `equals`. To compare the `password` string with the `userInput` string, you preface `.equals` with either of the two string objects. In Listing 18-5, I preface `.equals` with the `password` object:

```
if (password.equals(userInput))
```

Each string object has an `equals` method of its own, so I can achieve the same effect by writing

```
if (userInput.equals(password))
```

But Java has another class named `Integer`, and the whole `Integer` class has a static method named `parseInt`. If someone hands you a string of characters, and you want to turn that string into an `int` value, you can call the `Integer` class's `parseInt` method. Listing 18-6 has a small example.

Listing 18-6   More Chips, Please

```java
class AddChips
{
    public static void main(String args[])
    {
        String reply;
        int numberOfChips;

        System.out.print("How many chips do you have?");
        System.out.print(" (Type a number,");
        System.out.print(" or type 'Not playing') ");
        reply = DummiesIO.getLine();

        if (!reply.equals("Not playing"))
        {
            numberOfChips = Integer.parseInt(reply);
            numberOfChips += 10;

            System.out.print("You now have ");
            System.out.print(numberOfChips);
            System.out.println(" chips.");
        }
    }
}
```

Some runs of the code in Listing 18-6 are shown in Figure 18-8. You want to give each player ten chips. But some party poopers in the room aren't playing. So two people, each with no chips, may not get the same treatment. An empty-handed player gets ten chips, but an empty-handed party pooper gets none.

Figure 18-8:
Running
the code in
Listing 18-6.

```
C:\JavaPrograms>java AddChips
How many chips do you have? (Type a number, or type 'Not playing') 30
You now have 40 chips.

C:\JavaPrograms>java AddChips
How many chips do you have? (Type a number, or type 'Not playing') 0
You now have 10 chips.

C:\JavaPrograms>java AddChips
How many chips do you have? (Type a number, or type 'Not playing') Not playing

C:\JavaPrograms>_
```

So in Listing 18-6, you call my `DummiesIO.getLine` method, allowing a user to enter any characters at all — not just digits. If the user types `Not playing`, then you don't give the killjoy any chips.

If the user types some digits, then you're stuck holding these digits in the string variable named `reply`. You can't add ten to a string like `reply`. So you call the `Integer` class's `parseInt` method, which takes your string, and hands you back a nice `int` value. From there, you can add ten to the `int` value.

Java has a loophole that allows you to add a number to a string. The problem is, you don't get real addition. Adding the number 10 to the string `"30"` gives you `"3010"`, not 40.

Don't confuse `Integer` with `int`. In Java, `int` is the name of a primitive type (a type that I use throughout this book). But `Integer` is the name of a class. Java's `Integer` class contains handy methods for dealing with `int` values. For instance, in Listing 18-6, the `Integer` class's `parseInt` method makes an `int` value from a string.

Formatting Numbers

In Chapter 17, Listing 17-1 adds tax to the amount of a purchase. But a run of the code in Listing 17-1 has an anomaly. Look back at Figure 17-1. With five percent tax on 20 dollars, the program displays a total of 21.0. That's peculiar. Where I come from, currency amounts aren't normally displayed with just one digit beyond the decimal point.

If you don't choose your purchase amount carefully, then the situation is even worse. For example, in Figure 18-9, I run the same program (the code in Listing 17-1) with purchase amount 19.37. The resulting display looks very nasty.

Figure 18-9:
Do you have change for 20.33850000 0000003?

```
C:\JavaPrograms>java ProcessData
Amount: 19.37
Taxable? (true/false) true
Total: 20.338500000000003
```

With its internal zeros and ones, the computer doesn't do arithmetic quite the way you and I are used to doing it. So how do you fix this problem?

Well, the Java API has a class named `NumberFormat`, and the `NumberFormat` class has a static method named `getCurrencyInstance`. When you call `NumberFormat.getCurrencyInstance()` with nothing inside the parentheses, you get an object that can mold numbers into U.S. currency amounts. Listing 18-7 has an example.

Listing 18-7   The Right Way to Display a Dollar Amount

```java
import java.text.NumberFormat;

class BetterProcessData
{
    public static void main(String args[])
    {
        double amount;
        boolean taxable;
        double total;
        NumberFormat currency =
            NumberFormat.getCurrencyInstance();
        String niceTotal;

        System.out.print("Amount: ");
        amount = DummiesIO.getDouble();
        System.out.print("Taxable? (true/false) ");
        taxable = DummiesIO.getBoolean();

        if (taxable)
            total = amount*1.05;
        else
            total = amount;

        niceTotal = currency.format(total);
        System.out.print("Total: ");
        System.out.println(niceTotal);
    }
}
```

For some beautiful runs of the code in Listing 18-7, see Figure 18-10. Now at last, you see a total like $20.34, not 20.338500000000003. Ah! That's much better.

Figure 18-10:
See the
pretty
numbers.

```
C:\JavaPrograms>java BetterProcessData
Amount: 20.00
Taxable? (true/false) false
Total: $20.00

C:\JavaPrograms>java BetterProcessData
Amount: 20.00
Taxable? (true/false) true
Total: $21.00

C:\JavaPrograms>java BetterProcessData
Amount: 19.37
Taxable? (true/false) true
Total: $20.34
```

How the NumberFormat works

For my current purposes, the code in Listing 18-7 contains three interesting variables:

✔ The variable `total` stores a number, such as 21.0.

✔ The variable `currency` stores an object that can mold numbers into U.S. currency amounts.

✔ The variable `niceTotal` is set up to store a bunch of characters.

The `currency` object has a `format` method. So to get the appropriate bunch of characters into the `niceTotal` variable, you call the `currency` object's `format` method. You apply this format method to the variable `total`.

Look, more dots!

In Java, you can group a bunch of classes into something called a *package*. So the classes in Java's standard API are divided into about 140 packages. One of these packages is named `java.text`.

The package `java.text` contains about 25 classes, including the very useful `NumberFormat` class. Like most other classes, this `NumberFormat` class has two names — a full name and an abbreviated name. The class's full name is `java.text.NumberFormat`, and the class's abbreviated name is `NumberFormat`. You get the full name by adding the package name to the class's abbreviated name.

The formal term for what I call a "full name" is a *qualified name.* The formal term for what I call an "abbreviated name" is a *simple name.*

In Listing 18-7, you can use the full name of this `NumberFormat` class:

```
java.text.NumberFormat currency =
    java.text.NumberFormat.getCurrencyInstance();
```

But the *import declaration* at the top of Listing 18-7 lets you abbreviate the class's name. Instead of writing `java.text.NumberFormat` throughout your code, you can just write `NumberFormat` instead. With `import`, the Java compiler figures out where to look for the `NumberFormat` class.

Chapter 19

Creating New Java Methods

. . . .

In This Chapter

▶ Creating methods that work with existing values

▶ Creating methods that modify existing values

▶ Creating methods that return new values

. . . .

In Chapter 4, I introduce Java methods. I show you how to create a `main` method and how to call the `System.out.println` method. Between that chapter and this one, I make very little noise about methods. In Chapter 18, I introduce a bunch of new methods for you to call, but that's only half of the story.

This chapter completes the circle. In this chapter, you create your own Java methods — not the tired old `main` method that you've been using all along, but some new, powerful Java methods.

Defining a Method within a Class

In Chapter 18, Figure 18-6 introduces an interesting notion — a notion that's at the core of object-oriented programming. Each Java string has its own `equals` method. That is, each string has, built within it, the functionality to compare itself with other strings. That's an important point. When you do object-oriented programming, you bundle data and functionality into a lump called a class. Just remember Barry's immortal words from Chapter 17:

> A class describes the way in which you intend to combine *and use* pieces of data.

And why are these words so important? They're important because, in object-oriented programming, chunks of data take responsibility for themselves. With object-oriented programming, everything you have to know about a string is located in the file `String.java`. So if anybody has problems with the strings, they know just where to look for all the code. That's great!

So this is the deal — objects contain methods. Chapter 18 shows you how to use an object's methods, and this chapter shows you how to create an object's methods.

Making a method

Imagine a table containing the information about three accounts. (If you have trouble imagining such a thing, just look at Figure 19-1.) In the figure, each account has a name, an identification number, and a balance. In addition (and here's the important part), each account knows how to display itself on the screen. Each row of the table has its own copy of a display method.

	Account		
name	id	balance	display
Barry A. Burd	11010	$25.09	(method to display account info)
Jane Q. Public	24222	$131.27	(method to display account info)
Harold J. Wexler	88899	$12.35	(method to display account info)

Figure 19-1:
A table of accounts.

I need some code to implement the ideas in Figure 19-1. Fortunately, I have some code in Listing 19-1.

Listing 19-1 An Account Class

```
class Account
{
    String name;
    int id;
    double balance;

    void display()
    {
        System.out.print("The account with name ");
        System.out.print(name);
        System.out.print(" and id ");
        System.out.print(id);
        System.out.print(" has balance $");
        System.out.println(balance);
    }
}
```

The Account class in Listing 19-1 defines four things — a name, an id, a balance, and a display. So each instance of Account class has its own name variable, its own id variable, its own balance variable, and its own display method. These things match up with the four columns in Figure 19-1.

Examining the method's header

Listing 19-1 contains the display method's declaration. Like a main method's declaration, the display declaration has a header and a body. (See Chapter 4.) The header has two words and some parentheses:

✔ **The word** void **tells the computer that, when the** display **method is called, the** display **method doesn't return anything to the place that called it.**

Later in this chapter, a method does return something. For now, the display method returns nothing.

✔ **The word** display **is the method's name.**

Every method must have a name. Otherwise, you don't have a way to call the method.

✔ **The parentheses contain all the things you're going to pass to the method when you call it.**

When you call a method, you can pass information to that method on the fly. This display example, with its empty parentheses, looks strange. That's because no information is passed to the display method when you call it. That's okay. I give a meatier example later in this chapter.

Examining the method's body

The display method's body contains some print and println calls. The interesting thing here is that the body makes reference to the variables name, id, and balance. A method's body can do that. But with each object having its own name, id, and balance variables, what does a variable name in the display method's body mean?

Well, when I use the Account class, I create little account objects. Maybe I create an object for each row of the table in Figure 19-1. Each object has its own values for the name, id, and balance variables, and each object has its own copy of the display method.

So take the first display method in Figure 19-1 — the method for Barry A. Burd's account. The display method for that object behaves as if it had the code in Listing 19-2.

Listing 19-2   How the display Method Behaves When No One's Looking

```
//This is not real code:
void display()
{
    System.out.print("The account with name ");
    System.out.print("Barry A. Burd");
    System.out.print(" and id ");
    System.out.print(11010);
    System.out.print(" has balance $");
    System.out.println(25.09);
}
```

In fact, each of the three display methods behaves as if its body has a slightly different code. Figure 19-2 illustrates this idea for two instances of the Account class.

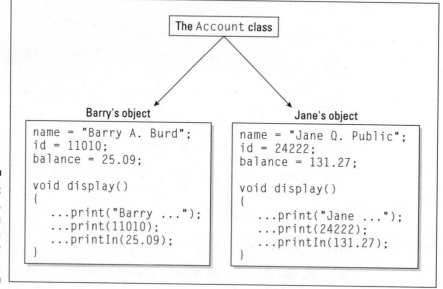

Figure 19-2: Two objects, each with its own display method.

Calling the method

To put the previous section's ideas into action, you need more code. So the next listing (see Listing 19-3) creates instances of the Account class.

Listing 19-3   Making Use of the Code in Listing 19-1

```
class ProcessAccounts
{
    public static void main(String args[])
    {
        Account anAccount;

        for (int i=0; i<3; i++)
        {
            anAccount = new Account();

            anAccount.name =
                DummiesIO.getString("accountData.txt") +
                " " + DummiesIO.getString("accountData.txt") +
                " " + DummiesIO.getString("accountData.txt");

            anAccount.id =
                DummiesIO.getInt("accountData.txt");
            anAccount.balance =
                DummiesIO.getDouble("accountData.txt");

            anAccount.display();
        }
    }
}
```

Here's a summary of the action in Listing 19-3:

```
Do the following three times:
    Create a new object (an instance of the Account class).
    Get values for the object's name, id and balance.
    Call the object's display method.
```

The first of the three display calls prints the first object's name, id, and balance values. The second display call prints the second object's name, id, and balance values. And so on.

A run of the code from Listing 19-3 is shown in Figure 19-3. This run uses the input data from Figure 19-4.

Figure 19-3:
Running
the code in
Listing 19-3.

```
C:\JavaPrograms>java ProcessAccounts
The account with name Barry A. Burd and id 11010 has balance $25.09
The account with name Jane Q. Public and id 24222 has balance $131.27
The account with name Harold J. Wexler and id 88899 has balance $12.35
```

Figure 19-4:
The account
Data.txt file.

The flow of control

Say you're running the code in Listing 19-3. The computer reaches the display method call:

```
anAccount.display();
```

At that point, the computer starts running the code inside the display method. In other words, the computer jumps to the middle of the Account class's code (the code in Listing 19-1).

After executing the display method's code (that forest of print and println calls), the computer returns to the point where it departed from Listing 19-3. That is, the computer goes back to the display method call and continues on from there.

So when you run the code in Listing 19-3, the flow of action in each loop iteration isn't exactly from the top to the bottom. Instead, the action goes from the for loop to the display method, and then back to the for loop. The whole business is pictured in Figure 19-5.

Using punctuation

In Listing 19-3, notice the use of dots. To refer to the name stored in the anAccount object, you write

```
anAccount.name
```

To get the anAccount object to display itself, you write

```
anAccount.display();
```

That's great! When you refer to an object's variable, or call an object's method, the only difference is parentheses:

✔ To refer to an object's variable, you don't use parentheses.

✔ To call an object's method, you use parentheses.

```
class Account
{
    yada, yada, yada ...
    void display()
    {
        system.out.print...
    }
}
```
3

```
class Account
{
    Blabitty, blah, blah,...

    for (int i=0; i<3; i++)
    {
        Blah, blah, blah,...

        anAccount.display();
    }
}
```
2

1

4

Figure 19-5:
The flow of
control
between
Listings 19-1
and 19-3.

When you call a method, you put parentheses after the method's name.
You do this even if you have nothing to put inside the parentheses.

Concatenating strings

The program in Listing 19-3 uses a cute trick. In Java, you can do two different things with a plus sign:

✔ **You can add numbers with a plus sign.**

For example, you can write

```
numberOfSheep = 2 + 5;
```

✔ **You can *concatenate* strings with a plus sign.**

When you concatenate two strings, you scrunch them together, one
right after another. For instance, in Listing 19-3, the expression

```
DummiesIO.getString("accountData.txt") +
" " + DummiesIO.getString("accountData.txt") +
" " + DummiesIO.getString("accountData.txt");
```

can scrunch together Barry, a blank space, A., another blank space, and Burd. The new scrunched up string is (you guessed it) Barry A. Burd.

Let the Objects Do the Work

Let me tell you . . . when I was a young object, I wasn't as smart as the objects you have nowadays. Take, for instance, the object in Listing 19-4. Not only does this object display itself, the object can also fill itself with values.

Listing 19-4   A Class with Two Methods

```
class BetterAccount
{
    String name;
    int id;
    double balance;


    void fillWithData()
    {
        name =
            DummiesIO.getString("accountData.txt") +
            " " + DummiesIO.getString("accountData.txt") +
            " " + DummiesIO.getString("accountData.txt");

        id = DummiesIO.getInt("accountData.txt");
        balance = DummiesIO.getDouble("accountData.txt");
    }


    void display()
    {
        System.out.print("The account with name ");
        System.out.print(name);
        System.out.print(" and id ");
        System.out.print(id);
        System.out.print(" has balance $");
        System.out.println(balance);
    }
}
```

I wrote some code to use the class in Listing 19-4. This new code is in Listing 19-5.

Listing 19-5   This Is So Cool!

```
class ProcessBetterAccounts
{
    public static void main(String args[])
    {
        BetterAccount anAccount;

        for (int i=0; i<3; i++)
        {
            anAccount = new BetterAccount();
            anAccount.fillWithData();
            anAccount.display();
        }
    }
}
```

Listing 19-5 is pretty slick. Because the code in Listing 19-4 is so darn smart, the new code in Listing 19-5 has very little work to do. This new code just creates a BetterAccount object, and then calls the methods in Listing 19-4. When you run all this stuff, you get the result shown in Figure 19-3.

Passing Values to Methods

Think about sending someone to the supermarket to buy bread. When you do this, you say, "Go to the supermarket and buy some bread." (Try it at home. You'll have a fresh loaf of bread in no time at all!) Of course, some other time, you send that same person to the supermarket to buy bananas. You say, "Go to the supermarket and buy some bananas." And what's the point of all this? Well, you have a method, and you have some on-the-fly information that you pass to the method when you call it. The method is named "Go to the super-market and buy some. . . ." The on-the-fly information is either "bread" or "bananas," depending on your culinary needs. In Java, the method calls would look like this:

```
goToTheSupermarketAndBuySome(bread);
goToTheSupermarketAndBuySome(bananas);
```

The things in parentheses are called *parameters* or *parameter lists*. With para-meters, your methods become much more versatile. Instead of getting the same thing each time, you can send somebody to the supermarket to buy bread one time, bananas another time, and birdseed the third time. When you call your goToTheSupermarketAndBuySome method, you decide right there and then what you're going to ask your pal to buy.

These concepts are made more concrete in Listings 19-6 and 19-7.

Listing 19-6   Adding Interest

```
class NiceAccount
{
    String name;
    int id;
    double balance;


    void addInterest(double rate)
    {
        balance += balance*(rate/100.0);
    }


    void display()
    {
        System.out.print("The account with name ");
        System.out.print(name);
        System.out.print(" and id ");
        System.out.print(id);
        System.out.print(" has balance $");
        System.out.println(balance);
    }
}
```

Listing 19-7   Calling the addInterest Method

```
class ProcessNiceAccounts
{
    public static void main(String args[])
    {
        NiceAccount anAccount;
        double interestRate;

        for (int i=0; i<3; i++)
        {
            anAccount = new NiceAccount();

            anAccount.name =
                DummiesIO.getString("bankData.txt") +
                " " + DummiesIO.getString("bankData.txt") +
                " " + DummiesIO.getString("bankData.txt");

            anAccount.id =
                DummiesIO.getInt("bankData.txt");
            anAccount.balance =
                DummiesIO.getDouble("bankData.txt");
```

```
        interestRate =
            DummiesIO.getDouble("bankData.txt");
        anAccount.addInterest(interestRate);

        anAccount.display();
      }
    }
}
```

In Listing 19-7, the line

```
anAccount.addInterest(interestRate);
```

plays the same role as the line goToTheSupermarketAndBuySome(bread) in my little supermarket example. The word addInterest is a method name, and the word interestRate in parentheses is a parameter. Taken as a whole, this statement tells the code in Listing 19-6 to execute its addInterest method. This statement also tells Listing 19-6 to use a certain number (whatever value is stored in the interestRate variable) in the method's calculations. The value of interestRate can be 5.00, 7.00, or whatever. In the same way, the goToTheSupermarketAndBuySome method works for bread, bananas, or whatever else you need from the market.

The next section has a detailed description of addInterest and its action. In the meantime, a run of the code in Listings 19-6 and 19-7 is shown in Figure 19-6. This run uses the bankData.txt file shown in Figure 19-7. If an account balance is $144.10, then the computer displays the ugly $144.1 amount. If you're aching to fix this ugliness, see the section on formatting numbers in Chapter 18.

Figure 19-6:
Running
the code in
Listing 19-7.

```
C:\JavaPrograms>java ProcessNiceAccounts
The account with name Barry A. Burd and id 11010 has balance $26.25
The account with name Jane Q. Public and id 24222 has balance $144.1
The account with name Harold J. Wexler and id 88899 has balance $12.84
```

Figure 19-7:
The bank
Data.txt file.

```
bankData.txt - Notepad
File  Edit  Format  Help
Barry A. Burd      11010   25.00    5.00
Jane Q. Public     24222  131.00   10.00
Harold J. Wexler   88899   12.00    7.00
```

Handing off a value

When you call a method, you can pass information to that method on the fly. This information is in the method's parameter list. Listing 19-7 has a call to the addInterest method:

```
anAccount.addInterest(interestRate);
```

The first time through the loop, the value of interestRate is 5.00. (Remember, I'm using the data in Figure 19-7.) So at that point in the program's run, the method call behaves as if it's the following statement:

```
anAccount.addInterest(5.00);
```

The computer is about to run the code inside the addInterest method (a method in Listing 19-6). But first, the computer *passes* the value 5.00 to the parameter in the addInterest method's header. So inside the add Interest method, the value of rate becomes 5.00. For an illustration of this idea, see Figure 19-8.

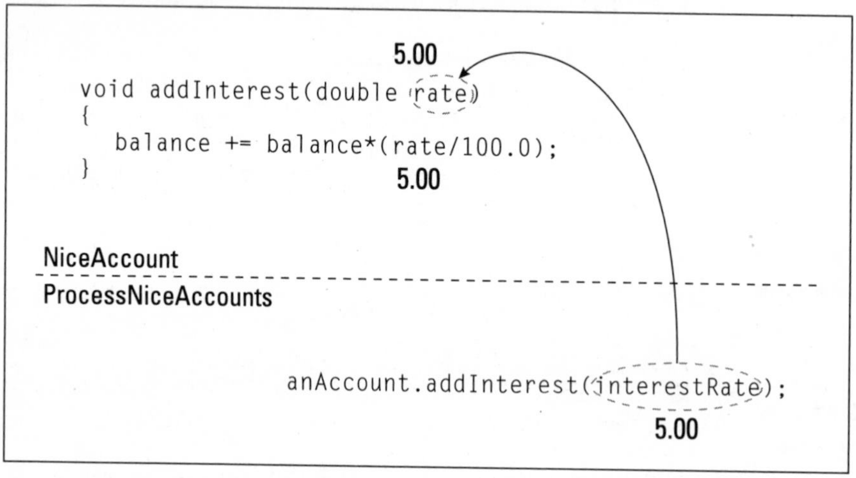

Figure 19-8:
Passing a value to a method's parameter.

Here's something interesting. The parameter in the method's header is rate. But, inside the ProcessNiceAccounts class, the parameter in the method call is interestRate. That's okay. In fact, it's standard practice.

In Listings 19-6 and 19-7, the names of the parameters don't have to be the same. The only thing that matters is that both parameters (rate and interestRate) have the same type. In Listings 19-6 and 19-7, both of these parameters are of type double. So everything is fine.

Working with a method header

In the next few bullets, I make some observations about the `addInterest` method header (in Listing 19-6):

✔ **The word** `void` **tells the computer that, when the** `addInterest` **method is called, the** `addInterest` **method doesn't send a value back to the place that called it.**

  The next section has an example in which a method sends a value back.

✔ **The word** `addInterest` **is the method's name.**

  That's the name you use to call the method when you're writing the code for the `ProcessNiceAccounts` class. (See Listing 19-7.)

✔ **The parentheses in the header contain placeholders for all the things you're going to pass to the method when you call it.**

  When you call a method, you can pass information to that method on the fly. This information is the method's parameter list. The `add Interest` method's header says that the `addInterest` method takes one piece of information and that piece of information must be of type `double`:

```
void addInterest(double rate)
```

  Sure enough, if you look at the call to `addInterest` (down in the `ProcessNiceAccounts` class's `main` method), that call has the variable `interestRate` in it. And `interestRate` is of type `double`. When I call `getInterest`, I'm giving the method a value of type `double`.

How the method uses the object's values

The `addInterest` method in Listing 19-6 is called three times from the `main` method in Listing 19-7. The actual account balances and interest rates are different each time:

✔ **In the first call, the** `balance` **is 25.00 and the interest rate is 5.00.**

  When this call is made, the expression `balance*(rate/100.0)` stands for 25.00*(5.00/100.00). See Figure 19-9.

✔ **In the second call, the balance is 131.00 and the interest rate is 10.00.**

  When the call is made, the expression `balance*(rate/100.0)` stands for 131.00*(10.00/100.00). Again, see Figure 19-9.

✔ **In the third call, the balance is 12.00 and the interest rate is 7.00.**

  When the `addInterest` call is made, the expression `balance*(rate/100.0)` stands for 12.00*(7.00/100.00).

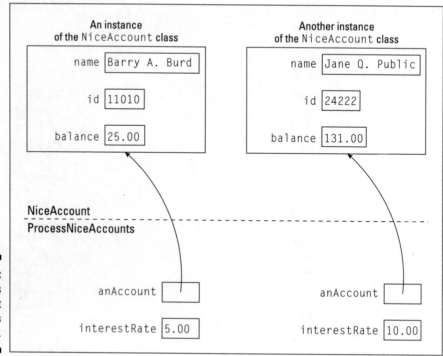

Figure 19-9:
Barry's
account
and Jane's
account.

Getting a Value from a Method

The last section had a story about sending a friend to buy groceries. I revisit that scenario in this section to see what treasures it holds.

You make requests for groceries in the form of method calls. You issue calls such as

```
goToTheSupermarketAndBuySome(bread);
goToTheSupermarketAndBuySome(bananas);
```

The things in parentheses are parameters. Each time you call your goToTheSupermarketAndBuySome method, you put a different value in the method's parameter list.

Now what happens when your friend returns from the supermarket? "Here's the bread you asked me to buy," says your friend. As a result of carrying out your wishes, your friend returns something to you. You made a method call, and the method returns information (or better yet, the method returns some food).

The thing returned to you is called the method's *return value,* and the type of thing returned to you is called the method's *return type.*

An example

To see how return values and a return types work in a real Java program, check out the code in Listings 19-8 and 19-9.

Listing 19-8   A Method That Returns a Value

```java
class GoodAccount
{
    String name;
    int id;
    double balance;


    double getInterest(double rate)
    {
        double interest;
        interest = balance*(rate/100.0);
        return interest;
    }


    void display()
    {
        System.out.print("The account with name ");
        System.out.print(name);
        System.out.print(" and id ");
        System.out.print(id);
        System.out.print(" has balance $");
        System.out.println(balance);
    }
}
```

Listing 19-9   Calling the Method in Listing 19-8

```java
class ProcessGoodAccounts
{
    public static void main(String args[])
    {
        GoodAccount anAccount;
        double interestRate;
        double yearlyInterest;

        for (int i=0; i<3; i++)
        {
```

(continued)

Listing 19-9 *(continued)*

```
        anAccount = new GoodAccount();
        anAccount.name =
            DummiesIO.getString("bankData.txt") +
            " " + DummiesIO.getString("bankData.txt") +
            " " + DummiesIO.getString("bankData.txt");

        anAccount.id =
            DummiesIO.getInt("bankData.txt");
        anAccount.balance =
            DummiesIO.getDouble("bankData.txt");

        anAccount.display();

        interestRate =
            DummiesIO.getDouble("bankData.txt");
        yearlyInterest =
            anAccount.getInterest(interestRate);

        System.out.print("This year's interest is ");
        System.out.println(yearlyInterest);
        System.out.println();
    }
  }
}
```

To see a run of code from Listings 19-8 and 19-9, take a look at Figure 19-10. The run in that figure uses the data from Figure 19-7.

Figure 19-10:
I want
my one
hundred-
trillionth
of a cent!

```
C:\JavaPrograms>java ProcessGoodAccounts
The account with name Barry A. Burd and id 11010 has balance $25.0
This year's interest is 1.25

The account with name Jane Q. Public and id 24222 has balance $131.0
This year's interest is 13.100000000000001

The account with name Harold J. Wexler and id 88899 has balance $12.0
This year's interest is 0.8400000000000001
```

The rates and balances in Figure 19-10 look ugly, but at least they're accurate. To make the rates and balances look nicer, check the section on formatting numbers in Chapter 18.

How return types and return values work

I want to trace a piece of the action in Listings 19-8 and 19-9. So for input data, I use the first line of values in Figure 19-7.

Here's what happens when getInterest is called (you can follow along in Figure 19-11):

- ✔ The value of balance is 25.00, and the value of rate is 5.00. So the value of balance*(rate/100.0) is 1.25 — a dollar and twenty-five cents.

- ✔ The value 1.25 gets assigned to the interest variable, so the statement

```
return interest;
```

has the same effect as

```
return 1.25;
```

- ✔ The return statement sends this value 1.25 back to the code that called the method. *At that point in the process, the entire method call in Listing 19-9 —* anAccount.getInterest(interestRate) *— takes on the value 1.25.*

- ✔ Finally, the value 1.25 gets assigned to the variable yearlyInterest.

```
double getInterest(double rate)
{
    double interest;

        1.25
    interest = balance*(rate/100.0);
    return interest;
}                     1.25


GoodAccount
ProcessGoodAccounts


    yearlyInterest = anAccount.getInterest(interestRate);
                                                    1.25
```

Figure 19-11: A method call is an expression with a value.

If a method returns anything, then a call to the method is an expression with a value. That value can be printed, assigned to a variable, added to something else, or whatever. Anything you can do with any other kind of value, you can do with a method call.

Working with the method header (again)

When you create a method or a method call, you have to be careful to use Java's types consistently. So make sure you check for the following:

✔ In Listing 19-8, the getInterest method's header starts with the word double. So when the method is executed, it should send a double value back to the place that called it.

✔ Again in Listing 19-8, the last statement in the getInterest method is return interest. So the method returns whatever value is stored in the interest variable, and the interest variable has type double. So far, so good.

✔ In Listing 19-9, the value returned by the call to getInterest is assigned to a variable named yearlyInterest. Sure enough, yearlyInterest is of type double.

That settles it! The use of types in the handling of method getInterest is consistent in Listings 19-8 and 19-9. I'm thrilled!

Chapter 20

Oooey GUI Was a Worm

. . . .

. . . .

There's a wonderful old joke about a circus acrobat jumping over mice. Unfortunately, I'd get sued for copyright infringement if I included the joke in this book.

Anyway, the joke is about starting small and working your way up to bigger things. That's what you do when you read *Beginning Programming with Java For Dummies*.

Most of the programs in this book are text-based. A *text-based* program has no windows, no dialog boxes, nothing of that kind. With a text-based program, the user types characters in the command prompt window, and the program displays output in the same command prompt window.

These days, very few publicly available programs are text-based. Almost all programs use a *GUI* — a *Graphical User Interface*. So if you've read every word of this book up to now, you're probably saying to yourself, "When am I going to find out how to create a GUI?"

I'm sorry, Skipper. Unless you use an integrated development environment, a Java program with a GUI takes some muscle to write. The code itself isn't long or ponderous. What's difficult is understanding how the code works.

So with these inspiring words of discouragement, please march ahead anyway. This chapter gives you a glimpse of the world of GUI programming in Java.

The Java Swing Classes

Java's *Swing* classes create graphical objects on a computer screen. The objects can include buttons, icons, text fields, check boxes, and other good things that make windows so useful.

The name "Swing" isn't an acronym. When the people at Sun Microsystems were first creating the code for these classes, one of the developers named it "Swing" because swing music was enjoying a nostalgic revival. And yes, in addition to `String` and `Swing`, the standard Java API has a `Spring` class. But that's another story.

Actually, Java's API has several sets of windowing components. An older set is called *AWT* — the *Abstract Windowing Toolkit*. The newer alternative is named *Swing*. Both AWT and Swing are part of a bigger cluster called *JFC* — the *Java Foundation Classes*.

Swing versus AWT

Here's a quick comparison of AWT and Swing (along with some interesting facts about both):

✔ When you create an AWT window, Java calls on your computer's operating system. Then the operating system spawns one of its own windows. For instance, if you're running Linux, then the Java Virtual Machine says, "Linux, please pop up a window of size 200 x 300." And Linux does it.

✔ To create a Swing window, Java draws the window on your computer screen. The underlying operating system thinks this is just a screen drawing of some kind.

✔ Because the AWT takes advantage of your operating system's built-in commands, the AWT classes run faster.

✔ Because Swing doesn't rely so much on your operating system's commands, Swing components are more portable. They run more or less the same way on Linux, Windows, Macs, or whatever. In fact, you can use Swing in Windows to create dialog boxes that have the Unix look and feel. How cute!

✔ Because Swing doesn't rely so much on your operating system's commands, Swing components are more versatile. For instance, a Swing button can have an icon on its face; an AWT button cannot.

✔ You can often tell when something is a Swing class by the thing's name. For example, the AWT has a class called `Frame` and Swing has a class called `JFrame`. The AWT has a class called `Button` and Swing has a class called `JButton`. Put a J in front of an AWT name, and you often get a Swing name.

Swing is called "lightweight" because its code uses less Windows, less Unix, less Mac, and more pure Java. But to use some of the Swing classes, you have to call on some of the old AWT classes. Go figure!

Showing an image on the screen

The program in Listing 20-1 displays a window on your computer screen. To see the window, look at Figure 20-1.

Listing 20-1   Creating a Window with an Image in It

```java
import javax.swing.*;
import java.awt.*;

class ShowPicture
{
    public static void main(String args[])
    {
        JFrame frame = new JFrame();
        ImageIcon icon = new ImageIcon("J2FD.jpg");
        JLabel label = new JLabel(icon);
        Container contentPane = frame.getContentPane();
        contentPane.add(label);
        frame.pack();
        frame.show();
    }
}
```

Figure 20-1:
What a nice
window!

The code in Listing 20-1 has very little logic of its own. Instead, this code pulls together a bunch of classes from the Java API.

Back in Listing 17-3, I create an instance of the Purchase class with the line

```java
Purchase onePurchase = new Purchase();
```

So in Listing 20-1, I do the same kind of thing. I create instances of the JFrame, ImageIcon, and JLabel classes with the following lines:

```
JFrame frame = new JFrame();
ImageIcon icon = new ImageIcon("J2FD.jpg");
JLabel label = new JLabel(icon);
```

Here's some gossip about each of these lines:

- A JFrame is like a window (except that it's called a JFrame, not a "window"). In Listing 20-1, the line

  ```
  JFrame frame = new JFrame();
  ```

  creates a JFrame object, but this line doesn't display the JFrame object anywhere. (The displaying comes later in the code.)

- An ImageIcon object is a picture. In my JavaPrograms directory, I have a file named J2FD.jpg. That file contains the picture shown in Figure 20-1. So in Listing 20-1, the line

  ```
  ImageIcon icon = new ImageIcon("J2FD.jpg");
  ```

  creates an ImageIcon object — an icon containing the J2FD.jpg picture.

- I need a place to put the icon. I can put it on something called a JLabel. So in Listing 20-1, the line

  ```
  JLabel label = new JLabel(icon);
  ```

  creates a JLabel object and puts the J2FD.jpg icon on the new label's face.

If you read the bullets above, you may get a false impression. The wording may suggest that the use of each component (JFrame, ImageIcon, JLabel, and so on) is a logical extension of what you already know. "Where do you put an ImageIcon? Well of course, you put it on a JLabel." When you've worked long and hard with Java's Swing components, all these things become natural to you. But until then, writing GUI code takes hours of trial and error (along with many hours of reading the API documentation).

You never need to memorize the names or features of Java's API classes. Instead, you keep Java's API documentation handy. When you need to know about a class, you look it up in the documentation. If you need a certain class often enough, you'll remember its features. For classes that you don't use often, you always have the docs.

For tips on using Java's API documentation, see this book's Appendix. To find gobs of sample Java code, visit some of the Web sites listed in Chapter 21.

Just another class

What is a JFrame? Like any other class, a JFrame has several parts. For a simplified view of some of these parts, see Figure 20-2. Like the String in

Figure 18-6 in Chapter 18, each object formed from the `JFrame` class has both data parts and method parts. For technical reasons too burdensome for this book, you can't use dots to refer to a frame's height or width. But you can call the methods in Figure 20-2 with those infamous dots. In Listing 20-1, I call the frame's methods by writing `frame.getContentPane()`, `frame.pack()`, and `frame.show()`.

JFrame

height	width	getContentPane	pack	show
153	116	(method for getting a content pane; that is, for getting a container)	(method to shrink wrap the frame)	(method to make the frame visible)

Container

components	add
label	(method to put stuff into the container)

Figure 20-2:
A simplified depiction of the JFrame and Container classes.

Here's the scoop on the three `JFrame` methods:

- You can't put an icon directly onto a `JFrame` object. In fact, you can't put a button, a text field, or anything else like that onto a `JFrame` object. Instead, you have to grab something called a *content pane,* and then put these widgets onto the content pane.

  In Listing 20-1, the call to `frame.getContentPane` grabs a content pane. Then the call `contentPane.add(label)` plops the label onto the pane. It seems tedious but, when you work with the Java Swing classes, you have to call all these methods.

- A frame's `pack` method shrink-wraps the frame around whatever has been added to the frame's content pane. Without calling `pack`, the frame can be much bigger or much smaller than is necessary.

  Unfortunately, the default is to make a frame much smaller than necessary. If, in Listing 20-1, you forget to call `frame.pack`, you get the tiny frame shown in Figure 20-3. Sure, you can enlarge the frame by dragging the frame's edges with your mouse. But why should you have to do that? Just call `frame.pack` instead.

✔ A frame's `show` method makes the frame appear on your screen. If you forget to call `show` (and I often do), when you run the code in Listing 20-1, you'll see nothing on your screen. It's always so disconcerting until you figure out what you did wrong.

What I call a "content pane" is really an instance of Java's `Container` class, and each `Container` instance has its own `add` method. (Refer to Figure 20-2.) That's why the call to `contentPane.add(label)` in Listing 20-1 puts the thing that holds the `J2FD.jpg` picture into the content pane.

Figure 20-3:
A frame that
hasn't been
packed.

Keeping the User Busy (Working with Buttons and Text Fields)

Without an integrated development environment, it takes some muscle to create a high-powered GUI program. First, you create a frame with buttons and other widgets. Then you write extra methods to respond to keystrokes, button clicks, and other such things.

In this book, I shy away from such methods. The next section contains some "take-my-word-for-it" code to respond to a user's button clicks. But in this section, the example simply displays a button and a text field. The code is in Listing 20-2, and two views of the code's frame are shown in Figures 20-4 and 20-5.

Listing 20-2   Adding Components to a Frame

```
import javax.swing.*;
import java.awt.*;

class MyLittleGUI
{
    public static void main(String args[])
    {
        JFrame frame;
        Container contentPane;
        JTextField textfield;
        JButton button;
        FlowLayout layout;
        String sorry;
```

```
        frame = new JFrame();
        frame.setTitle("Interact");

        contentPane = frame.getContentPane();

        textfield = new JTextField("Type your text here.");

        sorry = "This button is temporarily out of order.";
        button = new JButton(sorry);

        contentPane.add(textfield);
        contentPane.add(button);
        layout = new FlowLayout();
        contentPane.setLayout(layout);

        frame.pack();
        frame.show();
    }
}
```

Figure 20-4:
The frame in
Listing 20-2.

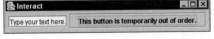

Figure 20-5:
The frame in
Listing 20-2
with the
button
pressed.

As with other programs that use classes from Java's API, Listing 20-2 comes with my litany of descriptions and explanations of the class' features. One way or another, it's all the same story. Each object has its own data and its own methods. To refer to an object's data or methods, use a dot. And to find out more about an object's data or methods, use Java's API documentation.

✔ Each frame (that is, each instance of the JFrame class) has a setTitle method. If you want, get a pencil and add a setTitle column to the JFrame table in Figure 20-2.

In Listing 20-2, I make the frame's title be the word Interact (as if interacting with this frame makes anything useful happen). You can see Interact in the frame's title bar in Figures 20-4 and 20-5.

✔ The JTextField class describes those long white boxes, like the box containing the words Type your text here in Figures 20-4 and 20-5. In Listing 20-2, I create a new text field (an instance of the JTextField class), and I add this new text field to the frame's content pane.

When you run the code in Listing 20-2, you can type stuff into the text field. But, because I haven't written any code to respond to the typing of text, nothing happens when you type. *C'est la vie.*

✔ The JButton class describes those clickable things, like the thing containing the words This button is temporarily out of order in Figures 20-4 and 20-5. In Listing 20-2, I create a new button (an instance of the JButton class), and I add this new button to the frame's content pane.

When you run the code in Listing 20-2, you can click the button all you want. Because I haven't written any code to respond to the clicking, nothing happens when you click the button. For a program that responds to button clicks, see the next section.

✔ Each Java container has a setLayout method. A call to this method ensures that the doohickeys on the frame are arranged in a certain way.

In Listing 20-2, I feed a FlowLayout object to the setLayout method. This FlowLayout business arranges the text field and the button one right after another (as in Figures 20-4 and 20-5).

For descriptions of some other things that are going on in Listing 20-2, see the "Showing an image on the screen" section, earlier in this chapter.

Taking Action

The previous section's code leaves me feeling a little empty. When you click the button, nothing happens. When you type in the text field, nothing happens. What a waste!

To make me feel better, I include one more program in this chapter. The program in Listing 20-3 responds to a button click. When you click the frame's button, any text in the text field becomes all uppercase. That's very nice, but the code is quite complicated. In fact, the code has so many advanced features that I can't fully describe them in the space that I'm allotted. So you may have to trust me (and trust Listing 20-3).

Listing 20-3   Responding to Button Clicks

```
import javax.swing.*;
import java.awt.*;
import java.awt.event.*;
```

```
class CapitalizeMe
{

   public static void main(String args[])
   {
      JFrame frame;
      Container contentPane;
      JTextField textfield;
      JButton button;
      FlowLayout layout;

      frame = new JFrame();
      frame.setTitle("Handy Capitalization Service");

      contentPane = frame.getContentPane();

      textfield =
         new JTextField("Type your text here.", 20);

      button = new JButton("Capitalize");
      button.addActionListener
         (new MyActionListener(textfield));

      contentPane.add(textfield);
      contentPane.add(button);
      layout = new FlowLayout();
      contentPane.setLayout(layout);

      frame.pack();
      frame.show();
   }
}


class MyActionListener implements ActionListener
{
   JTextField textfield;

   MyActionListener (JTextField textfield)
   {
      this.textfield=textfield;
   }

   public void actionPerformed (ActionEvent e)
   {
      textfield.setText
         (textfield.getText().toUpperCase());
   }
}
```

You can run the code in Listing 20-3. If you do, you see something like the
screen shots in Figures 20-6, 20-7, and 20-8. To get you started reading the
code, I include a few hints about the code's features:

✔ Java's API has a package named `java.awt.event`, which includes things like `ActionListener` and `ActionEvent`. Oddly enough, importing `java.awt.*` (on the second line in Listing 20-3) doesn't entitle you to abbreviate names from the `java.awt.event` package. To abbreviate these names, you need the additional `import java.awt.event.*` declaration.

✔ Calling `new JTextField("Type your text here.", 20)` creates a text field containing the words `Type your text here`. To allow more space for the user's typing, the new text field is 20 characters wide.

✔ The clicking of a button is called an *action event*. The call to `button.addActionListener` tells the Java Virtual Machine to make an announcement whenever the user clicks the button. The JVM announces the action to the code at the bottom of the listing.

✔ The JVM's "announcement" fires up the `actionPerformed` method, which in turn makes a call to the `toUpperCase` method. That's how the letters in the text field become uppercase letters.

Want to read more? I have a whole chapter about it in *Java 2 For Dummies* (written by yours truly and published by Wiley Publishing, Inc.).

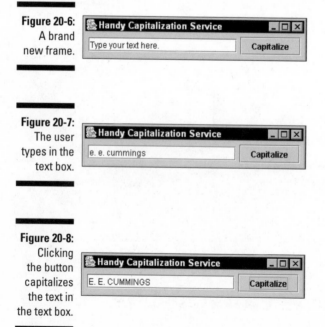

Figure 20-6:
A brand
new frame.

Figure 20-7:
The user
types in the
text box.

Figure 20-8:
Clicking
the button
capitalizes
the text in
the text box.

Part V

The Part of Tens

"Before I go on to explain more advanced procedures like the 'Zap-Rowdy-Students-who-Don't-Pay-Attention' function, we'll begin with some basics."

In this part . . .

Y
ou're near the end of the book, and it's time to sum it all up. This part of the book is your slam-bam two-thousand-words-or-less resource for Java. What? You didn't read every word in the chapters before this one? That's okay. You'll pick up a lot of useful information in this Part of Tens.

Chapter 21

Ten Sets of Web Links

*N*o wonder the Web is so popular: It's both useful and fun. This chapter has ten bundles of resources. Each bundle has Web sites for you to visit. Each Web site has resources to help you write programs more effectively.

The Horse's Mouth

Sun's official Web site for Java is `java.sun.com`. This site has all the latest development kits, and many of them are free. The site also has a great section with online tutorials and mini-courses. The tutorial/mini-course section's Web address is `developer.java.sun.com/developer/onlineTraining`.

Finding News, Reviews, and Sample Code

The Web has plenty of sites devoted exclusively to Java. Many of these sites feature reviews, links to other sites, and best of all, gobs of sample Java code. They may also offer free mailing lists that keep you informed of the latest Java developments. Here's a brief list of such sites:

✔ **Developer.com/Gamelan:** `www.developer.com/java`

✔ **JavaFile.com:** `www.javafile.com`

- ✔ **The Giant Java Tree:** `www.gjt.org`
- ✔ **The Java Boutique:** `javaboutique.internet.com`
- ✔ **FreewareJava.com:** `www.freewarejava.com`
- ✔ **JavaPowered:** `www.javapowered.com`
- ✔ **The JavaRanch:** `www.javaranch.com`
- ✔ **JavaToys:** `www.nikos.com/javatoys`
- ✔ **Java Shareware:** `www.javashareware.com`

Improving Your Code with Tutorials

To find out more about Java, you can visit Sun's online training pages. Some other nice sets of tutorials are available at the following Web sites:

- ✔ **Richard Baldwin's Web site:** `www.dickbaldwin.com/tocadv.htm`
- ✔ **IBM developerWorks:** `www-105.ibm.com/developerworks/education.nsf/dw/java-onlinecourse-bytitle`
- ✔ **ProgrammingTutorials.com:** `www.programmingtutorials.com`

Finding Help on Newsgroups

Have a roadblock you just can't get past? Try posting your question on an Internet newsgroup. Almost always, some friendly expert will post just the right reply.

With or without Java, you should definitely start exploring newsgroups. You can find thousands of newsgroups — groups on just about every conceivable topic. (Yes, there are more newsgroups than *For Dummies* titles!) To get started with newsgroups, visit `groups.google.com`. For postings specific to Java, look for the groups whose names begin with `comp.lang.java`. As a novice, you'll probably find the following three groups to be the most useful:

- ✔ `comp.lang.java.programmer`
- ✔ `comp.lang.java.help`
- ✔ `comp.lang.java.api`

Checking the FAQs for Useful Info

Has the acronym FAQ made it to Oxford English Dictionary yet? Everybody seems to be using FAQ as an ordinary English word. In case you don't already know, FAQ stands for *Frequently Asked Questions.* In reality, an FAQ should be called ATQTWTOSPOTN. This acronym stands for *Answers to Questions That We're Tired of Seeing Posted on This Newsgroup.*

You can find several FAQs at the official Sun Web site. You can also check out the FAQ for the `comp.lang.java` newsgroups that I discuss in the previous section. To read this wealth of information, go to `www.afu.com/javafaq.html`.

Opinions and Advocacy

Java isn't just techie stuff. The field has issues and opinions of all shapes and sizes. To find out more about them, visit `www.javalobby.org`. After you've hovered for a while and figured out the etiquette, you can even join the discussion.

Looking for Java Jobs

Are you looking for work? Would you like to have an exciting, lucrative career as a computer programmer? If so, check the SkillMarket at `mshiltonj.com/sm`. This site has statistics on the demand for various technology areas. The site compares languages, databases, certifications, and more. Best of all, the site is updated every day.

After you've checked all the SkillMarket numbers, try visiting a Web site designed specially for computer job seekers. Point your Web browser to `java.computerwork.com`.

Of course, it never hurts to mix and mingle. To hobnob and network with other Java professionals, visit `www.teamjava.com`. The site's mission is "... to promote and advance Java and assist Java consultants the world over in locating and completing contract work." Sounds good.

Becoming Certified in Java

These days, everybody is anxious to become certified. If you're one of these people, you can find plenty of resources about Java certification on the Web. Just start by visiting `www.jcert.org`. This site links to other interesting sites, including sites with practice certification exams.

Finding Out about Hot Technologies

The world of Java is constantly growing. When it started, Java programmers were big on applets. (An *applet* is a little Java program that you can include as part of a Web page.) Nowadays, applets are passé. Instead, people use things like Dynamic HTML and Flash animation to spice up their Web pages.

Currently, the hot acronyms in Java circles are J2EE and XML. (The letters J2EE stand for Java 2 Enterprise Edition, and the letters XML stand for Extensible Markup Language.)

For some relatively light reading on J2EE, visit `java.sun.com/j2ee/sdk_1.2.1/techdocs/guides/j2ee-overview/OverviewTOC.fm.html`. This site has a good hyperlinked document entitled, "What Is the Java™ 2 Platform, Enterprise Edition?" (It's not exactly light reading, but it's relatively light.)

To find out more about XML, visit `www.xml.org` and `xml.coverpages.org`.

Along with XML comes an emerging technology called *Web Services*. Some people in the know believe that, in the next few years, Web Services will change the way companies write and use software. To see some examples of Web Services, visit `www.xmethods.com` and `www.salcentral.com/salnet/webserviceswsdl.asp`.

Finding Out More about Other Programming Languages

It's always good to widen your view. So to find out more about some languages other than Java, visit the Éric Lévénez site: `www.levenez.com/lang`. This site includes a cool chart that traces the genealogy of the world's most popular programming languages. For other language lists, visit the following Web sites:

- **HyperNews:** `www.hypernews.org/HyperNews/get/computing/langlist.html`
- **Open Here!:** `www.openhere.com/tech1/programming/languages`
- **Steinar Knutsen's Language list page:** `home.nvg.org/~sk/lang/lang.html`

Finally, for quick information about anything related to computing, visit the `foldoc.doc.ic.ac.uk/foldoc` — the Free On-Line Dictionary of Computing.

Chapter 22

Ten Useful Classes in the Java API

In This Chapter
▶ Finding out more about some classes that are introduced earlier in this book
▶ Discovering some other helpful classes

I'm proud of myself. I've written around 400 pages about Java using less than twenty classes from the Java API. The standard API has about 2,700 classes, with at least 500 more in the very popular Enterprise Edition API. So I think I'm doing very well.

Anyway, to help acquaint you with some of my favorite Java API classes, this chapter contains a brief list. Some of the classes in this list appear in examples throughout this book. Others are so darn useful that I can't finish the book without including them.

For more information on the classes in this chapter, check Java's API documentation.

Applet

What Java book is complete without some mention of applets? An *applet* is a piece of code that runs inside a Web browser window. For instance, a small currency calculator running in a little rectangle on your Web page can be a piece of code written in Java.

At one time, Java applets were really hot stuff, but nowadays, people are much more interested in using Java for business processing. Anyway, if applets are your thing, then don't be shy. Check the Applet page of Java's API documentation.

Calendar

The Calendar class has some really nice methods. You can grab the current time and date from your system clock with the line Calendar now = Calendar.getInstance(). Then, if you display now.getTime(), you see something like Thu Feb 13 00:46:54 EST 2003. You can isolate things like the month or the day of the month with the calls now.get(Calendar.MONTH) and now.get(Calendar.DAY_OF_MONTH).

You can even travel forwards or backwards in time. For instance, to change now to what it was eighteen days ago, call now.add(Calendar.DATE, -18). This call changes what's stored in the now variable, but it doesn't change your system's clock. To change your system's clock, you need a statement like Runtime.getRuntime().exec("cmd /c time 08:19:00 A").

File

Talk about your useful Java classes! The File class does a bunch of the things that my DummiesIO class doesn't do. Method canRead tells you whether you can read from a file or not. Method canWrite tells you if you can write to a file. Calling method setReadOnly ensures that you can't accidentally write to a file. Method deleteOnExit erases a file, but not until your program stops running. Method exists checks to see if you have a particular file. Methods isHidden, lastModified, and length give you even more information about a file. You can even create a new directory by calling the mkdir method. Face it, this File class is powerful stuff!

Integer

Chapter 18 describes the Integer class and its parseInt method. The Integer class has lots of other features that come in handy when you work with int values. For example, Integer.MAX_VALUE stands for the number 2147483647. That's the largest value that an int variable can store. (Refer to Table 7-1 in Chapter 7.) The expression Integer.MIN_VALUE stands for the number -2147483648 (the smallest value that an int variable can store). A call to Integer.toBinaryString takes an int and returns its base 2 (binary) representation. And what Integer.toBinaryString does for base 2, Integer.toHexString does for base 16 (hexadecimal).

Math

Do you have any numbers to crunch? Do you use your computer to do exotic calculations? If so, try Java's Math class. (It's a piece of code, not a place to sit down and listen to lectures about algebra.) The Math class deals with π, *e*, logarithms, trig functions, square roots, and all those other mathematical things that give most people the creeps.

NumberFormat

Chapter 18 has a section about the NumberFormat.getCurrencyInstance method. With this method, you can turn 20.338500000000003 into $20.34. If the United States isn't your home, or if your company sells products worldwide, you can enhance your currency instance with a Java Locale. For example, with euro = NumberFormat.getCurrencyInstance(Locale. FRANCE), a call to euro.format(3) returns 3,00 € instead of $3.00.

The NumberFormat class also has methods for displaying things that aren't currency amounts. For instance, you can display a number with or without commas, with or without leading zeros, and with as many digits beyond the decimal point as you care to include.

String

Chapter 18 introduces Java's String class. The chapter describes (in gory detail) a method named equals. The String class has many other useful methods. For instance, with the length method, you find the number of characters in a string. With charAt, you can isolate a particular character within a string. And then there's replaceAll — one of my personal favorites. With replaceAll, you can easily change the phrase "my fault" to "your fault" wherever "my fault" appears inside a string.

StringTokenizer

I often need to chop strings into pieces. For instance, if you type 37 89 106, then my DummiesIO code has to send three separate numbers to your computer program. You hand me one big string (37 89 106), and I need three little strings — 37, 89, and 106.

Fortunately, the StringTokenizer class does this kind of grunt work. Using this class, you can separate 37 89 106 or 37, 89, 106 or even 37:89:106 into pieces. You can also treat each separator as valuable data, or you can ignore each separator as if it were trash. To do lots of interesting processing using strings, check out Java's StringTokenizer class.

System

You're probably familiar with System.out. It's a name for the command prompt window — the place where Java programs can display text. But what about System.getProperty? The getProperty method reveals all kinds of information about your computer. Some of the information you can find includes your operating system name, you processor's architecture, your Java Virtual Machine version, your classpath, your username, and whether your system uses a backslash or a forward slash to separate folder names from one another. Sure, you may already know all this stuff. But does your Java code need to discover it on the fly?

Vector

Chapter 16 introduces arrays. This is good stuff but, in any programming language, arrays have their limitations. For instance, take an array of size 100. If you suddenly need to store a 101st value, then you're plain out of luck. You can't change an array's size without rewriting some code. Inserting a value into an array is another problem. To squeeze "Tim" alphabetically between "Thom" and "Tom", you may have to make room by moving thousands of "Tyler", "Uriah", and "Victor" names.

But Java has a Vector class. A vector is like an array, except that vectors grow and shrink as needed. You can also insert new values without pain using a vector's insertElementAt method. Vectors are useful, because they do all kinds of nice things that arrays can't do.

Chapter 23

Ten Error Messages (And What to Do about Them)

In This Chapter

▶ Reading between an error message's lines

▶ Taking action when an error occurs

*W*hat could be worse than a chapter full of scary headings? You can keep headings like "The Monster That Ate Cleveland," or "The Body of Doctor Bloodletter." These headings don't scare me.

The things that scare me are the headings in this chapter — headings like "Cannot Resolve Symbol" and "NoClassDefFoundError." Fortunately, each heading in this chapter is followed by some helpful, calming advice — advice to help you solve the problem when you see one of these messages.

NoClassDefFoundError

You get this error when you're trying to run your code. So first ask yourself, did you attempt to compile the code? If so, did you see any error messages when you compiled? If you saw error messages, look for things you can fix in your .java file. Try to fix these things, and then compile the .java file again.

If you normally keep code in the JavaPrograms directory, make sure that you're still working in this JavaPrograms directory. (In Windows, make sure that the command prompt says JavaPrograms.)

Make sure you have an appropriately named .class file in your working directory. For instance, if you're trying to run a program named MyGreatProg, look for a file named MyGreatProg.class in your working directory.

Check your classpath to make sure that it contains the `.class` file that you need. For instance, if all your Java code is in your working directory, make sure that the classpath includes a dot.

NoSuchMethodError

When you encounter this error message, check for the misspelling or inconsistent capitalization of a method name. Check the capitalization of `main` (not `Main`).

When you issue the `java` command (or do whatever you normally do to run a program in your environment), does the class that you're trying to run contain its own `main` method? If not, then find the class with the `main` method and run that class instead.

Cannot Resolve Symbol

If you get an error message that includes `cannot resolve symbol`, check the spelling and capitalization of all identifiers and keywords. Then check again. (I always tend to miss these things the first few times I check.)

If the unresolved symbol is a variable, make sure that this variable's declaration is in the right place. For instance, if the variable is declared in a `for` loop's initialization, are you trying to use that variable outside the `for` loop? If the variable is declared inside a block (a pair of curly braces), are you trying to use that variable outside of the block?

Finally, look for errors in the variable's declaration. If the compiler finds errors in a variable's declaration, then the compiler can't resolve that variable name in the remainder of the code.

Expected ';' (Or Expected Something Else)

When you see an error message that says `';' expected`, go through your code and make sure that each statement and each declaration ends with a semicolon. If so, then maybe the compiler's guess about a missing semicolon is incorrect. Fixing another (seemingly unrelated) error and recompiling your code may get rid of a bogus `';' expected` message.

For a missing parenthesis, check the conditions of if statements and loops. Make sure each condition is enclosed in parentheses. Also, make sure that a parameter list (enclosed in parentheses) follows the name of each method.

For an <identifier> expected message, check your assignment statements. Make sure that each assignment statement is inside a method. (Remember, a declaration with an initialization can be outside of a method, but each plain old assignment statement must be inside a method.)

For the 'class' or 'interface' expected message, make sure you've spelled the word class correctly. If your code has an import declaration, check the spelling and capitalization of the word import.

Missing Method Body or Declare Abstract

You get a missing method body or declare abstract message when the compiler sees a method header, but the compiler can't find the method's body. Look at the end of the method's header. If you ended the header with a semicolon, then try removing the semicolon.

If the header doesn't end with a semicolon, then check the code immediately following the header. The code immediately following the header should start with an open curly brace (the beginning of a method body). If some code comes between the header and the body's open curly brace, consider moving that code somewhere else.

An 'else' without an 'if'

Compare the number of if clauses with the number of else clauses. An if clause doesn't need to have an else clause, but each else clause must belong to an if clause.

Remember, you enclose an if condition in parentheses, but you don't put a semicolon after the condition. Did you mistakenly end an if condition with a semicolon?

Look at all the lines between an if and its else. When you find more than one statement between an if and its else, look for curly braces. If the statements between the if and its else aren't surrounded by curly braces, you may have found the culprit.

Variable Might Not Have Been Initialized

If you see a message saying `variable might not have been initialized`, look for statements that use the values of variables. For instance, statements like `numberOfDonkeys++`, `numberOfDonkeys=numberOfDonkeys+1`, and `System.out.print(numberOfDonkeys)` use the `numberOfDonkeys` variable's value. Make sure that somewhere in your code (somewhere before any of the statements that use the variable's value) there's a statement that initializes the variable or assigns the variable a value.

When a variable's assignment statement is inside an `if` statement, the compiler may warn you about the variable's value not being initialized. (The compiler worries that the assignment statement can be bypassed.) The easiest (and often the best) thing to do is to decide what value the variable should have when the program starts running. Then add an initialization with that value to the variable's declaration.

Non-static Variable Cannot Be Referenced from a Static Context

Lots of things can give you a `non-static variable cannot be referenced from a static context` error message. But for beginning programmers, the most common cause is having a variable that's declared outside of the `main` method. It's no sin to declare such a variable, but because the `main` method is always `static`, you need some special help to make the `main` method refer to a variable that's declared outside the `main` method.

The quickest solution is to put the word `static` in front of the variable's declaration. But first, ask yourself why this variable's declaration isn't inside the `main` method. If there's no good reason, then move the variable's declaration so that it's inside the `main` method.

NumberFormatException

Are you using `Integer.parseInt`? If so, maybe the string in the method's parameter list doesn't look like an `int` value. For instance, calling `Integer.parseInt("77")` is okay, but calling `Integer.parseInt("Howdy")` is not.

For a call like `Integer.parseInt(myString)`, make sure the `myString` variable's value looks like an `int` value.

For a call like `Integer.parseInt(DummiesIO.getString())`, make sure that the value you type on the keyboard looks like an `int` value.

FileNotFoundException (The System Cannot Find the File Specified) or EOFException

If you encounter a `FileNotFoundException` message, check that the file named in your code actually exists. (Look for the file using your system's explorer or using the command prompt window.) Double-check the spelling in your code against the name of the file on your hard drive.

If you've found a correctly named file on your hard drive, make sure that the file is in the correct directory. (For a program running in your working directory, a typical data file is in the working directory also.)

If you're a Windows user, make sure that the system didn't add an extra `.txt` extension when you created the file. (Use the command prompt window to check the file's name. Windows Explorer can hide the `.txt` extension, and that always leads to confusion.)

For an `EOFException`, you're probably trying to read more data than you have in the file. Very often, a small logic error makes your program do this. So do a careful review of all the steps in your program's execution. Look for subtle things, like improperly primed loops or the reading of array values past the array's largest index. Look for conditions that use <= when they should use <. Conditions like these can often be troublesome.

Appendix

Reading and Understanding Java's API Documentation

· ·

In This Appendix

▶ Using the index to search for information

▶ Using the class list to search for information

▶ Transferring and reusing your documentation-reading skills

· ·

*B*efore Java was born, people judged programming languages solely by their structural features. Does an if statement do what you expect it to do? Are looping statements easy to use? Are methods implemented efficiently?

With Java, things are a bit different. Sure, Java has a whole collection of built-in language features. But Java is much more than just a big set of grammar rules. Java has a standard Application Programming Interface — a huge library consisting of at least 2,700 canned programs, each with its own functionality, its own limitations, and its own rules for effective use.

How do you figure out how to use all these programs? The answer is, you don't. You figure out how to use a few, and you read Java's API documentation. With this documentation, you can find information you need, when you need it.

Searching for a Term

You can find things in the API documentation in a number of different ways. Each way is convenient in one situation or another. For instance, in many of this book's listings, I call a method named System.out.println. The rest of this appendix describes two ways to look up the System.out.println method.

Using the index

Here's how to find something, such as `System.out.println`, by using the index:

1. **Download Sun's Java API documentation.**

   For more help on downloading the documentation, see Chapter 2.

2. **Open to the front page of the documentation.**

   When you download the documentation, you get several directories. In the top-level directory is a file named `index.html` (or `index.htm`). Open this file in your Web browser.

3. **Click the <u>API & Language</u> link, which is near the top of the front page, as shown in Figure A-1.**

   This takes you farther down on the same Web page.

Figure A-1: The front page of Sun's documentation.

Copyright 1993-2002 Sun Microsystems, Inc. Reprinted with permission.

4. **Click the <u>Java 2 Platform API Specification</u> link, as shown in Figure A-2.**

   The browser transports you to the start of the API pages, which are shown in Figure A-3.

Figure A-2: A link to the API specification.

API & Language Documentation

Java 2 Platform API Specification (NO FRAMES)   *docs*

Note About sun.* Packages   *website*

Copyright 1993-2002 Sun Microsystems, Inc. Reprinted with permission.

5. **Click the <u>Index</u> link at the top of the page to open the index, as shown in Figure A-4.**

A list of letters is near the top of the index. Click the P link to go to the section with `println` in it.

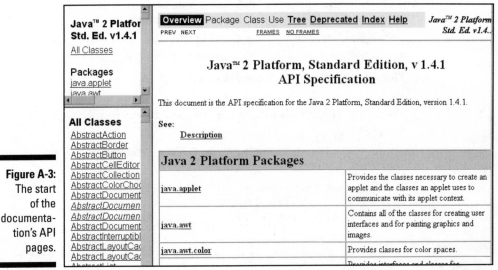

Figure A-3:
The start
of the
documenta-
tion's API
pages.

Copyright 1993-2002 Sun Microsystems, Inc. Reprinted with permission.

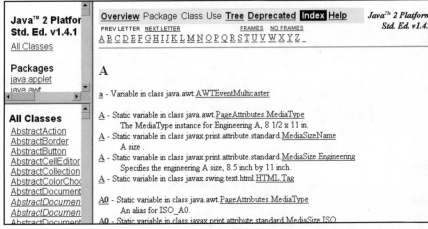

Figure A-4:
The API
documenta-
tion's index.

Copyright 1993-2002 Sun Microsystems, Inc. Reprinted with permission.

6. In the P section, do a search for `println` to find the `println` entries.

Most Web browsers enable you to search for something like `println` in the text of a page. Here's how:

A. Make sure the browser knows that you want to search in the big frame that takes up most of the page (and not in the smaller frames on the left side of the page). To do this, click your mouse inside the big frame. (Don't click a link. Click on some neutral white area of the frame.)

B. Open the browser's Find dialog box. On most browsers, pressing Ctrl+F coaxes the Find dialog box out of hiding.

C. When you see the Find dialog box, type **println** in the text box and click the box's Find or Find Next button.

7. **Pick one of the** `println` **entries.**

The P section has a big boatload of `println` entries, as shown in Figure A-5. The entries differ from one another in two ways:

- Each entry says `println(int)`, `println(String)`, or `println(someOtherTypeName)`. The type name can differ from one entry to another.

- Each entry says that `println` is a method in class `java.someStuff.someMoreStuff`. The class can differ from one entry to another.

Figure A-5: Some println entries in the API documentation's index.

At this point, it pays to poke around. If you're trying to print something like "Hello world!", you want one of the println(String) entries. On the other hand, if you're trying to print the value of amountInAccount, you'll probably choose a println(double) entry.

Now, suppose you've decided on println(String). You can choose from three println(String) entries. One says it's a method in class java.io.PrintStream, the next is a method in class java.io.PrintWriter, and the third is a method in class java.sql.DriverManager. Which of these three entries do you choose?

Well, what you're really trying to call is something named System.out.println. If you go through the whole lookup rigmarole with System.out, you'll find that System.out has type PrintStream. (See Figure A-6.) So the entry you decide to choose is println(String) - Method in class java.io.PrintStream.

Figure A-6: The out variable has type PrintStream.

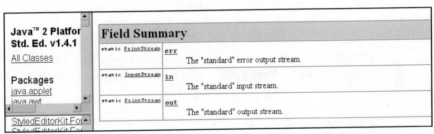

Copyright 1993-2002 Sun Microsystems, Inc. Reprinted with permission.

8. Click the link for the entry that you've chosen.

When you click the <u>println(String)</u> link, the browser takes you to a page that explains a println method, as shown in Figure A-7. The page tells you what println does ("Print a String and then. . . .") and points to other useful pages, like the page with the documentation for String.

Figure A-7: A description of the println method.

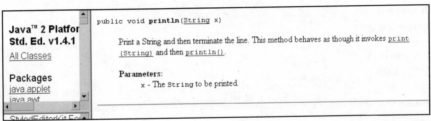

Copyright 1993-2002 Sun Microsystems, Inc. Reprinted with permission.

Using the list of classes

Here's how to find an entry in the API by starting in the list of classes:

1. **Navigate to the start of the documentation's API pages.**

   To do this, follow the first four steps in this appendix's "Using the index" section.

2. **Find the page that documents the** `System` **class.**

   You're looking for documentation that explains `System.out.println`. So you look up `System`, work your way to `out`, and from there, work your way to `println`.

   To find a link to `System`, look in the lower frame on the left side of the page. (See Figure A-8.) For hints on finding text on the page, see Step 6 in the "Using the index" section.

   Clicking the <u>System</u> link makes your browser display the documentation page for the `System` class, as shown in Figure A-9.

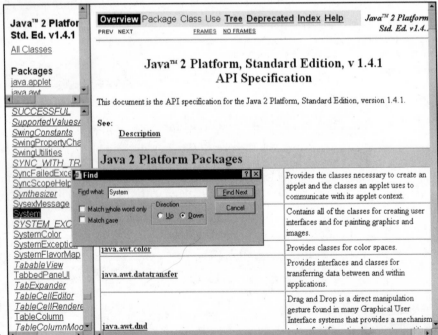

Figure A-8:
Finding a
link to the
System
class.

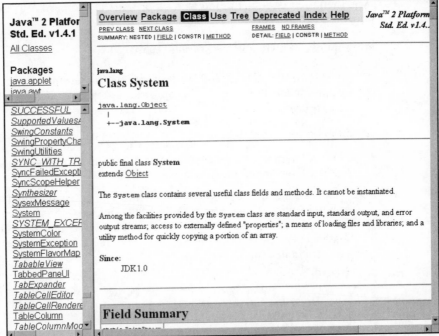

Figure A-9:
The System
class's
documenta-
tion.

3. **On the documentation page for the** System **class, find the** out **variable.**

   If you use your Web browser's Find dialog box, you have to click the Find Next button several times. (The word "out" is so common, it appears several times in several different contexts on the System documentation page.) When you've found what you're looking for, you see a table like the one shown in Figure A-6.

4. **In the table's** out **row, click the** __PrintStream__ **link.**

   According to the documentation, the out variable refers to an object of type PrintStream. This means that println is part of the PrintStream class. That's why you're clicking the PrintStream link.

5. **On the documentation page for** PrintStream, **find** println(String).

   You see an explanation like the one shown in Figure A-7.

You Can Do It Too

After following the steps in this appendix, you may be tempted to say, "Big deal, I can find println in the API docs, but I probably can't find anything else. And if people create documentation for stuff that they program on their own, then their documentation won't look like the standard API documentation. I'll be up a creek."

My response to all this is "Nonsense!" Here's why:

- ✔ Most of the tricks you need for finding things in the standard Java documentation are illustrated in this appendix's step-by-step instructions. If you can find `System.out.println`, you can also find `javax.swing.JButton` or any of the 2,700 programs in the standard Java API.

  And, as you discover more about Java and the relationships among classes, methods, and variables, this appendix's step-by-step instructions will feel much more natural.

- ✔ As for reading other people's documentation, you can scratch that problem right off your list. The standard API docs weren't typed by hand. They were generated automatically from actual Java program code. For instance, the code for `PrintStream.java` has a few lines that look something like this:

```
/**
 * Print a String and then terminate the line.
 * This method behaves as though it invokes
 * <code>{@link #print(String)}</code>
 * and then <code>{@link #println()}</code>.
 *
 * @param x   The <code>String</code> to be printed.
 */
```

To create the API documentation, the folks from Sun Microsystems ran a program called *javadoc*. The `javadoc` program took lines like these right out of the `PrintStream.java` file and used the lines to make the documentation that you see in your Web browser.

Other Java programmers — people who don't work for Sun Microsystems — do the same thing. In fact, everyone who writes Java code uses the `javadoc` program to generate documentation. So everyone's Java documentation looks like everyone else's Java documentation. When you know how read to the standard API documentation, you know how to read anybody's homegrown Java docs.

And yes, you can use the `javadoc` program too. When you download the Java SDK (see Chapter 2 for the details), you get the `javadoc` program as part of the deal. Although this book doesn't tell you how to use `javadoc`, you can experiment with the program and create your own nice-looking documentation.

Index

• B •

Notes

Notes

Notes

Notes

Notes

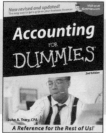
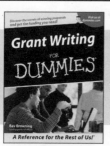

FOR DUMMIES®

A world of resources to help you grow

HOME, GARDEN & HOBBIES

Feng Shui
0-7645-5295-3

Gardening
0-7645-5130-2

Guitar
0-7645-5106-X

Also available:

Auto Repair For Dummies
(0-7645-5089-6)

Chess For Dummies
(0-7645-5003-9)

Home Maintenance For
Dummies
(0-7645-5215-5)

Organizing For Dummies
(0-7645-5300-3)

Piano For Dummies
(0-7645-5105-1)

Poker For Dummies
(0-7645-5232-5)

Quilting For Dummies
(0-7645-5118-3)

Rock Guitar For Dummies
(0-7645-5356-9)

Roses For Dummies
(0-7645-5202-3)

Sewing For Dummies
(0-7645-5137-X)

FOOD & WINE

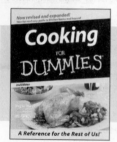

Cooking
0-7645-5250-3

Cookies
0-7645-5390-9

Wine
0-7645-5114-0

Also available:

Bartending For Dummies
(0-7645-5051-9)

Chinese Cooking For
Dummies
(0-7645-5247-3)

Christmas Cooking For
Dummies
(0-7645-5407-7)

Diabetes Cookbook For
Dummies
(0-7645-5230-9)

Grilling For Dummies
(0-7645-5076-4)

Low-Fat Cooking For
Dummies
(0-7645-5035-7)

Slow Cookers For Dummies
(0-7645-5240-6)

TRAVEL

Italy
0-7645-5453-0

Hawaii
0-7645-5438-7

Las Vegas
0-7645-5448-4

Also available:

America's National Parks For
Dummies
(0-7645-6204-5)

Caribbean For Dummies
(0-7645-5445-X)

Cruise Vacations For
Dummies 2003
(0-7645-5459-X)

Europe For Dummies
(0-7645-5456-5)

Ireland For Dummies
(0-7645-6199-5)

France For Dummies
(0-7645-6292-4)

London For Dummies
(0-7645-5416-6)

Mexico's Beach Resorts For
Dummies
(0-7645-6262-2)

Paris For Dummies
(0-7645-5494-8)

RV Vacations For Dummies
(0-7645-5443-3)

Walt Disney World & Orlando
For Dummies
(0-7645-5444-1)

Available wherever books are sold. Go to www.dummies.com or call 1-877-762-2974 to order direct.

FOR DUMMIES®

The advice and explanations you need to succeed

SELF-HELP, SPIRITUALITY & RELIGION

Sex FOR DUMMIES
0-7645-5302-X

Parenting FOR DUMMIES
0-7645-5418-2

Religion FOR DUMMIES
0-7645-5264-3

Also available:

The Bible For Dummies
(0-7645-5296-1)

Buddhism For Dummies
(0-7645-5359-3)

Christian Prayer For Dummies
(0-7645-5500-6)

Dating For Dummies
(0-7645-5072-1)

Judaism For Dummies
(0-7645-5299-6)

Potty Training For Dummies
(0-7645-5417-4)

Pregnancy For Dummies
(0-7645-5074-8)

Rekindling Romance For Dummies
(0-7645-5303-8)

Spirituality For Dummies
(0-7645-5298-8)

Weddings For Dummies
(0-7645-5055-1)

PETS

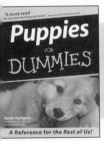
Puppies FOR DUMMIES
0-7645-5255-4

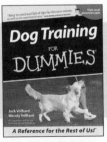
Dog Training FOR DUMMIES
0-7645-5286-4

Cats FOR DUMMIES
0-7645-5275-9

Also available:

Labrador Retrievers For Dummies
(0-7645-5281-3)

Aquariums For Dummies
(0-7645-5156-6)

Birds For Dummies
(0-7645-5139-6)

Dogs For Dummies
(0-7645-5274-0)

Ferrets For Dummies
(0-7645-5259-7)

German Shepherds For Dummies
(0-7645-5280-5)

Golden Retrievers For Dummies
(0-7645-5267-8)

Horses For Dummies
(0-7645-5138-8)

Jack Russell Terriers For Dummies
(0-7645-5268-6)

Puppies Raising & Training Diary For Dummies
(0-7645-0876-8)

EDUCATION & TEST PREPARATION

Spanish FOR DUMMIES
0-7645-5194-9

Algebra FOR DUMMIES
0-7645-5325-9

The ACT FOR DUMMIES
0-7645-5210-4

Also available:

Chemistry For Dummies
(0-7645-5430-1)

English Grammar For Dummies
(0-7645-5322-4)

French For Dummies
(0-7645-5193-0)

The GMAT For Dummies
(0-7645-5251-1)

Inglés Para Dummies
(0-7645-5427-1)

Italian For Dummies
(0-7645-5196-5)

Research Papers For Dummies
(0-7645-5426-3)

The SAT I For Dummies
(0-7645-5472-7)

U.S. History For Dummies
(0-7645-5249-X)

World History For Dummies
(0-7645-5242-2)

Available wherever books are sold. Go to www.dummies.com or call 1-877-762-2974 to order direct.

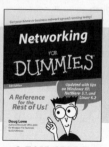